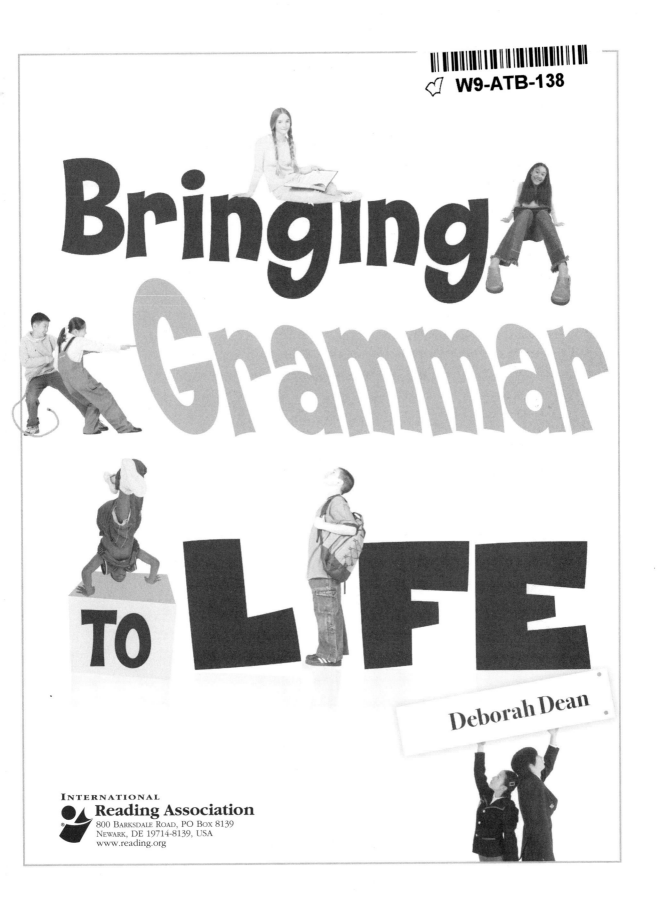

Bringing Grammar to LIFE

Deborah Dean

INTERNATIONAL
Reading Association
800 BARKSDALE ROAD, PO BOX 8139
NEWARK, DE 19714-8139, USA
www.reading.org

The International Reading Association attempts, through its publications, to provide a forum for a wide spectrum of opinions on reading. This policy permits divergent viewpoints without implying the endorsement of the Association.

Executive Editor, Books Corinne M. Mooney
Developmental Editor Charlene M. Nichols
Developmental Editor Tori Mello Bachman
Developmental Editor Stacey Lynn Sharp
Editorial Production Manager Shannon T. Fortner
Design and Composition Manager Anette Schuetz

Project Editors Charlene M. Nichols and Christina Lambert

Cover Design, Thomson Digital; Photographs © JupiterImags/Photos.com

Library of Congress Cataloging-in-Publication Data
Dean, Deborah, 1952-
  Bringing grammar to life / Deborah Dean.
    p. cm.
  Includes bibliographical references and index.
  ISBN-13: 978-0-87207-624-2
  1. English language--Grammar--Study and teaching (Secondary) I. Title.
  LB1631.D293 2007
  372.61--dc22

                                                                2007032552

CONTENTS

ABOUT THE AUTHOR

Deborah Dean is an associate professor in the English Department at Brigham Young University (BYU), Provo, Utah, where she teaches composition and courses on teaching writing, teaching grammar, and methods of teaching language arts to preservice English language arts teachers. Prior to coming to BYU, she taught junior high and high school in Washington state. She received her master's degree in education from City University, Bellevue, and her doctorate from Seattle Pacific University.

Deborah is the author of *Strategic Writing: The Writing Process and Beyond in the Secondary English Classroom* and numerous articles in *English Journal*, *Journal of Adolescent & Adult Literacy*, *Syntax in the Schools*, and *Voices From the Middle*. Her professional interests focus on helping teachers improve instruction, particularly instruction with writing and language—and to that end she has presented at national and international conferences, including the International Reading Association and National Council of Teachers of English annual conventions.

When she's not teaching (which she loves) or writing, Deborah likes to spend time with her children and grandchildren (reading books, making cookies, and pushing swings). She and her husband also enjoy traveling.

Author Information for Correspondence and Workshops

If you have grammar ideas you'd like to share with me or questions you'd like to ask about teaching grammar, please contact me at deborah_dean@byu.edu. As you use the ideas in the book, I hope you'll also let me know how they work for your students and in your classes. Share your stories with me. I would love it.

ACKNOWLEDGMENTS

First, I want to thank my students—of all ages—who have asked me questions for which I wanted to find answers and who have made me wonder and pay more attention to language. Those questions inspire my curiosity still and, in many ways, started me on the journey that is partly represented in this book. Without those students and their questions I wouldn't have learned nearly as much.

I must also thank the teachers (some of whom are also students) who have helped me learn. When you ask me to help, when you ask me how to teach something, I am better because of your wondering. You push me to articulate for myself and for others what I think. I learn from watching you teach and share with students your interest in language. Special thanks to Sonja Osborne and Gloria Nance, who first asked me to talk to teachers about teaching grammar, a request that pushed me to put my ideas in some sort of coherent form. Sonja and Gloria remain great models for me as I watch them implement ideas and work with teachers, and as they brainstorm ideas with me. Their energy and enthusiasm for students and learning inspire me. Also thanks to Raphael Johstoneaux and Don Norton, whose passion for language has inspired me and taught me. I will never forget debating the structure of a sentence diagram or visiting to ask about a specific construction to determine what it might be. You both have exemplified the kind of curiosity about language that I always want to have.

Thanks also to the readers, reviewers, and editors of this manuscript. My daughter, Julie (an English teacher), was the first reader of a pretty rough draft. Her comments along with those from the reviewers and the editors at the International Reading Association have helped shape and mold my original idea into the present (and, I believe, better) version. Thanks especially to Corinne Mooney and Charlene Nichols for their friendly assistance throughout the process. I appreciate all the help very much.

I can't finish without thanking my family, despite the jokes about the boredom level of writing a book about the semicolon (it's more than that, guys). They put up with inattention when my mind is in my writing and with disorder when drafts are spread over the table and counters. Finally and always, I give my appreciation to David. His support for me matters in countless ways—and makes possible anything I do.

INTRODUCTION

"When we engage with grammar as art, we allow ourselves to wonder, surrender, be tempted and overcome."

—MARY EHRENWORTH AND VICKI VINTON

"Mrs. Dean?"

I didn't recognize the young man who stopped me next to the giant bags of flour and sugar in Costco. Well, maybe his smile tugged at my memory...but, no, I didn't know him.

"You *are* Mrs. Dean, aren't you?"

"Yes. I'm sorry...."

When he said his name, I remembered. Trevor had been one of two students I had taught all three years of junior high. But that had been more than 10 years ago and in another state; he'd grown a lot from that slender, shorter than average junior high student I had known. He was just finishing college and had gotten married—to an English major, he informed me.

"Are *you* majoring in English?" I asked.

He laughed. Hard. "No way! But, thanks to you, I know grammar better than she does."

I don't know if that was a compliment or not. I taught Trevor in the beginning of my teaching career, poor guy. In those years, the school district required traditional grammar instruction, despite the fact that we were entering the last decade of the 20th century and publications for the previous 20 years had endorsed integrating grammar instruction and moving away from traditional approaches. I did what I was expected to do: I taught parts of speech and diagramming, although I modified our text's exercises because I wanted these students to be writers, not grammarians. When the district revised its expectations, asking teachers to teach grammar in context, I was happy to be able to give the time I'd devoted to grammar instruction to writing. But what I found is that I didn't know what "grammar in context" really meant. What was I supposed to do? How was it different?

I know that many of my fellow teachers just dropped grammar altogether. They were happy not to have to teach what they didn't like and what they thought students didn't enjoy. I had liked teaching grammar. I'd had fun—and I think my students had fun, too. We wrote clues for treasure hunts and stories, both consisting of only prepositional phrases, and police reports of absurd "crimes" full of adverbs. But teaching grammar in context? That was something I wasn't sure how to do—and no one I talked to seemed to know either.

I read what I could in professional journals and turned to minilessons connected to students' writing as my first try. But I think my minilessons were a lot like my traditional grammar instruction: using definitions of parts of speech to instruct and then giving students sample sentences from the textbook so they could practice the principles. I just assumed students would transfer such lessons to their writing. When they didn't, I started making more direct connections. That helped some. But I still didn't think this was what it meant to teach grammar in context. Shouldn't it be more integrated with the rest of the course, not just limited to revision days during a writing unit? And how was I to make those minilessons more applicable to writing?

I've learned a few things since those days. I've read more and practiced more ideas in my classes. My teaching didn't change overnight. It evolved—and I think it's still evolving. So now in my position as a teacher educator I think I do a better job when I try to help preservice teachers understand the importance of teaching grammar integrated with the whole language arts. That is, I think I do better until I observe them teach. They tend to teach grammar the way they were taught—either not at all or pretty traditionally. Then I realize that what I've explained doesn't make sense to them. They can't visualize integration.

When I talk with practicing teachers in workshops about integrating grammar into the rest of their course content, I say they should find language in all that their students read and write: "Grammar is all around us." I'm not the first to say it; in *Grammar Alive! A Guide for Teachers* (Haussamen, 2003), teachers are told, "You can use the literature the students are reading, as well as newspapers and other texts, to demonstrate or teach almost any grammar lesson" (p. 17). But the practice is harder to visualize than that exhortation (or mine) implies. Teachers still look at me with puzzlement: What does it *really* mean? What does it *look like* to do that?

Because of their questions, what threads through this book is a sample classroom dialogue that exemplifies what I think it means to integrate grammar into the content of a class. This dialogue portrays a class of ninth graders who are reading the novel *To Kill a Mockingbird* (Lee, 1960). The students' names and characters are a composite of students I have taught over the years. The words, obviously, are not actually what students said in any one single class. Rather, this is a compilation of classes and comments, very like parts of what happened in several classes. I hope "seeing" my class in action makes what it means to teach grammar in context more accessible for all teachers. I hope it shows that teaching grammar in context does *not* mean

- Waiting for students to bring up language issues
- Teaching language without preparation
- Teaching grammar only with writing

Instead, I hope it is evident that teaching grammar in context *does* mean

- Relating language to reading, writing, and student experience
- Planning an occasional minilesson on a grammar principle
- Encouraging talk about language as a part of class conversation

Chapter 1 sets the stage for teaching an integrated approach to language by briefly exploring the history of grammar instruction and clarifying what we as educators mean when we say we're "teaching grammar." It ends with my explanation of the five aspects of language I use throughout the book to address what I consider to be a comprehensive view of language instruction. Chapter 2 begins with an explanation of how language can be integrated with reading and ends with specific teaching examples that apply to each of the five aspects introduced in the first chapter. Chapter 3 mirrors the previous chapter except that it deals with integrating language with writing—again ending with specific teaching applications for each of the five aspects. Chapter 4 addresses two major issues that complicate the effective teaching of language for many teachers: concern for English-language learners and testing in our classes. The first part of the chapter explores questions and findings related to these concerns; the chapter ends with specific teaching applications that address these two areas for each of the five aspects of language. Chapters 2, 3, and 4 separate aspects of an integrated approach into discrete topics to make discussion possible; chapter 5 pulls all the strands back together, exploring how we can prepare for an integrated approach to teaching language—how we can plan for it and how we can assess it.

There are some other features in this book I should mention. Within the dialogues, "Thoughts From the Classroom" boxes explain what I'm doing with my class as a way to clarify the thinking and research I use to integrate and teach language—grammar. In addition, "Extending Your Knowledge" boxes accompany the information in the chapters themselves, extending the ideas for readers who want to know more. At the end of each chapter are reflective questions. I hope they provide a way for readers to begin to consider and adapt the ideas for individual classroom needs. In Appendix A, readers will find annotated references that they can use to learn more about the ideas in the different chapters. Appendix B provides some of my personal suggestions about basic grammar knowledge that teachers might consider to begin.

Together, I hope these features and the ideas in the chapters themselves will help you as you develop your own classroom dialogues—finding language in all you teach and sharing it with your students.

CHAPTER 1

What Is Grammar?

"Grammar is the skunk at the garden party of the language arts."

—Brock Haussamen

IN THE CLASSROOM...

Teacher (T): OK, let's get started. We're going to read chapter 20 today, the end of the trial—or at least Atticus's closing remarks; it starts on the bottom of page 199. Let's go over how chapter 19 ended, first, just to refresh our memories from yesterday. What had happened?

Tanner: Dill got upset and went out of the courthouse with Scout.

T: Why was he upset?

Beth: He didn't like how Mr. Gilmer was talking to Tom Robinson.

T: How he was talking?

Beth: Putting him down, like we talked about before. Using words to make it like he wasn't a person or someone to respect.

T: OK. Scout said Dill was "sick." Why do you think she used that word?

Justine: Well, I don't think she got what the deal was with Dill. I mean, like we talked about yesterday, she didn't seem bothered by the questioning, so just figured Dill must've had something else wrong with him, like being tired or hot or something.

T: Sure, and Dolphus Raymond finds them. Let's go back to page 160 to remind ourselves who Mr. Raymond is. What do we know about him?

Brady: He lives with the Negroes, has children with them.

Matt: And he drinks!

Brady: Yeah, out of a paper bag!

> ### THOUGHTS FROM THE CLASSROOM
>
> These comments refer to a prior discussion on the power of words to carry more meaning than just the denotative meaning. "The world is not simply the way it is, but what we make of it through language" (Romaine, 1994, p. 29). Helping students learn that language carries emotional weight is important for them to develop as responsible users and interpreters of language. It's also important that discussions on these topics occur repeatedly in the classroom, not just rarely.

T:	OK, then let's see what more we can learn about Mr. Raymond. Who wants to start the reading? Vanessa? [After reading to the bottom of page 201] Let's stop here and see what we learned.
Beth:	He's not really a drinker.
T:	No, he's not. Interesting.
Maria:	He pretends to be drunk so he can do what he wants.
James:	Yeah—and no one will hassle him 'cause they just think he's plastered.
T:	OK, what else do we know about Mr. Raymond?
Emily:	He isn't prejudiced, the way most of the town is.
Tiffany:	Yeah. He's more like Atticus in that way.
Trent:	He's more like the kids—at least that's what he says. He can tell the kids because they don't think the way the town does yet. Prejudiced.
T:	What can we tell about Mr. Raymond from his speech? What do you notice about his language?
Brady:	He kind of swears in front of the kids, like—"the hell with 'em."
Jon:	Yeah. Remember when Scout got in the fight with Cousin Francis? Afterward, Atticus said kids used bad language to get attention, like adults didn't do it—at least in front of people. And Atticus doesn't swear around the kids.
Sara:	He probably doesn't any time.
Jon:	Yeah, but other adults would talk that way.
T:	So, what does it mean if Mr. Raymond uses language that isn't what Atticus would use? [No responses] Let's look at some other word choices he makes and see if that can help us. Anything else unusual?
Trent:	Well, he uses words like the kids some of the time.
T:	What words?
Trent:	*Gotta*, *reckon*. Those words.
James:	And he says *'em* instead of *them*.

THOUGHTS FROM THE CLASSROOM

This discussion is also an extension of previous discussions. Crucial to students' understanding of the characters in the novel is their understanding that language is used purposefully, to show us character as well as to advance the plot. Thus, the fact that only certain characters use pejorative terms for Tom Robinson shows something about those characters. Furthermore, the Southern dialect may be unfamiliar to students—or they may be unaware of their attitudes toward it. Wolfram (1999) explains that "reflective interaction" can help students "confront the unjustified stereotypes and prejudices that often accompany our recognition of dialects" (p. 51). By looking at the characters' speech, students can begin to reflect on their own speech and their attitudes about speech.

T:	I also noticed how many contractions he uses: *things'll* instead of *things will* and *don't* for *do not*. *Ain't* for *haven't*. What kind of information do these words give you about Mr. Raymond?
Tanner:	Well, that's how we all talk.
James:	I don't say *reckon*. That sounds like a farmer or someone in a movie about the Old West.
Emily:	And my grandma would get real mad if I said *ain't*.
T:	Why do you think that is, Emily?
Emily:	Well, because she thinks it's like illiterate or something.
T:	Do any of the rest of you have family or friends that think that? Do you think it?
Several:	Yeah.
T:	It's interesting because it shows some things about the English language that we should pay attention to. It works as a contraction for *am not*—we don't have a contraction for that—and was used for a long time by educated speakers. But, somewhere along the line, someone decided it shouldn't be used—and enough people agreed—so now it's considered improper. If you use it in certain situations, you risk being considered uneducated. Still, I know educated people who do use it; it's just that because I know they're educated, I don't think anything about it. I guess the idea is that we have to be careful of certain words in certain situations because they carry some judgment with them—people will judge us based on our use of those words. Would that have been the case back in the 1930s, when this book was set?
James:	It probably wasn't a big deal back then, but it's just not right that people think stuff about you from your words.
T:	But you kind of thought that about *reckon*, didn't you? We all have language prejudices.
Several:	Language prejudices?
T:	Sure, you know, thinking things about ways of speaking that might not be true. Like the ones James and Emily mentioned. We just have to be aware of what they are so that we don't apply them unfairly. So we need to think about Mr. Raymond's choices in that way, too. Would they

> **THOUGHTS FROM THE CLASSROOM**
>
> It's important to talk about usage when it comes up in texts we are reading, too. While we, as teachers, don't have to go into length on the topic, just having students open their eyes to usage issues can benefit them as they continue their language learning. As Strong (2001) observes, "In actively investigating usage, students may well experience increased openness to language learning" (p. 51). Just getting students thinking about usage can be a beginning to that openness.

	be OK for his situation? Tanner, you said he talks like we all talk. What did you mean?
Tanner:	I meant more like the *won't* and *things'll*—those words.
T:	So what if we say *things will*, *do not*, *have not*, and so on?
Sara:	I *do not* like the way this is. I *don't* like the way this is. It seems kind of stuck-up to use the whole words.
Jon:	Yeah, more friendly to use the contractions.
T:	So he's being more informal. Why?
Beth:	To make the kids comfortable?
Emily:	Maybe that's just the way he is. Not everyone is really formal with language, are they? Just because they're adults?
T:	No. Although Atticus almost always is. See how few contractions Atticus uses on pages 204 and 205?
Several:	Hardly any.
T:	Sure, so some people use them more than others—and maybe some situations are better for them than others, informal ones rather than formal situations like speaking to a jury. Are there any ways Mr. Raymond's language is more like an adult's?
Matt:	Well, saying *hell* is still kind of adult.
T:	OK. Anything else?
Tanner:	Well, he does talk about instincts and reputation. Those are kind of like big ideas. I mean, kids would know what they are and stuff, but they are like adult ideas.
Maria:	And he seems to be trying to make his language simpler on purpose. See where he says, "Maybe things...."
T:	Where are you reading?
Maria:	Oh. Page 201, about the third paragraph. He says, "Things'll strike him as being—not quite right, say..."—I think he was going to use a bigger word and then changed for a simpler way to phrase it.
T:	What makes you think that?
Maria:	The dash seems like he changes his mind or pauses or something. And then what comes after it is kinda simple.

T:	So the dash, in this case, suggests a shift in the speaker's intent?
Emily:	Yeah, saying not exactly what he started to say. Was he going to say "wrong"?
T:	What do the rest of you think?
Jon:	It could be, or it could be "cruel."
James:	Or "prejudiced." No one really says that word in the book, do they?
T:	No, they don't, at least not in connection with their own behavior. Why do you think that is?
Angie:	They're kind of set in their ways.
Jason:	And they always think the other person is the bad one. They're the good ones.

T:	With that in mind, then, why do you think we have this little incident here? Why are Scout and Dill meeting this man? Why now in the story?
Tiffany:	Well, it's kind of like when we started the book and we talked about how Scout isn't all caught up in the society yet, she doesn't have a view that's opinionated yet. She knows stuff that's told to her, but mostly she knows stuff that she sees happening, but since she's a kid she either doesn't get it or she figures it in a way that might not be true.
Shannon:	Yeah, she's innocent, so her view would be innocent, too.
Brady:	But I want to know why here. I mean, I was a little bummed to have the trial interrupted. I don't know why we had to have stuff about Dolphus Raymond here.
Jon:	Me either.
T:	Any ideas? [No responses] Well we're going to read on, so maybe while we read you can think about why we had this interruption first, OK? Who wants to read? Jon?

I collect old grammar books. An odd hobby, I know, but one that helps me get a sense of the history of grammar instruction beyond the summaries I can read in other books. The preface in one grammar text from 1880 is interesting in how it reveals grammar teaching history and issues. The author, Albert Raub, asserts that "the principles underlying and regulating the use of the English language are best taught by an inductive process" (p. 3). After contrasting his belief with that of what he perceives as the norm—deductive, scientific, and unsuccessful—Raub states that his "design is to teach first the idea, then the name, and lastly the definition" (p. 3). Despite his intent, the book is a series of exercises focused on definitions (that students would have to know before they did the exercises)—nothing so dissimilar from other methods of that time, according to his own description, and certainly not so dissimilar from methods that persisted through most of the next century. Still, it's interesting that even in 1880 the awareness of the challenges of teaching grammar was evident.

Despite pronouncements from the National Council of Teachers of English (NCTE) as early as 1936 and concerns expressed by authors such as Raub, traditional grammar instruction—based on Latin and Greek models and involving memorization of definitions and identification of parts of a sentence—was central to modern education in the United States; that is, it was until the repercussions of *Research in Written Composition* (Braddock, Lloyd-Jones, & Schoer, 1963) hit. That report contains the following passage, so often repeated as almost to have become a mantra:

> In view of the widespread agreement of research studies based upon many types of students and teachers, the conclusion can be stated in strong and unqualified terms: the teaching of formal grammar has a negligible or, because it usually displaces some instruction and practice in actual composition, even a harmful effect on the improvement of writing. (pp. 37–38)

Braddock and colleagues' report started a controversy that was argued in journals for the next two decades. In fact, in 1985 Hartwell made the observation that both sides argued from the same research but that "prior assumptions about the value of teaching grammar" colored the interpretation of that research (p. 106)—people saw what they wanted to see. Hillocks's 1986 findings, more than 20 years after Braddock et al.'s report, reinforced the earlier findings and contributed to spreading its perspective: "The study of traditional school grammar...has no effect on raising the quality of student writing.... Taught in certain ways, grammar and mechanics instruction has a deleterious effect on student writing" (p. 248). Since the mid-1980s, this conclusion has largely been accepted as the final word in the controversy: Teaching grammar in traditional ways does nothing to improve writing.

Hartwell's assertion about how teachers interpret research findings depending on their prior assumptions certainly seems apparent in the way teachers responded to the reports from Braddock and colleagues and, later, Hillocks. Some teachers saw the reports as an excuse to throw out grammar instruction: At last they could stop doing what they hated and what their students seemed to hate. Some teachers believed that if grammar instruction didn't help students develop as writers, there was no value in teaching it. Others didn't want to give the impression that students' home languages weren't of value. For whatever reason, in many classes, students received no grammar instruction.

Teachers holding a grammarian perspective, believing in the effects of traditional grammar instruction despite the reports' findings, continued to teach grammar. Battistella (1999) suggests that along with this persistent belief in the academic value of teaching traditional grammar was a moral element, a feeling that good grammar was somehow reflective of good character and therefore ought to be taught. Teachers who persisted in teaching traditional grammar, though, were often seen as out of step with current theory and practice, so they withdrew from local discussions and sometimes hid what they taught in the classroom. According to Wallace (1995), they were "driven underground" (p. 2).

One (possibly unintended) consequence of the pronouncements from Braddock and colleagues and Hillocks is that grammar was linked almost solely with writing instruction. Both reports state that traditional grammar instruction does not improve student *writing*—thus effectively limiting the application for any other language instruction. What developed from this narrowed perspective is an approach toward grammar instruction called "teaching grammar in context," which is a response to an emphasis on the writing process and popularized in the well-known book of the same name (Weaver, 1996a). Lobeck (2005) comments on the consequence of this limited view of grammar's value: "The popular idea of teaching grammar only 'in context' perpetuates a narrow view of the applications of grammatical knowledge to other areas of study in the K–12 curriculum" (p. 100). Grammar as helpful to reading, grammar as related to language attitudes, or grammar as anything other than punctuation and correction seemed to be ignored in the rush to contextualize grammar as part of writing process instruction.

With the new focus on grammar for writing, some teachers tried to do what seemed to be the logical outcome of the research—they tried to integrate grammar into writing instruction. But many teachers found this stance problematic in a number of ways. Because integrated grammar instruction necessitates individual application, there is little that can be given to teachers to use in class in the way of texts or planned lessons. Teachers have to develop minilessons that respond to students' needs. As a consequence, teachers need something that's in short supply in public schools: time. They need time to analyze students' needs and time to prepare materials that will help meet those needs. As a result, I see teachers resort to such strategies as daily oral and written practice using sentences from a book that students correct as a class. These sentences generally contain a range of errors from a lack of punctuation at the end of a sentence to the use of commas in restrictive and nonrestrictive clauses. If a student is having trouble with sentence boundaries, I can't imagine he or she would be ready to learn about the complexities of which clause is essential and which is not. Furthermore, the sentences reduce grammar to a hunt for errors—and in sentences that aren't even the students' own! In most classes I observe, teachers make no application beyond correcting the sentences with the students—and then consider their teaching of language to be addressed.

And new textbooks aren't always helpful either. An analysis of popular writing texts from the 1990s shows that they include significantly more about writing than previous versions and that those sections are in the front of the texts, emphasizing writing. These texts include some grammar lessons within the writing chapters, in addition to the traditional grammar section that has been moved to the back of the book. Despite the appearance of integration of grammar instruction with writing, these texts "miss what is essential in real integration: connection with the concerns that are actually occurring in students' writing" (Dean, 2002, p. 31). Instead, the texts include a lesson on pronoun agreement with descriptive writing, for example, even though pronoun agreement may not be what is needed for students who are writing descriptions. The texts give the appearance of integration in what is really an almost impossible task for a text, because integration relies on the teacher's recognition of individual students' needs with specific pieces of writing or reading. For some teachers, all these challenges are just too much. The result? "The 'right moment' hardly ever arose and grammar was simply not taught at all" (Hudson, 1999, p. 102).

The difficulties of time and texts are compounded by the pressure of large-scale testing, resulting in what appears to be a trend reverting to traditional grammar instruction—out of context but easier. A few years ago I attended a national literacy conference. I heard that every session on grammar was packed—and all the ones I attended dealt with traditional grammar instruction. Attendees were hungry for what the presenters gave them because testing has complicated the issues of integration: How do we contextualize grammar instruction *and* prepare students for tests?

The teaching of grammar has an interesting past, a complicated intertwining of conflicting goals and purposes. The issues of what research shows and what teachers should do about research findings seem to be—at least to some extent—resolved. In a recent themed issue on grammar in *Voices From the Middle*, the editor summarized the current thinking: "The question isn't *Do we teach grammar*, but instead *How do we teach grammar in context?*" (Beers, 2001, p. 4). Part of the answer to that question involves defining the term. What does *grammar* mean?

Well, that depends on whom we ask.

Hartwell (1985), in refining Francis's earlier "Three Meanings of Grammar," provides five meanings for grammar.

- Grammar 1: the patterns of language people all learn intuitively as they learn a language. Hartwell calls this the "grammar in our heads" and describes its "internalized" and "abstract" nature, as well as its connection to "the acquisition of literacy" (p. 111). He gives an example to show Grammar 1 by listing a series of words and noting how native speakers always know the way to order the words to achieve meaning.
- Grammar 2: the scientific aspect of language that analyzes and studies patterns of language. Hartwell notes that there are "a number of scientific grammars," so Grammar 2 cannot be considered a "stable entity" (p. 114). This grammar, he (and

others) argues, is not of much value in schools because it is more concerned with theoretical factors than reality.

- Grammar 3: what Francis termed "linguistic etiquette" (as cited in Hartwell, p. 109) and what Hartwell calls "usage." Grammar 3 deals with issues of language that may have social consequences. If a person breaks the rules of Grammar 3, he or she may be thought uneducated, probably unworthy, and, possibly, immoral.

- Grammar 4: school grammar. Although scientific grammar and school grammar are linked, Hartwell calls Grammar 4 unscientific because of its "inadequate principles": a concern with logic and a false connection to Latin (p. 110). In his further discussions of Grammar 4, he refers to the rules teachers teach about language as "incantations." Hartwell asserts that when people follow the "rules," they are really just "accessing tacit heuristics honed by print literacy" (p. 119). He argues that these rules make sense only if a person already understands the concept—that the rules themselves cannot teach the concepts—and he provides examples of possessives and fragments to make his point.

- Grammar 5: "stylistic grammar" or grammar as it relates to teaching writing, particularly at the sentence level (p. 111). Today, Grammar 5 might even be broader and considered as rhetorical grammar, which moves beyond the sentence level in most cases. Hartwell anticipated this move somewhat by noting that "writers need to develop skill at two levels. One, broadly rhetorical, involves communication in meaningful contexts.... The other, broadly metalinguistic rather than linguistic, involves active manipulation of language with conscious attention to surface form" (p. 125). Today, references to grammar as style might refer to either level.

Since Hartwell's article, others have presented alternate definitions of grammar in an attempt to ensure that when teachers talk about what we are teaching, we are talking about the same thing—and not simply focusing on issues of correctness. The recent definition in *Grammar Alive! A Guide for Teachers* (Haussamen, 2003) condenses Hartwell's five meanings into two:

> Grammar refers to two kinds of knowledge about language. One is subconscious knowledge, the language ability that children develop at an early age without being taught.... The other kind of knowledge is the conscious understanding of sentences and texts that can help students improve their reading and writing abilities by building on that subconscious knowledge. (p. xiii)

Although this definition is simpler, it isn't clear what the "other kind of knowledge" actually refers to—learned grammar, I assume, but is it school grammar, scientific grammar, or style grammar? The definition also doesn't address oral use of language in formal situations. Burke (2001), citing Kress and van Leeuwen as sources, provides an even broader definition: grammar as "patterns of experience...enabl[ing] human beings to build a mental picture of reality, to make sense of their experience of what goes on around them and inside them" (p. 60). For the purposes of this book, I use *grammar* and *language* interchangeably, but my use is intended to embrace the three perspectives I've presented here: Grammar involves learning about language from a variety of perspectives to help students read, write, and speak in meaningful ways in a variety of contexts.

Why Should We Teach Grammar?

Weaver (1996a) cites nine reasons often given for teaching grammar, including the following: to train the brain, to aid in learning a second language, to help students score well on large-scale tests, to help them speak in socially prestigious ways, and to help them improve as writers and readers. After she discounts these reasons as invalid or ineffective because of research findings, she still suggests teaching grammar as a means of improving writing. Her recommendation to eliminate traditional grammar instruction in order to allow more time for writing seems to address the conflicting issues raised in research. This highly endorsed perspective—that we limit the focus of instruction to a few concepts and that we teach grammar primarily to improve student writing—is dominant in published literature on grammar instruction.

However, other educators and researchers make different arguments for studying language. Penha (2006) says we don't need a reason, that "by definition" that is what we do as English teachers (p. 20). Donna (1999) echoes this point when she compares goals for studying history or math with those of teaching language: "In stark contrast to other disciplines, the formal study of language in our schools too often ignores these four goals, doing little to establish basics, inspire wonder, train useful skills, or support advanced study" (p. 67). Her point makes a good case for incorporating language study into other aspects of a language arts course: to expose students to ideas about language and to generate interest in its issues. When I've approached grammar this way—as a way to inspire curiosity and interest in language—my experience has been that students are fascinated to learn more about something that is so integral to their daily lives. Noden's (2006) response to the question of why teach grammar is poetic:

> ### EXTENDING YOUR KNOWLEDGE
>
> Ehrenworth and Vinton (2005) affirm the position that the goal of grammar instruction should be "to teach knowledge of conventional usage...to increase power, opportunity, and voice; to teach habits of fluency, inquiry, and experimentation; and to engage students in such a way that this knowledge and these habits are sustaining and flexible" (p. 15).
>
> Postman (1995) makes a different but no less compelling argument for other reasons to study grammar: "[L]anguage habits are at the core of how we imagine the world...to the degree that we are unaware of how our ways of talking put...ideas in our heads, we are not in full control of our situation" (p. 176).
>
> Power and control: two good reasons to teach grammar.

I teach grammar because it is the doorway to the human soul.
Its intricacies trigger our laughter, our tears, our dreams. Grammar is the secret muse of all expression, the portrait painter of life's emotions.... Nothing in life is more essential, more sensitive, more intrinsic to the human soul.... How could we not teach grammar? (p. 19)

I have to echo Noden: How could we not?

What Aspects of Grammar Should We Teach?

Several educators try to answer this question. Noguchi (1991) reminds us that teaching grammar for writing is different from (although possibly overlapping with) teaching grammar for academic purposes. If we are to teach grammar for writing, he says, we should consider those aspects of grammar that most affect the teaching of style in writing, particularly those that address "syntactical, morphological, and punctuation errors" (p. 19). He considers the following four topics as inclusive of most of those errors: sentence, subject, verb, and modifiers. Weaver (1996a) presents her own list of what she labels "a minimum of grammar for maximum benefits" (p. 142). The items she suggests should be taught include the following (pp. 142–144):

- Concepts of subject, verb, sentence, clause, phrase, and related concepts for editing
- Style through sentence combining and sentence generating
- Sentence sense and style through the manipulation of syntactic elements
- The power of dialects and dialects of power
- Punctuation and mechanics for convention, clarity, and style

Like Weaver, Noden (1999) suggests using only minimum terminology for focused grammar instruction, not expecting memorization of a definition from a book or even, for that matter, complete definitions. So, for example, Noden defines *participle* as "an *ing* verb tagged on the beginning or end of a sentence" (p. 4). I interpret these admonitions to mean that students will not be tested on naming the parts of sentences or the terms for stylistic elements so much as they will be expected to use them effectively in their writing, and I agree with this perspective if my goal is to help students improve their writing.

Such a practice can have its challenges. In one remedial writing class I taught, I introduced appositives as a way to both improve writing and enhance comprehension during reading. After looking at several examples, students defined an appositive as a group of words that comes after a noun and says it another way. In Justine's writing log, where she was expected to note strategies authors used to enhance their communication of ideas, she wrote a sentence from her reading with this explanation: "Its an example of a positive [sic]." I read her sentence several times wondering "a positive *what*?" I finally asked my husband to listen as I read aloud her sentence, assuming he might help me figure out the meaning. As soon as I read the words aloud, her meaning was clear. She was identifying appositives in her reading; because I had only named the structure and hadn't stressed its spelling, she was doing the best she could. She could identify and use appositives—but she couldn't spell or define them. That's one possible consequence of this approach, one not entirely negative.

The International Reading Association (IRA) and NCTE (1996) present the following standards that also suggest a range of answers to the question of what we are to teach about grammar:

- Standard 4: Students adjust their use of spoken, written, and visual language (e.g., conventions, style, vocabulary) to communicate effectively with a variety of audiences and for different purposes.
- Standard 6: Students apply knowledge of language structure, language conventions (e.g., spelling and punctuation), media techniques, figurative language, and genre to create, critique, and discuss print and nonprint texts.
- Standard 9: Students develop an understanding of and respect for diversity in language use, patterns, and dialects across cultures, ethnic groups, geographic regions, and social roles.
- Standard 12: Students use spoken, written, and visual language to accomplish their own purposes (e.g., for learning, enjoyment, persuasion, and the exchange of information). (n.p.)

Generalizing from these standards, we should teach language (grammar) for both oral and written communication, and we should teach students that the use of language varies depending on the context and purpose for that communication—moving beyond simply oral and written styles to involve genre and audience considerations. Students should know something about language, its structure and its conventions, so that they can use that knowledge to help them read and interpret language in a variety of texts. Students should learn about language diversity—and the history of the language as well as something about language change that is inherent in that knowledge—so that they might become respectful of variety in language use.

Using these standards along with others' suggestions, I have come up with my own list of what we should teach. I recognize that any list I develop will not address everything. I am guided by a sense of language and grammar as more than just an influence on writing; I see it as an aspect of living, both in and out of the classroom. I'm certain that readers may want to add or delete some items. However, in looking at traditional concerns as well as linguistic concerns with language, in thinking about what we hope to achieve with language instruction in the classroom, and in considering what a language arts teacher could feasibly learn and address, I feel these areas are the most encompassing and pertinent. All are meant to be addressed in the context of the other activities in the classroom, not just with writing:

- Traditional Grammar
- Editing
- Usage
- Language Change
- Rhetorical Grammar

Traditional Grammar

Before anyone closes the book at this first item, I need to differentiate what I'm including from what is normally called traditional grammar, which is known for worksheets, memorizing definitions, diagramming, and so forth—all separated from anything else in the curriculum. There are many reasons to avoid teaching traditional school grammar (what Hartwell labeled as Grammar 4). Haussamen (2003) notes an important one: "Instead of helping students to focus on real literature or on the actual paper they are writing, traditional grammar pedagogy requires students to divert their attention to the isolated and often contrived sentences in a text book" (p. xiii). Even more fundamental, however, is the fact that traditional grammar instruction involves defining terms—and the definitions don't really work. Calvin makes that point in the conversation in the cartoon shown in Figure 1. Schuster (2003) makes the same point central to his book *Breaking the Rules: Liberating Writers Through Innovative Grammar Instruction*:

> The thesis of this book is that traditional school grammar has left a heritage of definitions that do not define and rules that do not rule (in usage, writing, and punctuation). These inadequate definitions and mythrules hamper students rather than help them in their development as speakers and writers. (p. 191)

He provides multiple examples in case anyone reading this text isn't convinced. And our own experiences as teachers should add weight to these claims. I can't say how many times I've been frustrated or have frustrated students who don't understand some aspect of grammar by using a definition to help them learn. My experience supports what Hillocks and Smith (2003) assert: "Traditional school grammar presents definitions that cannot function with desired results unless the person using them has more information about language than the definition provides" (p. 723). That is certainly the case when I try to teach sentence boundaries to some students using only the "definition" of a sentence.

So, if we are all clear on the negative aspects of traditional grammar, why do I include it here? I do so primarily for the sake of concept and vocabulary. Students need to know the concepts of sentences and parts of speech. Respected writers on the subject,

FIGURE 1. Calvin and Hobbes Cartoon: Pronouns

including Weaver, Noguchi, and Noden, use grammatical terms such as *adjectives*, *subjects*, *verbs*, *clauses*, and *phrases* when they discuss language and writing. And in chapter 8 of *Grammar Alive! A Guide for Teachers* (Haussamen, 2003), which provides a great overview of linguistic grammar, some traditional terms are used along with other terms. Some words just are necessary to talk about language, and the traditional terms are more universal. I am *not* saying we should teach these terms by definition and ask students to memorize them and identify them in sentences for a test (unless you have to practice that for state testing—but that's in another chapter) or that students should know the parts of a sentence so that they can diagram them in exercises from textbooks. But being able to generalize about the terms we use so that students can connect them to their innate knowledge of language concepts and use them to improve their abilities with activities that involve language (reading, writing, speaking) is important for the other things students do in classes.

Going back to Grammar 1, I think students develop very early a sense of parts of speech. In other words, they sense that certain words name things and other words explain what those things do and other words describe either the thing or the action. Most students possess this kind of sense about words, and it's evident even when we hear toddlers speaking that they comprehend the idea of how words function. What I'm suggesting is that we use that Grammar 1 knowledge as a foundation for a common vocabulary that will allow us to talk about language in the classroom. In the same way Noden (1999) describes an appositive as a "noun that adds a second image to a preceding noun" (p. 7), we can use a few basic terms from traditional grammar to aid us in language discussions with students. I want to make clear that I am not advocating diagramming sentences (although I personally like the challenge of it) or memorizing definitions or testing students' ability to identify parts of speech in sentences in textbooks. What I am advocating is that some of the terms—for want of anything better—can be useful to us as we talk to students about language and what it does.

And I don't think we have to rely only on the traditional definitions when we talk about the few terms we want to use. Because they don't work completely anyway and because students often have a sense of what the concepts are, let them help define the terms. Even if they don't get a definition that will explain every instance, the generalization will stick with them. If I want to talk about the verbs in a text or in my students' writing, I can have students decide what verbs are and what they do from students' own experience and from investigation of the texts in front of us—not to identify every verb (a traditional grammar kind of thing to do) but to discover how verbs make the author's intent clear or make the text more inviting to read. Then we could discuss how these ideas about verbs could be helpful to them as writers.

> ### EXTENDING YOUR KNOWLEDGE
>
> In *Sin and Syntax: How to Craft Wickedly Effective Prose*, Hale (1999) describes verbs this way: "Verbs add drama to a random grouping of other words, producing an event, a happening, an exciting moment. They also kick-start sentences: without them, words would simply cluster together in suspended animation, waiting for something to click" (p. 55). Students might not be as creative as this in their definitions, but allowing them to try to generalize about language will make a difference in their learning.

Other educators have written their suggestions for additional ways to explore some of the traditional aspects of grammar that teachers need to address without relying on the traditional definitions that don't work. Noguchi (2002) offers suggestions for finding the subject of a sentence through questioning. Schuster (2003) recommends several ideas for investigating parts of speech, including test frames for prepositions and an activity that helps students understand the differing effects of coordinating and conjunctive conjunctions. Using terms from traditional grammar does not mean a return to memorization of definitions or worksheets or diagramming. We can talk about language with those terms but teach them and use them in much more varied ways that have application to the rest of the work we do with students in our classes.

Editing

I remember my brother-in-law telling me about a job he'd interviewed for. The interviewer told him that more than 200 applicants had applied for that one position. The first cut was made on the basis of editing: If an application had a punctuation or grammatical error, it was tossed. Because this was an engineering job, I was surprised. I guess I thought those things mattered only to English teachers—at least that's what I hear all the time.

Writers haven't always been concerned with punctuation. It wasn't necessary in earliest written texts (at least in Western civilization) because the texts were read aloud anyway. Scribes who wrote the speeches were mostly concerned with accurately representing the words of the speaker. In fact, the words were written without breaks between them, let alone markings to indicate any other pause. But, according to Parkes (1993), since the sixth century, when reading silently started to be more of an expectation, conventions to aid the reader were developed and refined to address the changing needs of readers over time.

At first, since most of the texts were religious, scribes and monks were concerned that the markings to help readers should support orthodox interpretations (Parkes, 1993), showing even very early that writers understood how punctuation could affect meaning. Early punctuation marks were not standardized, the size was often in relation to previous words or letters, and changes occurred in what the punctuation represented over time. One example I find interesting is the use of the ivy leaf. In the 800s, it was used by Anglo-Saxons to differentiate text from commentary. By the 1800s, it was only a printer's ornament. So it went from being functional to decorative. I'm sure some of our students wish commas or apostrophes would make the same switch.

From the 12th century, we are more likely to see punctuation similar to today's—and we can thank Irish and Anglo-Saxon scribes because they developed many of today's conventions as they worked with Latin (another language) and tried to create smaller texts. Even with similar marks, however, Schuster (2003) notes that "punctuation conventions are always in flux" (p. 151), and anyone who reads e-mails knows that is true.

Schuster, in an analysis of a grammar book from 1762, notes that at that time "writers typically used about three times more punctuation than we do today" (p. 151). Our students should be happy to know that fewer marks mean fewer chances for error.

Despite the popularity of the book *Eats, Shoots & Leaves: The Zero Tolerance Approach to Punctuation* (Truss, 2003) and a sense that differing attitudes about punctuation are only modern, feelings about what punctuation should do for writers go back to attitudes and philosophies of the 17th and 18th centuries. At that time, John Locke's philosophy, represented in the view that language "ought to be subjected to a process of careful regulation with a view to achieving correctness and precision for the expression and communication of ideas" (as cited in Parkes, 1993, p. 91), countered a rhetorical view (supported by elocutionists like Thomas Sheridan) that written language should be more like speech, that punctuation should help reflect the speaker's emphasis and inclinations. That argument is still one we see today—the conflict between strict adherence to rules and a kind of flexibility that allows writers to shape meaning through punctuation marks.

By the term *editing*, I mean gaining an understanding of the use of punctuation not only for correctness but also for meaning and style. I have taught punctuation both ways, and, although knowing the "rules" is sometimes useful, I really believe it isn't as effective as learning punctuation by paying attention to how it affects meaning in texts— our own and others': *With your comma here, I group these ideas together and separate them from this idea. Is that what you want me to do?* But students also need to have a sense of how others read punctuation—the rules—so that they can interpret texts effectively. Just as drivers "read" a red light as a signal to stop, readers know from the "rules" what different forms of punctuation signal. It's a balancing act, to know how much "rule" and how much "sense" we should teach, and Ehrenworth and Vinton (2005) describe the tension well: Students "need to own the rules of grammar, not be enslaved to them" (p. 88). How to accomplish both tasks is the hard part.

One way to accomplish the balance is recommended by Atwell (2002), among others: minilessons, short, teacher-directed lessons focused on a specific topic related to students' current writing. In responding to the concern that students don't pay attention to even minilessons on punctuation, Atwell asserts (and I agree) that "students will respond to punctuation lessons when the content is relevant—when they need the information to strengthen their writing" (p. 238). She introduces punctuation concerns with an interesting lesson on the history of punctuation that provides an effective overview of the "why" of punctuation and allows students to apply the lesson by inventing their own punctuation. I've tried the same lesson and find it engages students and makes them more aware of punctuation as a way to guide readers; furthermore, it makes them more receptive to minilessons on the "rules."

Ehrenworth and Vinton (2005) describe how they read aloud—not only to show intonation but also as they say the punctuation—to show students the effect of punctuation choices in texts. They collect sentences and texts that provide strong examples for the discussions they have in class to showcase the punctuation they are learning. As they describe it,

> to get students to engage in grammar this way, we need to make it seductive, something they can't resist. We need to make them want to play with it, to dig in and get their hands dirty. We need to stop imposing it on them and invite them to explore it with us, discovering for themselves why the rules are there and what meaningful purpose they serve. (p. 89)

Editing is an important skill for students to learn. As teachers, we can help them learn through their writing, but we don't always need to wait until students are ready to polish a piece of writing to address editing concerns. We can address issues related to punctuation in our reading and in our talking, too. We can find examples for teaching punctuation all around us—in advertisements, in music, in e-mails. When students become sensitive to this aspect of language, they gain immeasurably in preparation for their lives outside of school as well as in their reading and writing.

Usage

We're all aware that usage is the aspect of grammar most people expect us to teach and to monitor. When strangers find out we're English teachers, they often respond, "Oh, I'd better watch my grammar around you." They don't mean their punctuation; they mean their usage. Usage issues evoke deep emotions about language. Out of respect for students' home languages, some teachers avoid addressing issues of usage altogether, considering that what is taught under the category of usage demeans the home language and perpetuates the power inherent in standardized forms of the language.

> **EXTENDING YOUR KNOWLEDGE**
>
> Mulroy (2003), in his defense of grammar teaching, asserts that ignoring usage doesn't serve anyone well, arguing that although "schoolmarms may be faulted for spreading an exaggerated notion of the inferiority of dialectical speech...their efforts make it possible for people born on the wrong side of the tracks to rise to...levels of wealth and influence" (p. 87).
>
> Still, he objects to what he sees as a purely mercenary reason for learning socially accepted usage; for him it should be more about effective and precise speech than improving economic standing.

But Ehrenworth and Vinton (2005) make a strong case for the opposite: "As teachers, we do our students a disservice not to apprise them of the standards and rules of written English that dominant society endorses—and that they, themselves, might be judged by" (p. 4). And to answer the concern that we are being too restrictive if we address usage, they note that knowledge of usage is essential to effective decision making: "Teaching students the language of power does not necessarily mean asking them to conform to it. It means giving them the knowledge they will need to make informed and meaningful language choices" (p. 6).

In fact, Ehrenworth and Vinton note that ignoring the issues of power inherent in language usage actually works against students' agency: "We hearken to Delpit's plea that 'to act as if power does not exist is to ensure that the power status quo remains the same'" (p. 52). Indeed, *Code-Switching: Teaching Standard English in Urban Classrooms* (Wheeler & Swords, 2006) is based on this premise of giving students options, different ways to use language in different situations. These educators, differing in approaches and philosophies, seem to agree on the unavoidable conclusion: usage matters. For me, this category of instruction deals with aspects of language use that shift for different purposes and audiences—and that often carry social weight in their choice.

To begin to explore usage issues, we can help students clarify the difference between descriptivism and prescriptivism. *Descriptivism* focuses on what language users actually do with language; *prescriptivism* is about what language users should do. Bex and Watts (1999) add to this simple description: "Prescriptivists tend to start from the premise that there are certain forms which are correct because they best express the meanings intended...[and] represent an ideological force which equates language use with social behaviour [sic] and correct usage with good citizenship" (p. 7). Descriptivists may observe different varieties of language, but they don't "enforce one variety for use in all situations regardless of medium" (p. 8).

Edlund (1995) describes Bakhtin's metaphor of the two: Prescriptivism is a rainbow, or language in its ideal state, while descriptivism is a stream, or language as it changes and flows among users, "to contain not only currents and eddies of ongoing linguistic change, but also mud and wreckage, unseen obstacles, and the other debris of life" (pp. 90–91). Students might wonder why the distinction matters. Wolfram (1998) provides several answers: Descriptivist perspectives help us "understand how language is structured and how it may be examined in a systematic, rigorous way" (p. 83). He adds that understanding the descriptive view helps us respect diversity in language and understand that the distinction can clarify "the essential difference between linguistic grammaticality and social acceptability" (p. 83)—or the rules compared with the feelings about language. Recognizing the distinction can also help students gain what Lobeck (2005) thinks is more important: "Students will need more than by-the-book grammar to succeed in the world. They will need to be innovators and creative thinkers, problem solvers and pioneers, or else they risk being marginalized again, condemned to the ranks of the functional" (p. 87). If students understand the concepts of descriptivism and prescriptivism, they can begin to be critical thinkers about language issues.

Some educators help students learn the ideas underlying usage issues by asking them to be descriptivists themselves and discover aspects of language use in the world around them. Students do this first by observing the discrepancy between any usage rule and the actual use of language with regard to that rule and then by drawing conclusions from their observations. Strong (2001) has his students create surveys and conduct field research, so that they "become experts in a domain of usage" (p. 50). Wolfram (1998) describes an activity where students judge sentences on a combination of linguistic grammaticality and social acceptability: Sample sentences are (a) grammatical and socially acceptable, (b) grammatical but socially unacceptable, (c) ungrammatical but socially

> ### EXTENDING YOUR KNOWLEDGE
> Williams (2004) describes the tension between descriptivists and prescriptivists as a class battle between "conservatives on one side who are afraid that the structures that provide our security are in danger of collapse and radicals on the other who seem willing to embrace any new fad that promises utopia" (p. 64). The battle, as he sees it, is between "Snobs and Slobs," the title of his essay.

acceptable, or (d) ungrammatical and socially unacceptable. This activity can help students discern the difference between prescriptive and descriptive approaches to language as it begins to develop their sensitivity to usage issues and how they are situational.

Related to prescriptivism is the notion of a standard version of English. Haussamen (2003) defines "Standard English" as "the variety of English that many people in the economic mainstream and predominant social culture of the United States speak and write" (p. 4). He notes that it is not standard because of any inherent superiority but because it "is the widely recognized and codified version of English" (p. 4). Most of the time, that recognition and codification relate to issues of power, education, or money. Trudgill (1999), writing from a British perspective, lists what Standard English is not: not a language, accent, style, or register. He says it is a dialect, "the most important dialect" (p. 123) and "a purely social dialect" (p. 124).

However, the idea of a standard variety of language isn't as clear cut as it may appear. Instead, Schuster (2003) sees "degrees" in Standard English (p. 57), Haussamen sees the concept as flexible (2005), and Lobeck (2005) calls it an "idealization" (p. 102). There isn't one Standard English. In fact, Wheeler and Swords (2006), referring to *The Stories of English* (Crystal, 2004), note "nearly sixty popular varieties of international Standard Englishes" (p. 127). So, the concept of Standard English is not simple. Whether it's written or spoken makes some difference; the audience and purpose are other considerations. And place matters, too.

> ### EXTENDING YOUR KNOWLEDGE
>
> Recognizing that Standard English isn't singular, Birch (2005) identifies four "Standard dialects within Standard American English (SAE)":
>
> 1. Standard Spoken English: "the acceptable way of speaking that may not follow all grammar rules...composed of several local standards"
>
> 2. Standard Written English: "used in fiction and news reporting"
>
> 3. Academic English: "refers to a more formal style of SWE—passive voice...complex noun phrases...register common to the university"
>
> 4. Proper English: "little more than a myth. —In PE, every grammatical rule that has come down through the ages must be strictly observed, and any deviations are strictly censure" (pp. 4–5).

Williams (2003) summarizes the issue effectively: "Here's the point: We must reject the notion that observing the rules of Standard English makes anyone intellectually or morally superior. That belief is not just factually wrong; in a socially diverse democracy, it is destructive" (p. 14). But it is not an uncommon belief. Once I wrote a thank-you note to a neighbor and gave it to him with a plate of cookies. Later, I was shocked when he expressed surprise that as an English teacher I would have used a double negative in my note. I was surprised that as a magazine editor he couldn't see that I had used it to create an effect. But I learned a lesson about Standard English: Audience matters even when the genre is informal. With even a limited exposure to these ideas, students can understand that the concepts related to usage are crucial for them as readers, speakers, and writers. Raising their awareness of these issues can help them make good choices in their own use of language, as well as become more flexible in their judgments about others' usage.

Tightly connected to usage issues is an understanding of language variety in all its forms: dialects, levels of formality, cultural differences. At the very least, teachers need to help students realize that language varies among people, among situations, and for different purposes. Even more, we should help students come to understand and appreciate this variety.

I enjoy Schuster's (2003) introduction to dialects: "I speak a dialect, you speak a dialect, all God's children speak dialects, because as linguist John McWhorter (2001) says, dialects are all there is/are/be" (p. 62). Schuster then relates a personal story of his own acquisition of standard dialect while retaining—and using when effective—the dialect he learned growing up. Dialects, especially those that are not considered standard, arouse responses in listeners. We attach judgments because of those responses.

I will never forget what I learned as a new college student. I attended a guest lecturer who was to speak about his book on the origins of colloquial phrases. After a laudatory introduction, he began to speak, but not in the dialect of academia I had expected. He used a rural Appalachian dialect instead. In the first place, I had trouble understanding some of what he said; in the second, I wondered what he had to say that could be of value to me. I guess I had forgotten the credentials mentioned in the introduction—and I was ready to walk out. Suddenly, he switched dialects and began speaking in the one I expected for the situation. In shock, I realized the trap I had fallen into, judging him based on his dialect.

Milroy and Milroy (1991) note that

> although public discrimination on the grounds of race, religion and social class is not now publicly acceptable, it appears that discrimination on linguistic grounds *is* publicly acceptable, even though linguistic differences may themselves be associated with ethnic, religious, and class differences. (p. 3)

I know from my experience and from comments my students make that this is the case: Attitudes about language use, especially negative ones, persist. To put these attitudes in perspective, Birch (2005) describes four language attitudes that fall along a continuum from language equality to language prejudice:

1. Language equality: This perspective is almost "anything goes"; as Birch puts it, this attitude asserts that "people have right to speak the way they want" (p. 6).

2. Language description: This perspective tries to be objective and neutral, to see language as something that should be described, not prescribed. As Birch notes, this stance is "not totally satisfying because society holds teachers accountable for their learners' language usage" (p. 7).

3. Prescriptive: This perspective, as the label implies, attempts to set rules for language use and is "based on the belief that dialectical variation is a changeable human characteristic (as opposed to race, gender, ethnicity, sexual orientation, and so on) and therefore that people may choose to adapt their dialects if they can" (p. 7).

4. Language prejudice: This perspective carries the prescriptive approach to another level and "permits and even encourages judgment of the individual or social group whose language or variety differs from the standard" (p. 8).

In explaining these varying attitudes, Birch notes that "few people hold only one coherent attitude toward variation" (p. 8). In other words, people might feel more tolerant toward some dialects than others. These attitudes can be attributed to what Wolfram (1999) calls the myths and folklore about language differences that he argues are "deeply rooted in our educational system and society at large" (p. 48). He urges educators to address these misconceptions and prejudices. We can do that in a number of ways.

Recognizing what dialects are is a start. Students should understand that dialects have grammar, that they follow rules, and that they are simply a variety of language. Wheeler and Swords (2006) explain that "since any language variety is like a fully stocked kitchen, any dialect...has the wherewithal to express whatever speakers need" (p. 13). In other areas of their lives students appreciate variety and self-expression. Just ask them about the issue of wearing uniforms to school. Students always bring up self-expression as a primary reason against any policy restricting their clothing. In a similar way, students can come to appreciate and understand the benefits that language diversity can add to their own lives as well as to their world.

EXTENDING YOUR KNOWLEDGE

Lobeck (2005) uses this definition (originally from *The Language Files*, published by The Ohio State University's Linguistics Department) to explain a dialect: "A dialect is any variety of a language spoken by a group of people that is characterized by systematic differences from other varieties of the same language in terms of structural or lexical features" (p. 102). Using this definition, students can consider how many dialects they speak.

Teachers can address misconceptions and prejudices about language by helping students become aware of the attitudes and responses associated with dialects, helping them recognize others' attitudes as well as their own. Lobeck (2005) suggests that knowledge of the history of English can aid in this awareness, as many of our attitudes toward language variation have their origins in the development of the language. Because, as she explains, "dialects are identified based on shared oral, rather than written patterns" (p. 102), students can examine the dialects they use and discover that most speakers shift among several dialects in adjusting to audience, purpose, and context. Calpurnia exemplified this shifting for contextual reasons in *To Kill a Mockingbird*: She used one dialect at church and a different one at the Finch household (Lee, 1960, p. 37). Students can identify their own dialects by considering how they speak in different situations and with different people. I recently overheard a ninth-grade student's comment to a friend: "I speak three languages: Utah, Pig Latin, and English. I could be an English teacher." He was obviously aware, at some level, of the ways he used language differently in different situations. When students realize that they are multidialectal, they should consider how certain audiences might respond to some of their dialects as a way to begin thinking about attitudes toward dialect.

Making sure students get exposure to dialects through reading is valuable, too, as wider exposure can help them develop understanding of the value of dialects. Alvarez (1998) recognizes this importance:

> When the voices of those with darker skins, less money, funny accents, and different religious affiliations or sexual preferences are excluded from our curriculums, when they are not on the shelves in libraries, when they are refused entry into our cannons or our understanding of ourselves as a nation, then we have less than the full story of who we really are. (p. 39)

Many of the novels and short stories students read in school contain characters who speak in dialects; these pieces of literature allow us to address issues of language variety with our students as they explore the richness of language available to all of us through dialects.

As teachers, we can use literature to help students understand how language may be used to reflect issues of power. As Graff and Birkenstein (2006) report, "the language scholar Geneva Smitherman mixes African American vernacular phrases with more scholarly language in order to suggest...that black English vernacular is as legitimate a variety of language as 'standard' English" (p. 119). Traugott (1999) suggests that a narrator's ideology can be expressed by choosing to have characters speak in dialect, asserting that "nonstandard Englishes and other languages over the years have become increasingly important in fiction, especially in developing awareness of and empathy with multicultural voices" (p. 176). Certainly many of the novels we read in English classes today—*To Kill a Mockingbird* (Lee, 1960); *Roll of Thunder, Hear My Cry* (Taylor, 1976); and *Their Eyes Were Watching God* (Hurston, 1937/1998), to name a few—can provide avenues for discussion of dialects and what they represent about culture and power as well.

Another aspect of usage has to do with levels of formality. According to Hagemann (2003b), linguist Martin Joos categorized five levels of formality: (1) intimate, (2) casual, (3) consultative, (4) formal, and (5) frozen. Although informality reigns in popular culture, there are still some places where the use of informal language can be problematic. Students need to consider audience and purpose when making choices about levels of formality, especially because those considerations can change. For example, in an English handbook for college freshmen, Graff and Birkenstein (2006) note that "academic writing today is no longer the linguistic equivalent of a black-tie affair" (p. 121). There is wiggle room in this aspect of language use. My students tell me that some teachers expect very formal academic language use in the writing for their classes, while others are OK with less formal language. Not many teachers find the informality of text

---

EXTENDING YOUR KNOWLEDGE

In speaking about her mother's English, author Amy Tan (2000) makes this observation:

> Like others, I have described it as "broken" or "fractured" English. But I wince when I say that. It has always bothered me that I can think of no way to describe it other than "broken," as if it were damaged and needed to be fixed, as if it lacked a certain wholeness and soundness. I've heard other terms used, "limited English," for example. But they seem just as bad, as if everything is limited, including people's perception of the limited English speaker. (pp. 114–115)

In this part of her essay, Tan is referring to her own abilities to shift dialects but also addresses how even the labels people attach to dialects reflect attitudes students need to be aware of.

messaging appropriate for classroom writing, however. Students need to be aware of expectations and levels of formality in order to make effective choices.

Usage issues—standards, dialects, levels of formality—address aspects of language that can have social consequences. Helping students realize that they already have a sense of many of these issues of usage, that in some cases they already shift usage unconsciously to adjust to situation, can help them develop not only a more conscious use of these varieties of language but also a more flexible attitude toward language in general—an attitude that helps them see that language adapts to purposes and audiences in many beneficial ways.

Language Change

I find Winchester's (2003) description of the changeable nature of English very compelling:

> And though George Orwell might have longed for an Anglo-Saxon revival, though John Dryden loathed French loanwords, despite Joseph Addison's campaigns against contractions such as *mayn't* and *won't*, and although Alexander Pope pleaded for retention of dignity and Daniel Defoe wrote of his hatred of the "inundation" of curse-words and Jonathan Swift mounted a life-long attempt to "fix our language forever"—no critic and advocate of immutability has ever once managed properly or even marginally to outwit the English language's capacity for foxy and relentlessly slippery flexibility.
>
> For English is a language that simply cannot be fixed, nor can its use ever be absolutely laid down. It changes constantly; it grows with an almost exponential joy. It evolves eternally; its words alter their senses and their meanings subtly, slowly, or speedily according to fashion and need. (p. 29)

Even though students might find that first sentence challenging to understand—and may not understand the implications of the names Winchester lists—the sense of how many people have sought to stop changes to English should be clear. Understanding the changeable nature of language helps students make the transition to understanding language variation. In differentiating between change and variation, Denham (2005) says the old maxim of "majority rules" is the best judge: "When a substantial number of speakers have adopted the variation as their own accepted pronunciation or grammatical form, then we say that the language has changed" (p. 150). To develop awareness of language change, students could identify words that are currently finding their way into the English language—or teachers could introduce them to the idea of language change by telling them which words have been adopted for dictionaries each year.

Change is a fascinating aspect of language, so in addressing language change, it's important for students to realize that change isn't a bad thing, that it doesn't mean that language is getting worse. Instead, it is an important indicator that language is alive and meeting the needs of its users. As an example, in the preface to the grammar book *An A.B.C. of English Usage*, Canby (1937) makes this observation after lamenting the inevitable acceptance of *contact* as a verb (as in *I contacted him*): "Nothing is more characteristic of the peculiar genius of English than the ease with which it has always expanded by using nouns as verbs, verbs as adjectives, and more rarely adjectives as nouns" (p. 7). In Figure 2, Calvin addresses just such shifting. His comments can help students consider their own expansions of language. William Shakespeare was a master at such expansion, and students can be directed to some of the ways his innovative use of language contributed to how we use language today. Comparing words older people use to those students now use can provide useful insights on helping students recognize that language change does not diminish the language.

Denham (2005) addresses language death with her students, noting that scholars predict that "in this century as many as 95% of the estimated 6,000 languages currently spoken in the world may become extinct" (p. 154). This indicates the highest language death rate ever. Students might not care, thinking that their language isn't dying. But helping students consider how identity and language are closely tied can help them understand their own language better as well as have concern for other languages. One way I've had students explore this idea is to consider color words. I bring in some paint samples and ask students to name the colors. Girls tend to have more color words in their vocabulary than boys do. For *blue*, girls name *navy*, *sky blue*, *cerulean*, *aqua*, *azure*, *turquoise*, *indigo*, *powder blue*, and *midnight*—to name a few. Boys want to know why it makes a difference—girls can tell them it allows them to be much more specific and precise. Raised in Alaska, I'd heard that the natives had many more words for *snow* than we did; Bryson (1990) confirms it: "fifty words...crunchy snow, soft snow, fresh snow, and old snow, but no word that just means snow" (p. 14). Bryson also gives examples of

> **EXTENDING YOUR KNOWLEDGE**
>
> Ehrenworth and Vinton (2005) suggest that, because language changes, we have to pay attention to the way it is used:
>
> > There is work to do in considering part of the responsibility of teaching as the labor of paying close attention to language and to literature. Contemporary writers are shifting the norms of language all the time.... And so none of us can ever rest on what we have already learned. Always, we look outward. (p. 160)
>
> That looking, that watching how we see language being used in new and interesting ways, can help our students see the wonder of language study.

FIGURE 2. Calvin and Hobbes Cartoon: Verbing

words that other languages have that English doesn't, concluding that these words reveal something about the cultures that developed them. Helping students see how language is connected to identity by finding ways their own language reflects their identity can help them appreciate language death as well as language change.

Even a brief introduction to the history of English can help students gain understanding about language change. A number of books—and one very interesting video—on the history of English are available (see Table 1 for some examples). Atwell (2002) has a good "brief history of the English language" that she uses in a minilesson (pp. 209–212). Bryson's book *The Mother Tongue* (1990) has a fascinating first chapter that provides great examples about English as a way to engage students' interest in their language. He provides examples for the aspects of English that set it apart: the richness of vocabulary, its flexibility, its conciseness, (arguably) its ease of spelling and pronunciation. He says its most notable trait, however, is "its deceptive complexity" (p. 19). All of these aspects relate in some way to the history of the language; I know from experience that even a little background on that history can help students understand aspects of language that they might otherwise find confusing or miss altogether.

One aspect of language change that has immediacy for students is related to spelling and irregular verbs. An understanding of the history of English with its influences from other languages can help students see why some words don't follow the spelling rules we learn in elementary school. Irregular plurals are left over from Old English patterns (e.g., *oxen, mice, geese*), words that haven't yet followed the tendency to regularize that other words did (Denham, 2005). Curzan (2005) explains that other spelling irregularities also derive from historical events. Because scribes originally used the Latin alphabet to write in English, we have 26 letters but more than 40 sounds—so "we have letters doing 'double time'" (p. 143). That complicates spelling. Sometimes, Curzan explains, words have changed in pronunciation but not in spelling—so the spelling reflects the older way of speaking, as in words like *knight*. Because of interest in classical periods, "Renaissance scholars sometimes made efforts to change English spelling to conform to the Latin forms of the words" that English had borrowed from French, as in *debt* (p. 144). Borrowing from other languages, something English does often, complicates spelling because those words don't follow English spelling patterns either. In some cases, there's even double borrowing, further complicating spelling issues; *colonel* is one example of

TABLE 1. Sample Titles That Can Provide Background on the History of English

Bragg, M. (2004). *The adventure of English: The biography of a language.* New York: Arcade.
Cran, W. (Director). (2001). *The story of English* [video recording]. United States: Homevision.
Crystal, D. (2004). *The stories of English.* Woodstock, NY: Overlook Press.
McCrum, R., Cran, W., & MacNeil, R. (2003). *The story of English* (3rd ed.). New York: Penguin.
Mugglestone, L. (Ed.). (2006). *The Oxford history of English.* New York: Oxford University Press.

this, borrowed from both French and Italian so that we have the French pronunciation and Italian spelling. Then, we should add, there is Webster, who wanted to use American spellings as a way to reinforce independence from England—so we have some spelling changes (*theater* instead of *theatre*, for example) from that period and some spellings that stayed the same as England's. Still, Crystal estimates that "80% of the English lexicon is spelled according to regular patterns, and only 3% is so irregular that speakers must learn the spellings individually" (as cited in Curzan, 2005, p. 142), so the problem with spelling isn't insurmountable. Knowing the history of the language at least makes it understandable.

As students address ideas of language change, it's only natural that they should confront ways that some users of language manipulate it to their advantage. Because many advertisements use language in persuasive ways that students might be unaware of, exploring connotation and denotation of words is an important aspect of being a critical reader and a critical viewer. Recognizing this aspect of language is an important part of understanding language change, especially as it affects critical thinking among consumers and citizens in a democracy. As Alvarez (1998) reminds us,

> Misusing the language is something that dictatorships and totalitarian governments know all about. One of the first things such a regime does is to seize control of the media, to censor the stories of the people, to silence dissenting opinions. I grew up where there was only one story—the official story. In the dictatorship of Rafael Leonidas Trujillo in the Dominican Republic, 1930–1961, books were rewritten to tell his truth, and his truth only on pain of death. In a school not far away from where I attended classes, a young teacher corrected a student's essay on Trujillo by suggesting that there had been other "liberators" of the country. That night, the teacher, his wife, and two children disappeared. (p. 39)

As teachers, we can help students understand this aspect of language change when we have them read and analyze political speeches (past and present) as well as advertisements and editorials. When students are aware of the difference between denotation and connotation, when they understand how words can shape attitudes and feelings, they can show responsible use of that knowledge in their own reading and writing for public purposes.

The idea that words have meanings that can be manipulated is only one part of language change. In the preface to the new translation of *Night* (2006), Elie Wiesel addresses another aspect of language that students should understand: Language changes when our words become inadequate to express human emotions or conditions. As he writes,

> I had many things to say, I did not have the words to say them. Painfully aware of my limitations, I watched helplessly as language became an obstacle. It became clear that it would be necessary to invent a new language. But how was one to rehabilitate and transform words betrayed and perverted by the enemy? Hunger—thirst—fear—transport—selection—fire—chimney: these words all have intrinsic meaning, but in those times, they meant something else. Writing in my mother tongue—at that point close to extinction—I would

pause at every sentence, and start over and over again. I would conjure up other verbs, other images, other silent cries. It still was not right. But what exactly was "it"? "It" was something elusive, darkly shrouded for fear of being usurped, profaned. All the dictionary had to offer seemed meager, pale, lifeless. (p. ix)

Helping our students appreciate this sensitive issue related to language change is important. For example, in *To Kill a Mockingbird* (Lee, 1960), it's important for students to recognize the mistake Tom Robinson made when he said he felt "sorry" for Mayella Ewell. It was a word that, as a Negro in the South in the 1930s, he wasn't allowed to use in relation to a white woman. As a real-world example, I learned that there's a trend in the courts in the United States to limit the words witnesses can use when they are testifying. Certainly that is a case of language change. When words don't work for us, when they are restricted to certain groups, when they become inadequate because of our experiences, language changes—or society does—to accommodate the needs. If students understand that, they are really learning about grammar and language at its most sensitive levels.

Rhetorical Grammar

This aspect of grammar instruction is probably the most familiar to teachers today; it is the grammar that relates to effective (not simply correct) writing, sometimes also called stylistic grammar. To me, rhetorical grammar is the way students apply what they know about language at all levels, not only at the level of correctness but also at the level of meaning and sense—abilities they will gain from a language program that treats grammar in all its forms: as parts of speech and editing, yes, but also as variation and usage and meaning. All aspects of language come into play in teaching rhetorical grammar.

Many teachers and writers who work with rhetorical grammar promote the use of what Ehrenworth and Vinton (2005) call "mentor texts," pieces of writing that students can read for ideas to implement in their own writing (p. 129). I like the term *mentor* rather than *model* because of the implications: Mentors guide, advise, and support; models are a likeness, pattern, or copy. I want the texts my students study to serve as possibilities, not constraints. Teaching students how to use them as such is important for their learning rhetorical grammar, so showing them how to question, consider, and choose when to use ideas from mentor texts is an important part of teacher work. Having students use and then reflect on the effects of their language choices in their writing is also the key to developing their rhetorical grammar.

Schuster (2003) relies heavily on professional texts as a way to learn which rules of writing really matter. In sampling published writing, students (and the teacher) investigate what constitutes effective writing. For example, in exploring the admonition to vary sentence beginnings, Schuster examined numerous classic and modern essays to conclude that "the advice to vary sentence openings is *very bad advice* indeed. Professional writers open sentences with their subjects approximately two-thirds of the time"

(Schuster, 2003, p. 122). Tufte's (2006) assessment is the same: Two thirds of English sentences begin with the subject, and about one quarter begin with an adverbial construction. Not a lot of variety. Students can use mentor texts to investigate all aspects of language use: usage, conventions, dialects, genre, and more.

Sentence imitation and sentence combining are additional ways to learn rhetorical grammar. Sentence imitation has a long history. Students imitate the structure of sample sentences with their own content. Usually this helps extend students' repertoire of grammatical structures. Depending on the sample sentences, students can learn how to use appositives, participial phrases, subordinate clauses, or parallel structure (among others) in their writing. They don't have to know the names of the structures—in fact, I started teaching imitation by naming the parts of the sentence ("The sentence starts with an infinitive phrase...") and just about destroyed my students' interest before I learned that they could imitate without naming anything. Once they understood the idea of imitation, they became avid imitators, bringing in sentences for me to use with the class and sharing their imitations generously. Sometimes they didn't always use them effectively in their writing, failing to match the structure to the tone of the writing, as one girl did who wrote about skateboarding while imitating several sentences from former U.S. President John F. Kennedy's Inaugural Address (1999). To me that is part of the learning process, and she, like others, figured out what needed to be done to make sentences rhetorically as well as structurally effective.

> ### EXTENDING YOUR KNOWLEDGE
> Oakley (1999) reminds us that writers develop the skill to create meaning for readers by becoming observant about the way others use language: "[W]riters need not only to be virtuoso performers of something to a reader, they also need to become astute observers of language, dispassionately and disinterestedly analyzing the rhetorical effects of their own and others' writing" (p. 130).
>
> That is, at the heart, what rhetorical grammar can teach students.

Sentence combining can contribute to students' learning of rhetorical grammar in similar ways. Despite some resistance to it during the 1970s and 1980s, sentence combining is one of the few instructional methods that has research supporting its effectiveness (Graham & Perin, 2007; Hillocks, 1986). Students combine short kernel sentences into longer sentences, either with cues or without. The problem I've seen with sentence combining is in how some teachers use it: to focus on correctness. They have students share their sentences and then decide if they're "right" or not. Instead, I ask students to combine the kernel sentences in at least two different ways and then decide which they like better and why. When we share, I ask for several responses so that we can discuss the effects of combining one way over another: Why do they like one sentence more than another? What difference in meaning do the various combinations create? This work with sentences shouldn't be about right and wrong; it's about rhetorical effectiveness and helping students understand how to achieve it.

In addition to sentence combining and sentence imitation, Johnson (2003) advocates lessons on stylistic devices, lessons that, he argues, not only help students revise their writing but also generate new ideas about their topics. Johnson explains that "stylistic devices are not merely *fun*, not just toys for writers, but tools by which writers can create certain effects on readers, physical feelings of comprehension and power, knowledge and connection" (p. 37). He uses minilessons and exercises to acquaint students with devices of rhythm and balance and sound (asyndeton, antithesis, alliteration, for example), but, he explains, his purpose is not to get students to write "heavily stylized language" (p. 40). Instead Johnson wants them to "practice these devices as a kind of interim measure toward listening to and thinking about their prose more carefully" (p. 40). His ultimate goal is for students to feel a sort of pleasure from their writing and to become more confident, thoughtful "participant[s] in the world" (p. 61). I've tried some of his methods, too, and found that my students gained a better awareness of what language can do and what they can do with language—just what we want from rhetorical grammar.

Well, that's my list and my explanations. I'm well aware that there are problems inherent in presenting any type of schema for a subject as broad as this subject is. Some might disagree with my choices; that's OK. At least that means we're all thinking about teaching language and what it means and what students need. One limitation to the schema I've presented is how it plays out when I talk about it in this book. It's hard to separate grammar integrated with reading completely from grammar for writing or speaking. It seems that as we work with language during reading, students will gain knowledge that could—and should—find its way into their writing and speaking—and vice versa. So, the chapter divisions I present artificially separate what wouldn't be separated in the classroom. I hope readers can see that these chapters peer more deeply into what's seen on the surface in the classroom dialogue that threads through the book and are separated only for the sake of convenience. That's how they're meant to be seen.

QUESTIONS FOR REFLECTION

1. If you had to decide what aspects of grammar would be taught, what would be on your list? How would it differ from the list presented in this chapter? What rationale do you have for your own list?

2. What are some ways you can already envision integrating these aspects into your own classroom? How do you see this integration benefiting your students?

3. What do you need to do to prepare to integrate the aspects you would like to use but don't know enough about? Make a plan (a list of readings, a timeline, a suggestion for courses to take) for how you will accomplish your preparation.

CHAPTER 2

Reading and Language

"Why are we reading, if not in the hope of beauty laid bare,
life heightened and its deepest mysteries probed?"

—ANNIE DILLARD

BACK IN THE CLASSROOM...

T:	[Students have read aloud to the top of page 203 in *To Kill a Mockingbird*] OK, let's stop here. Now this is really shocking to Scout and Jem. Atticus has loosened his clothes—in front of the jury and the judge and all the spectators. Something he doesn't even do at home. He's so formal all the time, even at home—and then this. Why does he do it?
Beth:	Well, he could be, like, getting down to work. You know: Here's the hard part, so let's loosen our tie?
T:	Sure, that makes sense. Could it be anything else?
Brady:	He's like changing his character, you know? Changing his appearance to be someone else?
James:	Yeah.
T:	Why would he want to be a different character? A different person?
Tiffany:	Well, he is—normally—a very different person from most of the people in the town, isn't he? He talks different and he acts different. Isn't that kind of what Miss Maudie meant that time she was talking to the kids about Atticus?
T:	So why would he want to be different now?
Tanner:	To be more like the rest of the people in the town?
James:	But why?
Emily:	Maybe because he wants them to think of him not like a lawyer with a lot of big words and a lot of education. Maybe he wants to be like them so they'll agree more with what he says?

T: Why might that matter now?

Jon: Well, he wants to win the case. So he'd want the jury to be more like "Hey, he's like us so what he says makes sense."

T: So he changed his appearance to make his words more appealing to his audience?

Several: Yeah.

T: Do you ever do that—change something so that whatever you're saying will be more acceptable to the person you're talking to?

William: Oh yeah. All the time. I mean, I can't say the same stuff to my friends that I say to my dad, especially when I want something from him. Then it's like, I try to say polite things and not just the kinds of words I say to the guys I hang with. [Murmurs of assent] I can't call him names or dis him the way I do my friends; even joking around is different.

> ### THOUGHTS FROM THE CLASSROOM
> Kolln (2003) defines rhetorical grammar as language that responds to the "rhetorical situation—the audience, purpose, and topic—[and] determines the grammatical choices you make" (p. 2). Getting students to think about how people adjust language for rhetorical situations, even a little, can help them make connections to their own language use in speaking and writing.

T: So why doesn't Atticus just change how he talks, like Mr. Raymond seemed to with Scout and Dill?

Beth: I don't know if he could, you know, really change how he talks as easily. It'd be easier to change how he looks, more casual-like.

Jeremy: Yeah, that's what I think, too. It's harder to change your language.

T: OK, then let's watch what he does with language in this final, really important speech to the jury.

Tanner: Wait. I have an idea. You asked us why we had the Dolphus Raymond part right in the middle of the trial. See, with that there we don't get to read Mr. Gilmer's final speech to the jury. All we get to hear is Atticus giving his. So, it kind of makes us think just about his part, not how the people who think Tom's guilty would think. Is that right?

T: I don't know, but it sounds like a possibility. Writers get to choose what they put in and what they leave out—and they make those choices for reasons. That's certainly one possibility. Good idea. Any others? OK, then. We'll read on; I'll read so you can pay attention to what Atticus says in his speech. [Reads to end of chapter] OK, before we discuss, take out a piece of paper. Now, write your prediction for how the jury will respond to Atticus's final speech to them. Was he effective or not—to the jury—and why do you think what you think? Take a few minutes. OK, how many of you think his speech was effective, that it was convincing to the jury? [A few hands go up] Leslie, tell us why you think so.

Leslie: Well, he went over the stuff from the trial that would help them see that Tom Robinson wasn't guilty. He reminded them about Tom's arms—that he could only use the right one but that Mayella was hit by a left-handed person and that Mr. Ewell is left-handed.

Trent: Yeah, and he said it wasn't really a hard case, that there wasn't a lot of evidence to consider. He went over the events that they can all agree on.

Beth: And he tried to say how even if the people were prejudiced outside of the courtroom, they should still be fair inside the courtroom. So he was kinda reminding them to do the right thing.

T: Who thinks it wasn't effective? [A few hands go up] Tanner? Why do you think it wasn't?

Tanner: Well I just think these are really just the same people who'd come to the jail to lynch Tom. I mean, not the exact same people, but you know what I mean. If they feel like that, how can they be convinced, really? No matter how good his speech is.

T: So you think their real lives are too powerful to be swayed by his speech? You think that his speech works but just not enough for this jury?

Tanner: Yeah. I mean, it's a good speech and I would be convinced, I just don't think anything like a person talking is going to change how these people act. Look at history. It took a lot more—I mean, we read about the Scottsboro Boys. And I've read about Emmett Till. [Referring to well-known trials involving circumstances in which white women accused black men of sexual harassment or rape] A few good speeches by themselves just don't change people.

Jon: I see what Tanner means, it took a lot of speeches to change how people acted. And it took riots and laws and other stuff, too.

Maria:	Sometimes they still act that way, even with all the other stuff.
T:	So it seems to me that what we're saying is that the speech is a strong one, but that the people's beliefs and culture are strong, too?
Several:	Yeah.
T:	Let's just look for a minute at the speech then, to see what makes it a strong one. When we really want to make something or someone change, we have to use very effective strategies. If the strategies Atticus uses are powerful ones, they would be useful to you, too, when you want to make a point or try to change someone's opinion. First, everyone take two sticky notes and put them by two parts of the speech that you think are the strongest or two sentences you think are the most powerful. Shelby, do you have a spot you picked out to share with us?

Shelby:	Well, I don't know if this is what you mean. I just thought it was interesting that he repeats words all through the speech.
T:	What words? Can you give us some examples?
Shelby:	*Pity*, *guilt*, *lie*, *all*, *some*—those words.
T:	Good. Let's start there. Where do you see *pity* repeated?
Sara:	It's twice in that middle paragraph on page 203: "I have nothing but pity in my heart" and "but my pity does not extend."
William:	I see it in the next paragraph, too. "But I cannot pity her."
T:	What connects all these repetitions?
Emily:	They're all his pity for Mayella. Like he's feeling sorry for her.
James:	Hey! That's the same as Tom Robinson said in the trial: He felt sorry for Mayella.
T:	What do you think it means? Why did Atticus make this point? Jenny?
Jenny:	He's making himself like Tom?
Matt:	Yeah, like trying to make Tom's statement not such a bad thing. He's saying, we should all feel sorry for her. I get it.
T:	What about the repetition of *guilt* on this page?

Tiffany:	It's all right there together with the "pity" parts: "get rid of her own guilt. I say guilt, gentlemen, because it was guilt that motivated her."
T:	What do you notice that connects this repetition?
Matt:	It's the same thing! It's all about Mayella being guilty, not Tom.
T:	I just want to point out some things Atticus does that matter in language to emphasize words. Certain placements make some words get emphasized more than others. Can you guess where in a sentence would get the most attention? Adam?
Adam:	The first part?
T:	The beginning of a sentence can be an important part—it kind of depends on what's there. Anywhere else?
Maria:	I think it could be the end, too.
T:	Sure. Look at the sentence that is the whole paragraph: "I have nothing but pity in my heart for the chief witness for the state, but my pity does not extend so far as to her putting a man's life at stake, which she has done in an effort to get rid of her own guilt." What words do you notice most?
Sara:	*Pity.*
William:	*State* and *stake.*
Brady:	*Guilt.*
Others:	Yeah.
T:	So putting the word *guilt* at the end of the long sentence can make it stand out. There are other things we can do to make people pay attention to words in the middle. One is to make a pause.
William:	Like the comma after *state* and *stake*?
T:	That's one way. Or right before or after the word we want emphasized we can use an interrupter surrounded by commas, as Atticus did when he said "I say guilt, gentlemen, because it was guilt that motivated her." He used *gentleman* as an interruptor to focus on *guilt*. Another is to use structures that take attention away from the first part of the sentence and put it somewhere else. For example, when we say "There is the ____" or "It was ____," we delay the focus word until later in the sentence. In this case, Atticus uses both these strategies to help us focus on guilt as it relates to Mayella. First, he says "I say guilt, gentlemen," which emphasizes the word *guilt* through the structure "I say ____" and through the pause after it,

"gentlemen." Then, right away, he comes back to the delaying structure, "because it was ____" to emphasize the guilt. Nice work on his part. Good job noticing it, Jenny. Before we go on to look at some of the sentences others have picked out, let me have you notice one other thing on this page that might be a good strategy. Remember at the beginning of the book when we talked about names, about how the names of the people in the town became associated with behaviors? We talked then about how important names are, so I want you to look at this first part of Atticus's speech and see whose names are brought up. What do you see?

Sara: Only Tom is mentioned by name.

Vanessa: Yeah, Atticus just says "witness" and "she" over and over again.

T: Look on the next page. Does Atticus ever use the Ewells' names?

William: Just for that one paragraph, the second one on page 204.

Brady: Yeah, it's almost all Tom's name.

T: What do you think the effect of that is on the jury—or at least could be?

Maria: Could it be that it makes Tom more important? Using his name and not theirs?

T: What do the rest of you think?

Leslie: Well, if someone says "she," it's kinda like they aren't a real person, you know? A name makes a person real. "She" can be anyone.

T: Why would that be an important idea for Atticus to plant in the jury's mind—at least along with the other ideas of pity and guilt?

Emily: I wonder, because the culture valued whites over blacks, if Atticus was trying to make Tom equal, at least as equal as he could, you know, by saying his name and not the Ewells'?

Several: Yeah.

T: I wonder that, too.

> **THOUGHTS FROM THE CLASSROOM**
>
> I'm introducing the "there transformation" and the "it-cleft transformation" (Kolln & Funk, 2006, pp. 332–333), both important grammatical concepts. However, because I want students to focus on the effects of the structures, I don't use the technical terms here.

> **THOUGHTS FROM THE CLASSROOM**
>
> Here, although I'm talking about pronouns, I'm doing it in a way that isn't separated from discussion of the text. What I want students to understand is not how to identify pronouns but how pronouns can be used—correctly, of course, but more important, to create an effect. I want students to be aware of how pronouns can work in ways beyond just filling in for a noun—at the same time, though, they are identifying pronouns. I agree with the statement from *Grammar Alive! A Guide for Teachers* that "knowing grammatical terminology is not an end in itself but a means toward greater awareness of how language and literature work" (Haussamen, 2003, p. 23). That's what I want this discussion to help students understand.

Someone told me a story about being on a jury. One point of evidence—a statement by a witness—was a point of contention in the jury room. The foreman, an English teacher, used grammar (explaining subordinate clauses) to help the rest of the jury accurately interpret the statement. Knowing something about language and grammar can help us read and understand better. Many publications by educators suggest using reading (i.e., mentor texts) to teach grammar and language for writing, and that's a great suggestion. But this chapter, focusing on the language of the IRA and NCTE (1996) standard connected to reading, centers on teaching grammar as a way to help students develop as readers and language users. Although many more teachers and researchers have written about using grammar to teach writing, some have also addressed its use with reading. In fact, in his case for teaching grammar, Mulroy (2003) asserts that "we increasingly encounter students who can speculate about the 'hidden meanings' of literary texts but miss their literal sense" (p. 17). He argues that the reason for this inability to comprehend the literal meaning is students' lack of knowledge about grammar, and he contends that grammar can help clarify meaning in texts. Particularly, he adds, "the study of grammar helps us to understand the great literature of the past" (p. 79). Certainly Doniger (2004) agrees when he describes how he uses grammar—"inverted word order and unexpected word usage," and "apposition, hyperbole and redundancy"— to aid students in their comprehension of plays written by William Shakespeare (p. 8).

Benjamin (2004) also uses grammar to help students become more effective readers. Although she uses grammar terms in her teaching of literature, she doesn't worry about how well the students know those terms: "You can't wait until students come to you already knowing what it is you wish to teach them.... Just start talking. Infuse the basics along with some more sophisticated concepts" (p. 3). Some teachers might worry that students won't "get" what the lesson is if they don't know the terms first. My experience is that students have enough general knowledge to understand the gist of the concepts, and they will learn what they need. The point is that this use of the terminology isn't about teaching grammar through literature as much it is teaching literature through grammar. A different goal means we focus on different things.

> **EXTENDING YOUR KNOWLEDGE**
>
> Standard 3: Students apply a wide range of strategies to comprehend, interpret, evaluate, and appreciate texts. They draw on their prior experience, their interactions with other readers and writers, their knowledge of word meaning and of other texts, their word identification strategies, and their understanding of textual features such as sound–letter correspondence, sentence structure, context, and graphics. (IRA & NCTE, 1996, n.p.)
>
> This standard encourages a broad approach to literature instruction that uses language as an integral part of that instruction.

Benjamin (2004) summarizes her approach as using "grammar as the flashlight to illuminate literature" (p. 5). I like that simile. Keeping that focus in mind helps give the language we discuss with our reading a purpose: Students will learn about grammar, about language, *and* about the texts we are reading. But Benjamin's admonition is clear: Use the grammar for the goals of improved comprehension, evaluation, and appreciation of the texts (as the IRA and NCTE standard urges) rather than for the goal of knowing the terminology.

What follows are some teaching suggestions for each of the five concepts discussed in chapter 1. Although the texts that are used as examples may not be ones used in your classroom, the ideas can be adapted to other texts and to a variety of grade levels.

Traditional Grammar

Grammar and Tone

I can never decide if I would rather have Halloween fall on a school day or not. The day after is often worse. There is no getting around the fact that the first major holiday after school starts has an impact on students, no matter what grade level they're in. I've tried ignoring the fact that I'm trying to teach Homer or William Shakespeare to a group of fully costumed ghouls, pirates, rock stars, babies, or bunnies. Instead, I've decided to embrace the day. I found a book that I can use to address the costumes and still feel as though I'm teaching students. The book, *Halloween Pie* (Tunnell, 1999), tells the story of a witch who bakes a pie and then casts a spell on it as she leaves it to cool on her windowsill. The regular Halloween cast—a vampire, a ghoul, a ghost, a banshee, a zombie, and a skeleton—catch the scent and eat the pie. What happens to them lets readers know what the spell is. It's a fun story, and it uses a lot of grammatical elements to make it work. So, as a class, we talk about grammar in the context of the book—how the story is enhanced by the grammar.

One thing I like about using *Halloween Pie*—or any picture book—is that students often have the mistaken belief that picture books are easy to write, that they aren't necessarily crafted in the same way longer stories or books are. Although the language is more accessible than that of Charles Dickens or William Shakespeare, the authors of picture books use just as much care to craft effective texts as other authors do. Although our discussion doesn't necessarily help students access complicated content, it does help them understand the care with language that all writers take to enhance the tone or message of their writing.

1. Begin by reading aloud the story—and showing the pictures—so that students know the plot. Then, go back to specific parts to explore the story through grammar. For instance, when the creatures get to the witch's house, they all yell for the pie, "Give me some pie!" But the dialogue tags are different: "called," "bawled," "sighed," "cried," "groaned," and "moaned." The verbs rhyme, but they also match the speaker (ghoul, banshee, and so forth). Discuss the author's choice to have each speaker say the same line: Is six times too many? Why or why not? How do the different tags help individualize the characters, especially when the dialogue is the same?

2. Eventually, the spell begins to take effect, and all the pie eaters fall asleep. Tunnell uses a series of six short sentences to describe this development, but each sentence uses a different verb and a different prepositional phrase to indicate where the crea-

ture slept: "fell asleep before the fire," "dreamed in an empty drawer," "dozed behind the door." Discuss the author's choices in using sentences of the same length and parallel structure and in varying the verbs used for the same action. Have students try to rewrite this section and see if combining the ideas is more or less effective. Focus the discussion on how the author's choices enhance a story in a picture book but might not be effective in other kinds of writing, such as research papers.

3. Later, when the witch returns home and finds the pie gone, she finds something else instead: "Loafing before the fire was a perfectly shaped pumpkin.... Scattered inside the drawer was a smidgeon of salt. Swinging from the rafters was a sack of sweet sugar" (n.p.). All the ingredients the witch needs to make a new pie—and all where the creatures had fallen asleep. After I tell students that the structures that begin the sentences are part of the verb phrase, we look at the sentence patterns. It's clear that the subject of the sentence is the last word or last part of the sentence. We talk about how we normally would say the sentences: "A perfectly shaped pumpkin was loafing before the fire," for example. Why did the author choose to rearrange the order? What is the effect? Students notice that the inverted order requires me to slow the reading down, thus focusing on plot and giving students a chance to make connections, because we didn't know what spell the witch had cast. Other students notice that the word order emphasizes where the ingredients are, linking the locations to the characters that had fallen asleep in those places. Sentence structure helps tie the sections of the story together, making it clearer for the reader.

Alternative Suggestion: If you don't have access to *Halloween Pie*, use another picture book, such as *Dear Fish* (Gall, 2006). In that book, most pages have a series of four words—verbs or nouns, although many of the nouns are gerunds—that add details to the story. Read the story without the repetition of the rhyming nouns and verbs, and then read it again with them included so that students see how the rhyming words add detail and depth to the story. Students could try adding detail to their own writing by inserting a series of verbs or a series of nouns, including gerunds—*ing* words acting as nouns. The secret is if you can put an article in front of it, *the* reading or *a* snorting, then it is acting like a noun. Students might experiment with the effect created, noticing how the repetition of specific parts of speech creates different tones.

This way of using discussions about parts of speech to look at textual effects could also be used with traditional (nonpicture) books. For example, the first few chapters of *A Tale of Two Cities* (Dickens, 1997) lend themselves to a discussion of how grammar enhances meaning. In the second chapter, for instance, the repeated use of conjunctions creates an interesting effect:

He walked uphill in the mire by the side of the mail, as the rest of the passengers did; not because they had the least relish for walking exercise, under the circumstances, but because the hill, and the harness, and the mud, and the mail, were all so heavy, that the horses had three times already come to a stop, besides once drawing the coach across the road, with the mutinous intent of taking it back to Blackheath. (pp. 15–16)

Whew! Don't we feel as tired as the passenger (did we forget this sentence was initially about that one man?) did? The repeated use of conjunctions slows the passage down; add in commas, prepositional phrases, and unusual word order, and the whole sentence begins to feel as if it, too, were climbing a hill through mud.

Thus, investigating grammar can help students comprehend their reading in ways that don't necessarily require them to know the terms of the structures they explore. Although I think this idea can be applied to almost any text, many of the historical texts we teach benefit from this application of grammar: *Wuthering Heights* (Bronte, 1988), *Pride and Prejudice* (Austen, 2005), *Great Expectations* (Dickens, 1963).

Grammar and Description

Referred to earlier in this chapter, Benjamin's (2004) example of using traditional grammar to help students better understand a text provides a good model. Her process is as follows:

1. She introduces *The Grapes of Wrath* (Steinbeck, 2002) by giving students a copy of the first paragraph—without modifiers. Students discuss the language and the mood that is being established.

2. Then she shows them the same paragraph with adjectives and adverbs, to help them feel "Steinbeck's use of color and texture" (Benjamin, 2004, p. 4).

3. Finally, she gives them the complete first paragraph with prepositional phrases added. "At this point, the text blossoms for us with its full intended effect, an effect so much more powerful because we withheld the detail" (p. 4).

Benjamin's process can work with different texts. For example, the beginning of *Where the Red Fern Grows* (Rawls, 1961) describes a dog fight in language that contains a lot of participles—more than are found in other parts of the chapter. There's a reason for that, and students can understand how the language itself adds to the meaning of the passage.

1. Begin the lesson with a short introduction to participles. They are words that look like verbs but act like adjectives. Although participles can end in *-ed* or *-ing*, the *-ing* forms are the easiest for students to understand, so those are the ones I begin with. In his book *Image Grammar: Using Grammatical Structures to Teach Writing*

Noden (1999) explains that "participles evoke action," and that "using single participles creates rapid movement, while expanded phrases add details at a slower, but equally intense pace" (pp. 4–5). Students can see how these concepts work in this passage from the novel. First, have students read the following passage without the participles:

I was trying to make up my mind to help when I got a surprise. Up out of that mass reared an old redbone hound. For a second I saw him. I caught my breath. I couldn't believe what I had seen.

He fought his way through the pack and backed up under the low branches of a hedge. They formed a halfmoon circle around him. A big bird dog, bolder than the others, darted in. The hedge shook as he tangled with the hound. He came out so fast he fell over backwards. I saw that his right ear was split wide open. It was too much for him and he took off down the street.

A big ugly cur tried his luck. He didn't get off so easy. He came out with his left shoulder laid open to the bone. He sat down on his rear and let the world know that he had been hurt.

By this time, my blood was boiling. It's hard for a man to stand and watch an old hound fight against such odds, especially if that man has memories in his heart like I had in mine. I had seen the time when an old hound like that had given his life so that I might live.

I waded in. My yelling and scolding didn't have much effect, but the coat did. The dogs scattered and left. (Rawls, 1961, p. 2, with parts deleted)

2. Ask students what they can see and hear in the passage. Most of the time, they have some answers; often, though, they'll have questions. After they share their responses, have students read the original passage, included below with participles and participial phrases italicized:

I was trying to make up my mind to help when I got a surprise. Up out of that *snarling, growling, slashing* mass reared an old redbone hound. For a second I saw him. I caught my breath. I couldn't believe what I had seen.

Twisting and slashing, he fought his way through the pack and backed up under the low branches of a hedge. *Growling and snarling,* they formed a halfmoon circle around him. A big bird dog, bolder than the others, darted in. The hedge shook as he tangled with the hound. He came out so fast he fell over backwards. I saw that his right ear was split wide open. It was too much for him and he took off down the street, *squalling like a scalded cat.*

A big ugly cur tried his luck. He didn't get off so easy. He came out with his left shoulder laid open to the bone. He sat down on his rear and let the world know that he had been hurt.

By this time, my *fighting* blood was boiling. It's hard for a man to stand and watch an old hound fight against such odds, especially if that man has memories in his heart like I had in mine. I had seen the time when an old hound like that had given his life so that I might live.

Taking off my coat, I waded in. My yelling and scolding didn't have much effect, but the *swinging* coat did. The dogs scattered and left. (p. 2)

3. Now ask students the same question: What can they see and hear? They'll have more to say now with the participles added. Students should also note, however, that along with adding sensory details, the participles—those "-ing words" that we deleted in the first version—actually intensify the ferocity of the fight. The words themselves, their meanings and their sounds, help to create the action in and movement of the fight: twisting and slashing, growling and snarling.

4. In order for students to see the effect of the participles in creating action, have students add to participles or take away from them and compare the effect. For instance, look at the participial phrase that ends the second paragraph—*squalling like a scalded cat.* What is the effect if we say only "squalling"? It's faster. Have students add details to the other participles and then consider the effect: "Twisting *his red body* and slashing *at the dogs with his paws,* he fought his way through the pack.... Growling *deep in their throats* and snarling *through their teeth,* they formed a halfmoon circle around him." The effect is very different. Slower. Not as tight or quick as the scene that's written in the book—or the scene as it was taking place.

5. Have students read the rest of the first chapter, looking for participles and participial phrases. Students should notice that there aren't very many. Have them speculate why that might be. They should see that the presence of the participles, especially the one-word kind, aren't as necessary in this chapter for the ideas that have to do with healing and that show a slower, less intense pace. When students approach the end of the book, help them review this lesson by looking again for participles in the scene where the narrator and his dogs are attacked by a mountain lion. In that passage (pp. 225–228) many participles and participial phrases are used to show action and create intensity.

   In their enthusiasm, students sometimes confuse verbs that end in -ing with participles. That's something teachers should anticipate and is a distinction they should be ready to clarify: Although the two look alike, when the word is the action, it's a verb. When it's describing the actor, it's a participle. Students also sometimes notice that some verbs ending in -ing act like nouns, as *yelling* and *scolding* do in the next to the last sentence. Those are gerunds. Although students might not care to know the name, it's a good idea to be prepared in case they identify them in their search.

Alternative Suggestion: This plan can be applied to any text that uses participles in the same way—to represent action or to create intensity. In the near final scene of *Lord of the Flies* (Golding, 1954), before the boys are rescued, Ralph is running from the fire and the "savage" (p. 184). That passage is full of participles and participial phrases that create an intense feeling of panic. In another text, *Mississippi Trial, 1955* (Crowe, 2002), longer participial phrases create intensity of emotion: "I wrapped my arms around Grampa's neck and hugged him while we cried together, mourning the loss of a wife and grandmother and friend, wondering how we could possibly survive without her" (p. 28). Students could rewrite the passage as three sentences, noticing the effect the use of the participial phrases creates in that significant moment. As we spot these structures in our reading, we can help students see how they are useful to understanding the text and the language that creates emotion for readers.

You can apply this process to any element of grammar. In *Mississippi Trial, 1955*, Crowe (2002) makes effective use of adjectives to set scenes:

> Ralph and Ronnie Remington even came over to pay their respects. Ronnie wore a black suit coat stretched to button across his wide belly; a limp bow tie hung cockeyed from the collar of his white shirt. Ralph wore a blue tuxedo jacket with navy blue pants, shiny at the knees. He carried a champagne bottle with a wide purple bow tied around its neck. Both men looked about as comfortable as cows in a slaughterhouse. (p. 29)

Using a process modeled after Benjamin's (2004), prepare copies of the text without the adjectives so that students can recognize how grammatical elements contribute to the mood and message of a text. Other books with passages that make use of specific verbs or unique adjectives to set a mood include *A Separate Peace* (Knowles, 1959, pp. 4–6, 22–23) and *Lord of the Flies* (Golding, 1954, pp. 7–8, 134–135).

Editing

Punctuation and Pausing

In *Eats, Shoots & Leaves: The Zero Tolerance Approach to Punctuation*, Truss (2003) establishes a base for explaining how punctuation can affect meaning: "On the page, punctuation performs its grammatical function, but in the mind of the reader it does more than that. It tells the reader how to hum the tune" (p. 71). When students hear passages with effective punctuation read aloud, they gain a sense of how punctuation matters, how it helps create meaning.

In *My Antonia* (Cather, 1954), the punctuation is especially effective when reading aloud. In the following passage, Cather uses commas to good effect, but she also makes use of dashes, semicolons, and colons to create pauses of different lengths and intensity.

1. Begin by having students close their eyes and listen as you read aloud the passage. Then have students follow along in the text as you read aloud the passage again.

When spring came, after that hard winter, one could not get enough of the nimble air. Every morning I wakened with a fresh consciousness that winter was over. There were none of the signs of spring for which I used to watch in Virginia, no budding woods or blooming gardens. There was only—spring itself; the throb of it, the light restlessness, the vital essence of it everywhere: in the sky, in the swift clouds, in the pale sunshine, and in the warm, high wind—rising suddenly, sinking suddenly, impulsive and playful like a big puppy that pawed you and the lay down to be petted. If I had been tossed down blindfold on that red prairie, I should have known that it was spring. (Cather, 1954, pp. 119–120)

2. During a third read-aloud, ask students to measure which marks of punctuation create the longest or most emphatic pauses—down to those that create the softest or shortest of the ones used in this passage. Then have students get into small groups to discuss their findings (they often argue about them) before holding a whole-class discussion of what they felt. Ask them to relate their findings to the effects the different pauses create in the text. How do longer pauses focus attention on what the writer wants the reader to focus on? How do softer pauses allow for less focus? Even if students don't agree on their findings, such a discussion helps students understand how punctuation marks matter to a piece of writing, how they help create meaning.

Alternative Suggestion: Any passage in a book that uses varying kinds of punctuation can be used in the same way to raise students' awareness of the connection between punctuation and reading and meaning. This is especially true of poetry, including poems by Emily Dickinson and Robert Frost.

Punctuation and Meaning

Another way to look at punctuation's influence on meaning is by analyzing how a writer uses a particular point of punctuation. I use an approach similar to one suggested by Petit (2003), but with "A Modest Proposal" (Swift, 1996).

1. Make sure that students have an understanding of satire and irony before reading the essay. After reading it, have students explore Swift's intent and meaning through discussion, possibly addressing some of the following questions, among others:

   • How does Swift establish his credibility in the essay? Why is it important that he do so?

- What kind of evidence does Swift use to support his assertions? Why are those types of evidence useful to him?
- Where is the evidence that Swift is being satirical and not serious?

It's important to help students understand the text (this or any other used in this application) before moving on to an analysis of the use of punctuation in helping to create meaning—because the point isn't so much the use of punctuation as it is its effect on the content.

> **EXTENDING YOUR KNOWLEDGE**
>
> In "The Stylish Semicolon: Teaching Punctuation as Rhetorical Choice," Petit (2003) describes her analysis of semicolons in Martin Luther King Jr.'s "Letter From Birmingham Jail." She asserts, "Only by exploring language in context, written for a particular time and place, can students discern the subtle ways that punctuation affects meaning" (p. 70). Having students work through this kind of analysis not only improves their reading abilities, but it also improves their abilities to think about and use punctuation effectively.

2. Have students work in small groups to identify sentences in the essay that use semicolons. Then, ask students to cluster the sentences they found into pairs or groups that use semicolons in the same way, as shown in the following examples:

The question therefore is how this number shall be reared and provided for; which, as I have already said, under the present situation of affairs, is utterly impossible by all the methods hitherto proposed. (Swift, 1996, p. 802)

But as to myself, having been wearied out for many years with offering vain, idle, visionary thought, and at length utterly despairing of success, I fortunately fell upon this proposal; which, as it is wholly new, so it hath something solid and real, of no expense and little trouble, full in our own power, and whereby we can incur no danger in disobliging England. (p. 808)

Or this example:

Some persons of a desponding spirit are in great concern about the vast number of poor people who are aged, diseased, or maimed; and I have been desired to employ my thoughts what course may be taken to ease the nation of so grievous an encumbrance. (p. 805)

And as to the younger laborers, they are now in almost as hopeful a condition: they cannot get work and consequently pine away for want of nourishment to a degree that if at any time they are accidentally hired to common labor, they have not strength to perform it; and thus the country and themselves are in a fair way of being soon delivered from the evils to come. (p. 806)

Or this example:

For we can neither employ them in handicraft or agriculture; we neither build houses (I mean in the country) nor cultivate land. (p. 802)

Thus the squire will learn to be a good landlord and grow popular among his tenants; the mother will have eight shillings net profit and be fit for work until she produces another child. (p. 804)

Students should be able to find several more examples for these patterns and at least one more pattern of semicolon use in the essay. When students have made the groups of sentences, have them give a name to the way the semicolon is used to combine ideas in each grouping. For instance, for the first pair I show, they might call it the "'which' combination." Students may develop different names for groups of sentences, and that's OK. Naming the groups is not an activity meant to measure correctness; it is simply a way for students to label what they've found in order to compare it more effectively with other constructions.

3. Next, have students look for nonexamples. That is, have them find sentences with the same structure that do *not* use the semicolon. So, for the first pair, I give students the following sentence: "I shall now therefore humbly propose my own thoughts, which I hope will not be liable to the least objection" (p. 803). They might say that the sentence has a first "part" followed by a second "part" that begins with *which*; they will probably not identify the parts as clauses, which is OK. Next, have students compare the examples with nonexamples and begin to generalize about the reason for the semicolon's use when it is used. For example, students might decide that the use of the semicolon in the "'which' combination" actually makes readers pay more attention to the two separate ideas than they would in the nonexample. The semicolon creates a more noticeable pause between the two parts; if a person were reading the sentences aloud (a good suggestion for this analysis), the voice tends to drop more, as it would for a sentence-ending punctuation rather than the slighter pause necessitated by the more common comma. Thus, we read the two parts with more emphasis on each part. Students should consider why Swift would want that emphasis in the examples and not in the nonexamples. As they do so, their insight on the satire and meaning of the essay increases.

Alternative Suggestion: This procedure can be used with any text (or parts of texts) that use punctuation in interesting ways. Thoreau's *Walden and Civil Disobedience* (1980), Wordsworth's "Ode: Intimations of Immortality" (1996), and Stoker's *Dracula* (1988) are such texts. But you can also use the process with other punctuation that provides insight on how a text is written (and, thus, how it carries meaning). For example, *The Woman Warrior* (Kingston, 1989) would serve as a noteworthy study of the use of dashes and the way they contribute to tone and meaning in a text.

EXTENDING YOUR KNOWLEDGE

Warne (2006) says that "punctuation imitates what our voices do when we speak" (p. 25). If we can help our students see that punctuation aids meaning when the speaker is absent, we can move them a long way toward understanding nuances of language.

Teachers with whom I have shared this process have found many texts that benefit from paying attention to punctuation as a way to delve more deeply into meaning. And when students are paying attention to punctuation in this way, even though they may not immediately apply it (although I would recommend such application—write a paragraph about the satire in Swift's essay and use semicolons at least once to create an effect as he did), they will still be developing sensitivity to aspects of language that are important to them as readers and writers.

Usage

Dialect and Emotion

In *Their Eyes Were Watching God*, Hurston (1998) uses dialect to help readers "see" characters' feelings in ways that Standard English might not allow. Such use of dialect points to limitations of Standard English rather than issues of power normally associated with usage. In fact, the novel's foreword includes an account of how the novel was unaccepted during the 1940s and acknowledges language as a contributor to that lack of acceptance: "The quieter voice of a woman searching for self-realization could not, or would not, be heard" (p. x).

1. Prepare students for the characters' language by reading aloud at least some of the book. By listening to the language as they follow along in their texts, students can feel and hear the rhythm of the language—and see how meaning is carried in more than the words alone. Hearing the voices aloud at first helps me to create the voices in my head so that later, while reading to myself, I can still hear those voices and their rhythm and usage. That's what I want to do for students, too.

2. As you read the book, notice places in the text (I'll identify two here) where the usage shifts—midparagraph—from more standard usage to the dialect of the characters. After students read these passages, ask them why they think the author constructed the passage the way she did.

So Janie began to think of Death. Death, that strange being with the huge square toes who lived way in the West. The great one who lived in the straight house like a platform without sides to it, and without a roof. What need has Death for a cover, and what winds can blow against him? He stands in his high house that overlooks the world. Stands watchful and motionless all day with his sword drawn back, waiting for the messenger to bid him come. Been standing there before there was a where or a when or a then. She was liable to find a feather from his wings lying in her yard any day now. She was sad and afraid too. Poor Jody! He ought not to have to wrassle in there by himself. She sent Sam to suggest a visit, but Jody said No. These medical doctors wuz all right with the Godly sick, but they didn't know a thing about a case like his. (Hurston, 1998, p. 84)

The thing made itself into pictures and hung around Janie's bedside all night long. Anyhow, she wasn't going back to Eatonville to be laughed at and pitied. She had ten dollars in her pocket and twelve hundred in the bank. But oh God, don't let Tea Cake be off somewhere hurt and Ah not know nothing about it. And God, please suh, don't let him love nobody else but me. Maybe Ah'm is uh fool, Lawd, lak dey say, but Lawd, Ah been so lonesome, and Ah been waitin', Jesus. Ah done waited uh long time. (p. 120)

Use questions like the following to guide discussion:

- What does it reveal to shift usage in these passages? What do these shifts represent in terms of the characters? In terms of plot? In terms of social and cultural relationships?
- What meaning might such shifts have in our own use of language?
- What does consideration of this shifting nature of language tell us about the social aspects of language, not only the language we use with others but the language we use in our most private thoughts?

In one response to these questions, the shifts seem to suggest the inadequacy of standard usage to represent our deepest feelings or emotions. Gates (1998) interprets this shifting between vernacular and the Standard English of the narrator's voice as "a verbal analogue" that represents being a "woman in a male-dominated world and...a black person in a nonblack [sic] world" (p. 203).

3. Have students consider how usage connects to our emotions and to the roles we play as we move through different situations in our lives. Have students reflect on their own more obvious shifts in usage—writing a text message versus writing an essay for school. These shifts also reflect roles and relationships in varying social situations.

4. Guide students to consider their own uses of language in connection with other passages from the novel that address issues of voice and language, passages such as this one: "There is a basin in the mind where words float around on thought and thought on sound and sight...there is a depth of thought untouched by words, and deeper still a gulf of formless feelings untouched by thought" (p. 24). Do we have feelings and thoughts that we don't have words for? Or note this one from the trial: "She felt them pelting her with dirty thoughts...were there with their tongues cocked and loaded, the only real weapon left to weak folks. The only killing tool they are allowed to use in the presence of white folks" (pp. 185–186). Considering these passages in connection to shifts in usage can help students understand social aspects of language in relation to the personal.

Alternative Suggestion: A favorite picture book of mine, *Show Way* (Woodson, 2005), works in a similar way, showing how dialect can open readers to emotion. The rhythm of the vernacular lets us into the feelings of the women in the book: "Had herself a baby girl and named that child Mathis Way. Loved that baby up so. Yes, she loved that baby up" (n.p.). If this passage were written in Standard English, readers would be unable to sense the emotion and personality communicated through the dialect.

Dialect and Character

One of the charms of *The Adventures of Huckleberry Finn* (Twain, 1988) is the use of dialect to reveal the characters. In the Explanatory Note preceding the text, Twain identifies the specific dialects he uses and indicates that he names them so that readers will notice the differences. Certainly there is some underlying message in the satirical tone, but with this note Twain opens the conversation about language and usage. What will readers expect to hear in the voices of this book? Students can predict—and as soon as they begin reading, they will see:

> EXTENDING YOUR KNOWLEDGE
>
> Bomer (2006) notes that good readers hear shifts in voices, hear the way different voices sound—including the narrator's voice: "To read...without hearing a shift in voice is to lose much of the pleasure of the text and is also probably a good sign that the reader is not making meaning" (p. 525). Helping our students learn to hear those different voices helps them improve as readers.

> You don't know about me without you have read a book by the name of *The Adventures of Tom Sawyer*; but that ain't no matter. That book was made by Mr. Mark Twain, and he told the truth, mainly. There was things which he stretched, but mainly he told the truth. That is nothing. I never seen anybody but lied one time or another, without it was Aunt Polly. (p. 1)

Right away we can see that this book offers language that is not the kind we expect from more formal situations. There are issues of standardized usage ("there was things" and "ain't") as well as dialectal issues ("without you"). As different characters speak throughout the novel, readers are able to see different levels of formality in their usage, which should encourage discussion as to what these uses of language reveal about the characters.

1. Begin by making sure students understand what is meant by levels of formality. I like a version that Strong (2001) provides. He identifies three style levels: high, middle, and low. For each style level he notes the voice, diction, syntax, and contexts associated with that level of formality. So, for instance, he notes that high style is formal and detached, uses abstract words or words that draw attention to themselves in long sentences and fully developed paragraphs. High style is used in contexts that are usually formal or ceremonial. By contrast, the low (informal) style is chatty and rambling, using slang words and contractions in syntax that mirrors speech. This style is more appropriate for journals and e-mails. If students think about word

choice, sentence complexity and style, and general tone, they are usually able to consider revising usage and then contemplating its effect in different situations.

2. Once students understand levels of formality, ask them to revise the beginning sentence (or more) of the novel so that it sounds formal or academic, perhaps like this: "Unless you've read *The Adventures of Tom Sawyer*, you might not know about me." That would be one way. Another would be this: "Unless you've perused *The Adventures of Tom Sawyer*, you may not be acquainted with me." That's even more formal. When students have created one or two more formal revisions of sentences from *The Adventures of Huckleberry Finn*, discuss the different effects: Why is the original sentence in the book more appropriate for that context? How would we interpret Huck's character if one of the other voices (from rewritten sentences) had been used?

3. Repeat this practice at different points in the book. Have students rewrite informal language in varying degrees of formality and have them determine the appropriate place for each level of formality. Examples such as the following are possible: In a conversation between Huck and the Judge in chapter 4, contrast the Judge's more formal language with Huck's; the Judge rarely uses contractions and his sentences tend to be more complex in structure than Huck's. Later in that chapter, we hear Jim's voice; it contrasts in formality with Huck's in a similar way as Huck's contrasted with the Judge's. Helping our students recognize the different voices and how making them all the same would detract from the characterization of the novel can also help them recognize the varying degrees of usage formality in their own lives—and see that questions of formal and informal usage are not questions of "right" and "wrong" so much as they are questions of appropriateness.

Alternative Suggestion: Other books that show characters using different dialects or levels of formality in language can be used for the same application. *Cold Sassy Tree* (Burns, 1984), *A Day No Pigs Would Die* (Peck, 1972), and *Monster* (Myers, 1999) are three options. In *The Catcher in the Rye* (Salinger, 1991), language is an issue; it is also reflective of character. When using any of these texts, have students consider how the different levels of language help to reflect the characters. How might the characters be differently represented if they were assigned the same usage—formal or informal, slang or dialect?

EXTENDING YOUR KNOWLEDGE	

EXTENDING YOUR KNOWLEDGE

"To help students discover grammar, you need to show them that they can discover grammar wherever they find language" (Haussamen, 2003, p. 16). This is especially true of levels of formality. Helping students see how language shifts for its myriad uses is part of teaching them grammar.

Certain picture books can also be used to help students understand how levels of formality help to create authentic characters. *The Perfect Pumpkin Pie* (Cazet, 2005) uses dialect to reveal character. From his first full sentence in the book, "I does love a perfect pie," Old Man Wilkerson reveals himself to be the ideal character to become an irascible ghost—unlike Grandma with her more standard language. Other picture books with similar traits include *Flossie and the Fox* (McKissack, 1986), where the dialogue alternates between vernacular and standardized dialects. Using books like these in the classroom can help students learn about the richness of the English language—in all its varieties—and how dialects help authors reflect character.

Also consider using newspaper articles or magazine articles that have quotations from people who may be using various levels of formality in their language. Following the same practice as above (rewriting the quotations in varying levels of formality), have students consider the same questions: How is language formality a function of situation? How does it reveal character?

Discussions could also occur with a number of pieces of literature that show language use differing from one group to another or from one situation to another. Calpurnia changes dialects in *To Kill a Mockingbird* when she takes the children to church—and she explains why she makes the shift: "Now what if I talked white-folks' talk at church, and with my neighbors? They'd think I was puttin' on airs to beat Moses.... It's not ladylike.... It aggravates 'em" (Lee, 1960, p. 126). In *The Bean Trees* (Kingsolver, 1988), when Lou Ann meets Taylor, she says, "You talk just like me" (p. 102). That observation provides an occasion to discuss the dialects of the two characters, especially what constitutes a dialect because, in some ways, the women's speech isn't very different from informal speech found in other areas around the United States.

Sensitive Language

Sometimes objections are raised to reading specific novels in the classroom because of their use of painful language, including racial slurs. It certainly is something I'm sensitive to when I teach those books.

1. Prepare students for understanding texts appropriately by helping them see why authors use such language—and it's not because they value it or want to perpetuate it. Mildred Taylor, in her "Note to the Reader" in *The Land* (2003), has this to say about her use of painful language in her novels:

    All of my books are based on stories told by my family, and on the history of the United States. In my writing I have attempted to be true to those stories and the history. I have included characters, incidents, and language that present life as it was in many parts of the United States before the Civil Rights Movement. Although there are those who wish to ban my books because I have used language that is painful, I have chosen to use the language that was spoken during the period, for I refuse to white-wash history. The language was painful and life was painful for many African Americans, including my family.
        I remember the pain. (n.p.)

    When we teach novels containing language that is painful—slurs, epithets, name calling—it's important to help students understand that such language is meant not to be emulated but to add knowledge of the situation. Sharing Taylor's note is a good way to begin.

2. Before reading *To Kill a Mockingbird* (Lee, 1960), ask students to watch for which characters use racial slurs. By doing so, they can begin to see why an author might choose to use the language as a way to portray characters as well as situations more effectively. As students read have them pay attention to why the slur is used and to the intent of the author in making use of a painful term. This is an ongoing observation. When students find the use of the word, they should ask, Who is speaking? What might be the author's intent in using these words in this place, with this character? When we've finished the novel, my students usually conclude that it's the ignorant characters—the Ewells or Miss Stephanie or, occasionally, children—who use such terms. Calpurnia, however, does use a racial slur once in a confrontation with another church member who objects to Jem and Scout being at the church (Lee, 1960, p. 119); Naylor's essay (1999) about the significance of context can help explain this case. She remembers that although she had heard a derogatory word before, its meaning was different when spoken by someone outside of her community: "The people in my grandmother's living room took a word that whites used to signify worthlessness or degradation and rendered it impotent" (p. 269). Calpurnia's use of the word, then, is different. Although Scout uses the term (repeating what she hears), she isn't aware of the pain attached to the word; in fact, when she uses other offensive words, her uncle concludes that she doesn't really "know the meaning of half she says" (Lee, 1960, p. 87). The characters that are meant to be respected—Atticus or Miss Maudie—do not use such terms. In this way, we are able to see how painful language provides insight on the novels we read, showing the trouble and hurt of the characters. The language, then, becomes not something to continue so much as something to avoid.

    I need to acknowledge that the use of this essay by Naylor has been challenged in at least one school district (deVise, 2007). However, the challenge seems to have developed from the way the teacher presented the essay: reading it aloud, "imitat[ing] stereotypical African American body language and elocution" (p. A01), and asking students to mark each use of the epithet. Certainly any discussion on such a sensitive topic needs to be handled with care and compassion. Too much of a focus—through extended discussion or repeated verbal use of hurtful terms—undermines the point of teaching students about hate speech.

    Alternative Suggestion: Other books, including *Roll of Thunder, Hear My Cry* (Taylor, 1976), *The Adventures of Huckleberry Finn* (Twain, 1988), or *Mississippi Trial, 1955*

EXTENDING YOUR KNOWLEDGE

Harmon and Wilson (2006) suggest that hate words "are so commonly spoken that persons who use them sometimes fail to see the depths of hate they convey and the damage they do" (p. 80). Helping students understand this can benefit them in and out of school. Harmon and Wilson also note that "members of groups have privileges not granted to members outside the group" (p. 83). Students can consider other terms they use within groups that they don't allow outsiders to use in the same way.

(Crowe, 2002), also use racial terms in ways that are meant to reflect the pain of some characters at the same time as they reveal the insensitivity or thoughtlessness of others. Discussing this sensitive issue from the position of an author's choice to present difficult situations helps students see the use of such language from a more positive perspective—and not as language they would want to use themselves.

Language Change

Names and Naming

In *Romeo and Juliet* (Shakespeare, 1969), Juliet suggests that names don't change identity in her famous line "A rose by any other name would smell as sweet" (act 2, scene 2, lines 43–44). However, most of us know that naming is a serious action—and we are aware that the names people use to label others for good or ill often stick. Sometimes those names are words that have been around for a long time but are now being used in new ways (two such names are *pimp* and *gay*), but the use of the names carries emotional baggage. Considering names and their associations with them can help students understand the power language has over people.

1. In *I Know Why the Caged Bird Sings* (Angelou, 1969), Marguerite's name is changed on a whim by Mrs. Cullinan, who feels the name Marguerite is too long. Have students read the passage aloud.

    Every person I knew had a hellish horror of being "called out of his name." It was a dangerous practice to call a Negro anything that could be loosely construed as insulting because of the centuries of their having been called niggers, jigs, dinges, blackbirds, crows, boots and spooks.
      Miss Glory had a fleeting second of feeling sorry for me. Then as she handed me the hot tureen she said, "Don't mind, don't pay no mind. Sticks and stones may break your bones, but words...." (p. 109)

    In the book, Miss Glory goes on to explain that 20 years earlier her name was changed from Hallelujah to Glory by Mrs. Cullinan. Of course Marguerite is stunned: "Imagine letting some white woman rename you for her convenience" (p. 109). Marguerite then does everything she can to get herself fired.

2. After reading this passage with students, discuss how names are significant. Does the adage about sticks and stones really hold true? How does language hurt, even when the names we are called are not the traditional ones that are considered hurtful? How does our name connect to our identity—and then how important is it to have people call us by our names and not mispronounce or misconstrue them?

Alternative Suggestion: Any book that deals with name calling or renaming in some way could be used for a similar discussion. *Freak the Mighty* (Philbrick, 2001) is one such option. Another book that addresses naming is *The House on Mango Street* (Cisneros, 1984).

Shakespeare's Words

New words come into the English language through numerous avenues: creating new words to meet new needs, borrowing from other languages, or processes such as shortening to acronyms and alphabetisms (Curzan & Adams, 2006, p. 484). Students could even consider how they now use *google* as a verb for searching on the Internet, where it originated as the name of a search engine, as an example of word change. One of the challenges for students when reading Shakespeare is the language—and not all of it is the syntax. Some of it is the vocabulary. Shakespeare is credited with creating more than 1,000 words (McQuain & Malless, 1998, p. viii), many that we still use today. He created most of his new words through "a handful of word-making practices" (p. ix): by using them as different parts of speech (using nouns as verbs and the reverse), by combining words never combined before, and by using prefixes and suffixes in unique ways. Part of understanding Shakespeare means understanding the language of his day, how it has changed since, and how the English language is changed because of him.

1. Introduce the topic of language in Shakespeare by having a discussion of a word common to many of his plays. In *Romeo and Juliet*, Gregory uses the word *marry* in a way that students find confusing. Read a passage where the word is found (e.g., act 1, scene 1, line 39), and ask students what it sounds like the term might mean without looking in the text notes. Most of the time, my students say it sounds like a swear word or some slang term. Notes in my text show they are close to the mark: It means "indeed (originally an oath to the Virgin Mary)" (1969, p. 15). Students can see that the spelling has already changed through time (*Mary* to *marry*), and we no longer use the word at all; we have a different one (*indeed*) instead.

2. Ask students to think of other words that are an abbreviated version or name of something else, which we use like slang—"John Doe" comes to mind as the name for someone we cannot identify.

3. Share with students the cartoon of Calvin and his mother using Shakespearean language shown in Figure 3. Have students translate the dialogue into modern language and discuss what differences they see. Then, have them take a different comic (one with character interaction) and rewrite it using Shakespearean language. Sharing these as a class can help students overcome some of the fear they feel and become more comfortable with Elizabethan language.

4. Prompt students to consider words they don't know from the perspective of language change as they continue to read the play: Are these words still in use today? If so, how are they changed? If not, what do we have to replace them? An example

FIGURE 3. Calvin and Hobbes Cartoon: Shakespearean Language

is the word *morrow*, which most students think means "tomorrow." According to the *Oxford English Dictionary (OED) Online*, it more likely meant "morning," but it can also mean "tomorrow." Because Shakespeare had the option of *morn* (more common in his day than *morning*) or *morrow* (more common in his day than *tomorrow*), why choose what he chose?

5. The following are words and phrases coined by Shakespeare to which teachers can draw students' attention in *Romeo and Juliet*. These terms show how language grows. Other words that we no longer use, found in the margins of most versions of the play, can be shown as examples of how language fades.

   • In act 2, scene 4, lines 71–73, Mercutio uses the phrase "wild-goose chase" to describe their witty exchange—coined to resemble the way one goose leads others in formation and only later connoting the idea of futility, according to McQuain and Malless (1998).

   • In act 1, scene 3, line 76, the Nurse uses the phrase "man of wax" in describing Paris to Juliet. In other words, he was a model figure, in those days made of wax (such as in a wax museum of famous people). My students are always intrigued by the term. Discuss who might qualify as a "man of wax" today— and what term(s) we use for such people today (McQuain & Malless, 1998).

   • I first heard the term "burning daylight" in a John Wayne movie. I thought it was a term used by cowboys. Imagine my surprise to find the term used in *Romeo and Juliet* (act 1, scene 4, line 43) and cited by *OED* as being coined by Shakespeare. The phrase means "to waste time," and Romeo's friends use it when they are on their way to the party where Romeo and Juliet will meet. Students can talk about why the term is used (relating to burning lamps) and why we might not use it so much today. Why was it more appropriate, say, for cowboys?

Alternative Suggestion: Reading any of Shakespeare's plays allows for plenty of talk about language change—both growth and decline. *The Scarlet Letter* (Hawthorne, 1986) and *The Crucible* (Miller, 1976) are two other works often taught in English classes that allow us to address language change because each text uses words that are no longer commonly spoken today. Giving students the opportunity to research the origins of words is also beneficial in helping them learn about language change—and see it as a natural process.

Rhetorical Grammar

Structure and Meaning

In *Night* (Wiesel, 2006), there is one passage in particular that can be used to exemplify the use of text passages to teach rhetorical grammar—that is, to show how texts can help students understand that rhetorical choices are important to meaning. This may be a more powerful example than some other texts contain, but all good pieces of literature have passages that can be studied for the rhetorical effects of the grammatical choices found therein. The processes for any passage would be similar; only the choices and effects would differ.

1. Begin by reading the passage with students.

   Never shall I forget that night, the first night in camp, that turned my life into one long night seven times sealed.
   Never shall I forget that smoke.
   Never shall I forget the small faces of the children whose bodies I saw transformed into smoke under a silent sky.
   Never shall I forget those flames that consumed my faith forever.
   Never shall I forget the nocturnal silence that deprived me for all eternity of the desire to live.
   Never shall I forget those moments that murdered my God and my soul and turned my dreams to ashes.
   Never shall I forget those things, even were I condemned to live as long as God Himself.
   Never. (p. 34)

2. After reading the passage, ask students how it makes them feel. This exploration of emotional response is important so that they can connect what they feel to the choices the writer makes. The passage comes right after Wiesel and his father think they are going to die but, at the last moment, are instead herded into the barracks. His father reminds him of the woman on the train who screamed about the fires; they had assumed she was insane. They knew now that she was not. This passage is a

powerful way of saying that what they experienced is beyond words, beyond description. It can only be conveyed through this moving commentary—and students feel the weight of the passage, even if they sometimes lack the words to describe their emotions.

3. Next ask students what they notice grammatically about the text. They generally notice what you expect they will: The repeated use of "Never shall I forget" at the start of every statement—and then "Never" by itself at the end. Ask them why Wiesel didn't say "I shall never forget" instead. Usually, students decide that putting the word *Never* first is more powerful than *I* would be. Wiesel wants the eternity of his memory to be emphasized, and his deliberate syntactical choices create that effect.

4. Students may ask about the use of "shall" instead of "will" in this passage. This is an interesting question. The "rule" is that *shall* is used in the first person—*I shall*—and *will* is used in second and third person—*you will, he will* to portray simple futurity. However, both my dictionary and my usage books suggest that this "rule" is rarely followed in actual speech, especially in the United States and especially among younger speakers. As such, sometimes students think its use here is formal or old fashioned. They wonder if that was intentional. Good question. In some cases, because the rule is so seldom followed in regular use, *shall* can also connote the inevitable or something that must occur. Because *Night* is a translation, it's not clear whether the translator adhered to usage rules, if the original had the sense of *shall* more than *will*, or if the speaker is being formal. Discuss the options with students—but it's hard to say for sure whether or not this is a rhetorical choice. We can discuss only the effects, not whether those effects were deliberately caused, which brings up another interesting point!

5. Sometimes students notice the formatting of the passage. Because the rest of the book is not formatted this way, but more like a novel, we can assume the formatting (indenting each statement as a paragraph) is deliberate. Discuss with students the effect of single-sentence paragraphs, even single-word paragraphs. Paragraphs are a concept students think they know by the time they read *Night*: Each contains five to seven sentences each, have a topic sentence, and are focused on a single idea. But, as Schuster (2003) notes, "The reality is that there is no such thing as *the* paragraph" (p. 144). Through examples he shows that paragraphing changes depending on what genre is being written. I tell my students that paragraphs are the writer's way to tell the reader to consider certain ideas together and then other ideas together and so on. It's a way to control how the ideas are connected in the mind of the reader. So, if Wiesel wants each sentence to be separate rather than connected, he is telling us something with that choice. Have students consider what that might be. They usually conclude that he wants each image to be considered separately, not as part of the whole. In that way, the experience becomes fragmented

but also more intense. Readers aren't allowed to crowd the whole experience into a neat package. It must be considered in this broken way.

6. Finally, ask students to notice, if they haven't already, the content of the statements. They sometimes have to be guided to discover that the images, after the first general statement, move from concrete to abstract: smoke, faces, flames, silence, moments, things. This, too, is a rhetorical choice, and students can consider why Wiesel would put the statements in this particular order. If necessary, read them in the reverse order, so students can feel the difference. Most of the time students decide that starting with the abstract is less powerful, that they need the concrete images first so that they have something to hold onto before they get to the *silence* and the *moments* and the *things*. This thinking about the levels of abstraction and how they create rhetorical effects is helpful to them both as readers and as writers.

7. In informal writing, have students reflect on how the rhetorical choices Wiesel made in this passage enhance the meaning of the passage and, ultimately, the book (at least to this point). Their reflections can aid them in understanding the text more fully.

Alternative Suggestion: Although the choices of rhetorical devices and effects change, many texts lend themselves to this type of questioning process as a way to understand texts better. Any passage that has emotional impact usually has devices and structures that contribute to that impact. Letting students discover those devices and structures in relation to the emotions they find in them builds their sense of rhetorical grammar. I have found *The House on Mango Street* (Cisneros, 1984) useful toward this end. The chapter titled "Those Who Don't" (p. 28) is a good follow-up to the *Night* passage because it uses repetition and both abstract and concrete images to express emotion. I find the chapter titled "My Name" (pp. 10–11) is also a good one to use to teach rhetorical grammar. Looking at the rhetorical choices in that chapter (the contrasting positive and negatives nouns and adjectives) helps students uncover Cisneros's feelings about her name and the way they are complicated by those feelings about her heritage and new environment. I have also used this process with *An American Childhood* (Dillard, 1987), particularly the moth passage (pp. 160–161). By asking students to stop and notice the repetition of *wings*, they see how Dillard uses that repetition to emphasize the damage done to the moth. The contrasting verbs *crawled* and *walked*, used against the repetition of *wings* (suggesting flight), give the passage much of its intensity. Usually, the key points of any well-written text benefit from this type of inquiry, and the inquiry helps students gain insight on the meaning of texts.

Sentence Type and Tone

Helping students understand how the choice of sentence types can create an effect in writing can help them avoid the common lapse into imperatives in analysis essays or other school genres. Such lapses suggest that students have not learned the idea that sentence types affect tone. A passage in *The Trumpet of the Swan* (White, 1970, pp. 47–48) allows teachers and students to explore this effect of sentence types and punctuation on tone.

1. To begin, students should have some idea of the four functions of sentences: declarative, interrogative, imperative, and exclamatory. Introduce the idea by asking students what we try do with sentences. Most students will say "tell someone something" or "ask questions." They might not see differences among explaining (declarative), giving directions (imperative), and expressing strong emotion (exclamatory), as these all seem to combine under a common idea of telling someone something. In fact, Tufte (2006) calls imperative, exclamatory, and even interrogative sentences "common reshapings of the basic declarative sentence" (p. 205). Some grammar books differentiate among the sentence types by talking about the punctuation that ends each type—but this seems too simplified and is going to be contradicted by the examples from *The Trumpet of the Swan*. It seems more logical to explain that the differences among sentence types have to do with the intent of the speaker, not the punctuation at the end of the sentence.

2. After students have a sense of the four sentence functions, ask them to consider how the sentences are spoken—that is, what they sound like when people use them. If you have a few examples such as the following, it might help if students read them aloud, emphasizing the emotion or sense of the sentence.

   - What did you say?
   - How are you getting to the game?
   - I didn't mean it!
   - Hooray!
   - I have to take a test in English class today.
   - I am not going to be able to go to the dance after school.
   - Get back in the car.
   - Put your books under your desk and take out a pencil.

3. From reading these aloud (and others the teacher or students might add), students begin to see the tonal qualities associated with different kinds of sentences. Students might benefit from a discussion of how the different sentences make them feel. How do they feel when all they hear is imperatives? "Get in your seat." "Take out your book." "Don't talk." "Read to page 47." On the other hand, does tone change when commands are phrased as declarative sentences? "It is time to get into your seat. You should have your book out. It's important that we are all quiet so everyone can study. The assignment is to read to page 47." Ask students, Is it the request or the way the request is made (the sentence construction) that makes a difference in tone?

4. Next, have students read the passage from the novel. It may be helpful to have this one passage prepared to display on a screen so that students can work on it together. On these pages, the cob is trying to help the cygnets fly.

"I think," said the cob, "the best plan is for me to demonstrate flying to you. I will make a short exhibition flight while you watch. Observe everything I do! Watch me pump my neck up and down before the takeoff! Watch me test the wind by turning my head this way and that! The takeoff must be into the wind—it's much easier that way. Listen to the noise I make trumpeting! Watch how I raise my great wings! See how I beat them furiously as I rush through the water with my feet going like mad! This frenzy will last for a couple of hundred feet, at which point I will suddenly be airborne, my wings still chopping the air with terrific force but my feet no longer touching the water! Then watch what I do! Watch how I stretch my long white elegant neck out ahead of me until it has reached its full length! Watch how I retract my feet and allow them to stream out behind, full length, until they extend beyond my tail! Hear my cries as I gain the upper air and start trumpeting! See how strong and steady my wingbeat has become! Then watch me bank and turn, set my wings, and glide down! And just as I reach the pond again, watch how I shoot my feet out in front of me and use them for the splashdown, as though they were a pair of water skis! Having watched all this, then you can join me, and your mother, too, and we will all make a practice flight together, until you get the hang of it. Then tomorrow we will do it again, and instead of returning to the pond, we will head south to Montana. Are you ready for my exhibition flight?" (White, 1970, pp. 47–48)

5. After reading the passage, ask students to discuss the tone of the paragraph. What does it feel like? Many should note that the passage feels demanding; they will soon see that this is created by the heavy dependence on imperatives. Students might also note the use of exclamation points, which add a sense of urgency to the passage. Go through the passage with the students and identify the kinds of sentences in it. There are three: The first two are declarative; then begins a series of three imperatives before another declarative is used; this pattern of three imperatives followed by a declarative is repeated. Many imperatives follow the repeated pattern before the final sentences, which are declarative and interrogative. When students have identified the sentences by purpose, they can begin to notice that even when imperatives don't begin with the verb, they still carry a commanding tone.

6. To further understand the effect, have students change most of the declaratives to imperatives, making the paragraph even more demanding. Then, have students change as many of the imperatives as they can to declaratives and discuss the different tone. (In order not to make this task too burdensome, have students work in

pairs on one sentence each. They get practice, and the class gets the new passage rewritten quickly so that discussion can focus on the effect more than the rewriting.)

7. At this point, students should also look at the punctuation's effect on tone. Most of the time we encourage students to use exclamation points sparingly. Have them consider why White chose not to follow that advice in this passage. They should also be directed to note that one declarative sentence also ends with an exclamation point (the long sentence that ends the second pattern of three imperatives). Ask students, What tone is created in this passage by the use of exclamation points?

8. Finally, contrast this passage with one from the preceding page where the cob is explaining flying. That passage has a very different tone (and predominant sentence type) than the passage where he is giving verbal directions for flying. Have students read both passages and explain the differences.

"True," replied the cob. "But flying is largely a matter of having the right attitude—plus, of course, good wing feathers. Flying consists of three parts. First, the takeoff, during which there is a lot of fuss and commotion, a lot of splashing and rapid beating of wings. Second, the ascent, or gaining of altitude—this requires hard work and fast wing action. Third, the leveling-off, the steady elevated flight, high in air, wings beating slower now, beating strongly and regularly, carrying us swiftly and surely from zone to zone as we cry ko-hoh, ko-hoh, with all the earth stretched out far below." (p. 46)

9. The tone of this passage is so different that students should be able to see that using declaratives (implied, at least) creates a different feeling for a reader than using imperatives does. Have them discuss the reasons for that difference. Finally, have students reflect on what thinking about these sentence types means for them as readers and as writers. Why might White have made the sentence choices he did? What effects did he want those sentences to have on his readers? How does it feel to read the different sentence types? What kind of writing has more or fewer of the different types? When can students use their understanding of sentence types to help them as readers? As writers?

10. Because other structures add to the tone of this last passage, be prepared to address the idea of fragments, appositives, absolutes, participles, and adjectival phrases that also contribute to this effective passage. Especially with regard to fragments (or what some call minor sentences), consider Schuster's (2006) review of the best essays in America, which showed that those writers use

> ## EXTENDING YOUR KNOWLEDGE
>
> In his article, Schuster (2006) identifies several reasons for using fragments. Some of those reasons include "to create a dramatic pause for emphasis," "to create intense emphasis and succinctness," "to emphasize the individual items in a list or series," "to achieve a more natural, conversational tone" (pp. 80–81). I find Schuster's argument compelling—and its application to student writing effective. Certainly, as Schuster explains, students should have a justification for their use of fragments, but if we're teaching them to consider published writing as mentor texts and then telling them to avoid some of the options available to them from that mentoring, our instruction seems weakened. Right?

such constructions frequently. He argues for teaching students the effective uses of fragments as possibilities, especially because they will find fragments used strategically in most of what they read.

Alternative Suggestion: This approach can be used with any text that has passages that vary sentence types to create different tones. Informational texts of different types (directions and explanations, for example) can be contrasted to emphasize the tonal qualities of sentence types. Students could also investigate the effects of the various sentence types in the description of Catherine's delirium in *Wuthering Heights* (Bronte, 1988). In that scene (chapter 12), the combination of different types of sentences—declarative, interrogative, imperative, and exclamatory—helps to create the sense of madness that lets us understand her condition.

Repetition and Tone

A Tale of Two Cities (Dickens, 1997) provides an effective way to teach about rhetorical devices and the effects they can have on the tone of a piece of writing. Although Myers (2006) argues that "reading symbolic meaning out of syntactic structures remains a sketchy and subjective business at best" (p. 18), rhetoricians from ancient times until today have written about the effects of such choices.

1. Read aloud the first two paragraphs and ask students what they notice about them. They should note the rhythm or repetition. On an overhead or display you prepare, have them look again at the passage and consider it line by line. This exercise should serve to emphasize both the parallelism and the antithesis.

It was the best of times,
It was the worst of times,
It was the age of wisdom,
It was the age of foolishness,
It was the epoch of belief,
It was the epoch of incredulity,
It was the season of Light,
It was the season of Darkness,
It was the spring of hope,
It was the winter of despair,
We had everything before us,
We had nothing before us,
We were all going direct to Heaven,
We were all going direct the other way.... (p. 13)

2. Ask students what effect the structure has on the tone. My students sometimes comment that they thought they weren't supposed to have any repetition, a belief that Bresler (2004) finds can lead to ridiculous uses of language, to a condition he calls "the synonym game" (p. 68). Help students understand that repetition can be carried to extremes, but that it can also be used effectively. In this passage, the repetition eventually ends with Dickens's statement "that things in general were settled for ever" (at least in some minds, p. 13). Students should consider both what the passage is saying as well as the way it is being said: Are things really settled forever? Is the world of the novel as ordered as these statements suggest? How does the structure of the passage add to the meaning of the passage? Tell them that scholars suggest that parallelism reflects logic and orderly thinking (Corbett & Connors, 1999) and ask how knowing that adds to what they think the structure contributes to tone.

3. After studying the effects of the sentences written as they exist, have students try to write the sentences in different ways and then contrast their versions with the original to understand further how the grammar contributes to meaning. They might write, "It was both the best and worst times" or "At the same time it was both good and bad, people were both wise and foolish." Then have them discuss how the structure of the sentences works to create different tones. After completing the novel, make sure students return to these initial paragraphs and reconsider the structure and tone: Now that they know the story, how are the emphasis and repetition in the beginning even more important to the meaning of the book?

Alternative Suggestions: Any text that has passages with strong parallelism or repetition could be used similarly. Presidential speeches (John F. Kennedy's Inaugural Address, for example) often use parallelism to create a tone of logic and stability—and an ethos of reliability for the speaker. Rylant's *Scarecrow* (1998) is also a good text for showing effective repetition, showing both anaphora (repetition of beginning words or phrases) and epistrophe (repetition of concluding words and phrases). Students can consider the way that repetition works to depict a particular tone in any piece and then decide whether or not it's appropriate for the passage.

> **EXTENDING YOUR KNOWLEDGE**
>
> In addressing the ridiculous lengths to which writers might go to avoid repetition, Bresler (2004) quotes from an article published in *The Boston Globe* about a "pumpkin-growing contest." The writer, trying to avoid the repetition of the word *pumpkin*, referred to "the huge, orange produce item" (p. 68). Although I know students can go overboard either with repeating or avoiding repetition, drawing attention to effective uses of repetition in their reading should go a long way in helping them see this as a valuable tool for reading and writing. Writers use repetition to make connections, to enhance meaning; our students can use it in those ways, too.

QUESTIONS FOR REFLECTION

1. What literature or reading material do you use in your classes? What plan can you make to reread them, looking for issues of language to incorporate in your teaching? How can you then translate these ideas about language into discussions and writing?

2. How can you add texts to your units—informational and functional texts, perhaps—that will allow you to expand students' view of language beyond its use in literary contexts?

3. How can you incorporate picture books or other reading materials that will build students' understanding of language change and diversity?

CHAPTER 3

Writing and Language

*"We seduce the students into grammar. We let grammar seduce us.
We assume that it is, in fact, seductive, and we search out those writers
who manipulate and exploit grammatical structures in their writing."*

—MARY EHRENWORTH

BACK IN THE CLASSROOM...

T:	Let's look at some of the sentences from *To Kill a Mockingbird* that you put a sticky note by. Isac?
Isac:	In the middle of page 205, "But there is one way in this country in which all men are created equal—there is one human institution that makes a pauper the equal of a Rockefeller, the stupid man the equal of an Einstein, and the ignorant man the equal of any college president."
T:	I like that one, too. Who else picked it? Trent? Why do you think it's powerful?
Trent:	I don't know. It just sounds, like, you know, like something a president would say or something.
Isac:	Yeah. I like how it kinda repeats. It sounds important that way.
T:	OK. We'll look at it a little more in a minute. What other sentences did you note?
Jenny:	The one above that, "We know that all men are not created equal in the sense some people would have us believe—some people are smarter than others, some people have more opportunity because they're born with it, some men make more money than others, some ladies make better cakes than others—some people are born gifted beyond the normal scope of most men."
T:	Good. Why do you think that's a powerful sentence?
Jenny:	I don't know. I just like it.

T: Liking it is a good sign that it is powerful. Did anyone else pick that sentence? Sarah, why do you think it's powerful?

Sarah: I don't know. I guess because it's, like, you know, true. I mean, we all know that some people do some things better, so it's kinda like he's contradicting what we say by pointing out what we know—and then he goes on to say that even with this inequality there should still be equality in the courts, so it kinda like makes the point better. I don't know.

T: I think you do know—you did a good job showing how this sentence sets up the main point Atticus wants to make. Let's talk about these two sentences for a minute. They have something in common that helps to make them powerful. Can you look at them and see what it is?

Jason: They're both long! [Laughing]

T: You're right. That's one thing they have in common. Anything else?

Tanner: Well they both have repeated parts. I mean, in the first sentence, "some people, some men, some ladies, some people," and so on, and in the second one it's like something is the equal of something else, repeated.

T: Good eye. There is repetition, but it's a different kind than the repetition we saw with "guilt" and "pity." This is more of a repetition of structure that we can see through the repetition of words. It's called parallel structure, and it's an important strategy to learn, especially for persuasion. People who study sentence structure and how it affects meaning say that parallel structure, because it's logical and patterned, suggests that the person using it is also logical—and therefore we can put more trust in what he or she says. Cool, huh? I want people who read what I write to think I know what I'm talking about. I think it's interesting, too, that you pick it out, even when you don't know what it is. You recognize its power, so you should be able to use it when you think it can help you persuade. You will certainly want a person you're trying to convince of something to think you are logical and trustworthy, won't you?

Look at these examples for a minute. I think they will help us figure out parallel structure. What do you notice is the difference between the non-parallel examples and the parallel ones?

> Nonparallel: My hobbies are skiing, shopping, and to read a good book.
>
> Parallel: My hobbies are skiing, shopping, and reading a good book.
>
> Parallel: My hobbies are to ski, to shop, and to read a good book.
>
> Nonparallel: The new student in our class was loud and made crude comments.
>
> Parallel: The new student in our class was loud and crude.
>
> Parallel: The new student in our class had a loud voice and made crude comments.

Vanessa: Well, the words are the same in the parallel ones and not the same in the not-parallel one. I mean, like, there's an *-ing* at the end of all the parallel ones or *to* something, *to ski*, *to shop*, *to read*. They're the same kinds of words.

T: OK. Anyone see anything else?

Matt: Does it always have to be a list? I mean, the first one has three things and the second example has two. So, does it like have to have a certain number to be parallel or something?

T: Good question. A good rule of thumb is any time you use a coordinating conjunction—a word from our short list—you should check to be sure the items, however many there are, are parallel. So, you can have two, three, even four or more items in a list. In fact, if you write a brochure or make lists in a vertical column, you should especially check for parallel structure.

Emily: I don't get the second example. I mean, the first one is so out there. Who would really say it like that? But the second one seems OK, even not parallel.

T: Good point, Emily. And it isn't strictly incorrect. If we wanted to, we could diagram the sentence—but we won't!—and show how the sentence could have two predicates: *was loud* and *made crude comments*. It's just that it's smoother, more effective this way. When we start a sentence with "The person was..." whoever is listening expects that we'll end with adjectives: *loud* and *crude*. When we start a sentence the second way, we have two similar kinds of verbs: *had* and *made*. That makes it a little better.

Jon: What if we just said "The new student made crude comments in a loud voice"? Would that work?

T: Sure, and it doesn't have to be concerned with parallelism because you've put one of the ideas in a prepositional phrase. Why might we choose to say it your way or the first parallel way? Why choose one over the other?

Tiffany: The two words—*crude* and *loud*—stand out more in the parallel example. They get less attention in Jon's example.

Vanessa: Yeah, I guess if you wanted to really make the point about how he was, that sentence would be better. But if you were, like, describing the class and saying stuff about a bunch of students, then Jon's sentence would be the best.

T: So we choose parallel structure to make a point, to create an effect, right? Let's try a few examples together to see how we do in fixing sentences that aren't parallel. Try the first one. The beginning of the sentence kind of sets up the two parts that should be parallel.

1. I can't decide which activity I prefer: to swim at the shore in July, when the sand is warm, or jogging along country roads in October, when the autumn leaves are at their colorful best.

2. The coach announced an extra hour of drill on Saturday and that the practice on Sunday would be canceled.

3. To reduce stress, Margie tried deep breaths, yoga, and to eat chocolate. (sentences 1 and 2 from Kolln & Funk, 2006, p. 229)

James: "To swim at the shore" and "to jog along country roads."

T: OK. That's parallel. Is there another way we could do it?

Jon: I don't know another way, but do you always have to have the other parts the same, too?

T: What parts?

Jon: The "when the sand is warm" and "when the autumn leaves are at their colorful best" parts.

T: Good question. What do the rest of you think?

Emily: Well it sounds kind of good, like it's the same thing again, so it's kinda like a double one, isn't it?

T: Good point, Emily. I'd say that you don't always have the option of having modifiers be the same kinds of structures, prepositional phrases or adjectives or whatever. The main parts that match up should be the same kind of structure, though. If you can keep the modifiers similar, that creates a nice effect, as Emily noticed. See the first part of the sentence? "*Swim* at the shore" or "*jogging* along country roads." Different words start the modifying phrases, but they are both the same kind of phrases. And you could have one with a modifier and one without, if you want, as long as the main structures are the same. See how the second one adds "in October"? Does that answer your question?

Jon: Yeah, I get it.

T: Are there any other options for making this sentence parallel?

William: What if you said "swimming at the shore...or jogging along country roads"?

T: It's parallel. What do the rest of you think?

Several: It's OK.

T: What's the difference? Is one better than the other?

Tanner: I like the -*ing* ones. They're shorter.

Vanessa: I don't see a difference really.

James: The one with "to swim...and to jog" seems more like writing. I think in talking we say *swimming* and *jogging* more.

T: So one sounds more formal?

James: Yeah.

T: So we choose sometimes between two correct versions to make a different effect, then. What about number 2?

Tanner: I can't figure it out.

T: OK. Let's try to underline the two parts that should be parallel. What is the set up? It's not as clear as in the first example, but it's there.

Shelby: "The coach announced two things."

T: So we'll underline what? The two things he announced were...?

Jenny: "An extra hour of drill on Saturday."

Several: "That the practice on Sunday would be canceled."

T: So how do we make these two parts the same?

Jon: You could start both of them with *that*.

T: What would the first part be then?

Matt: "That they'd have an extra hour of drill on Saturday"?

T: What do the rest of you think?

Several: Yeah.

Tanner: I don't like it—it makes the sentence too long.

T: How could we make the second part like the first part?

Sara: "A cancellation of Sunday's practice"?

Tanner: "A cancellation?" Who talks like that?

T: Well, then, Tanner, how could we say it in a way that is parallel and how a person talks?

Tanner: "No practice on Sunday"?

T: What do the rest of you think? "The coach announced *an extra hour of drill on Saturday* and *no practice on Sunday*." Is it parallel?

Sara: Yes.

T: Why?

James: Well, an extra hour and no practice. They're kind of the same, aren't they?

T: Sure, both are noun phrases. How does it sound?

Tiffany: Well, it's more like talking now, but I kind of liked the other one, too—the one with the *that*s.

T: Why?

Tiffany: I don't know. It sounds good to me.

Tanner: It's too long—and it sounds stuck up.

T: What if we wanted to create that formal effect, though. Would it be a better choice then?

Several:	Yeah.
Tanner:	OK, I get it. It's like I can say it like talking or say it like writing?
T:	Sure. It isn't just about making it right—it also has to be about the effect you create. Let's try number 3. I guess the short way first, right?
Shelby:	"Deep breaths, yoga, and chocolate."
T:	OK, that's parallel. What's another way to do it?
Sarah:	"Taking deep breaths, practicing yoga, and eating chocolate"?
T:	Sure. And what's the difference?
Tanner:	The first one's shorter.
Sarah:	But the second one's more exact, because you really are trying three different activities, not just three different things.
Tanner:	Yeah, but I know what is meant with the short one so why take time for the longer version?
T:	It comes down to meaning: What do we really want to say? And there's the effect, too. Personal choice is some of it.

> **THOUGHTS FROM THE CLASSROOM**
>
> Here, as earlier in the discussion, students explore the difference between oral and written speech. Gaining sensitivity about language variety—that it changes for situation—and about appropriateness is important for students to develop as effective speakers and writers. Ehrenworth and Vinton (2005) insist that "learning grammar must be linked to the process of discovery, to intellectual thought" (p. 17). I agree—and even brief discussions like this allow that discovery and thought to develop.

I believed what I read: Teaching grammar is useful for helping students fix their mistakes in writing. I knew the admonitions about connecting grammar instruction with writing, but the only place people talked about the connection seemed to be with the last part of writing, with editing. I was a little uncomfortable with the limitation, but what did I know? It just seemed logical to me that knowing about language could influence what comes before editing—when we are putting ideas down on paper, maybe even before that, when we are shaping ideas.

Since my early questioning, I've found others who've wondered about the same thing: Umbach (1999), speaking of the way handbooks present grammar, explains that "the message is clear. Grammar is what you use to clean up the mess that you make, that you will inevitably make" (p. 5). Ah. So, even if we do connect grammar to writing, if we do it only as a way to "clean up" writing, what does that say about grammar and language—and why would students be motivated to learn much about it? After all, computers pick up a lot of those messes.

Shouldn't grammar—language—have an impact on the *whole* writing process? It seems that it should help writers know the level of language to use with certain genres in specific situations, even as they begin drafting. If I write my draft of a research paper with the level of language appropriate for a text message, I probably will have a lot of trouble finishing an adequate paper. Knowing about genres and the language expectations associated with them is part of *starting* to write. And shouldn't language help writers find ways to express ideas more effectively? I need to decide when I write if the ideas I'm writing about are coordinate or subordinate to each other, don't I? It seems that an understanding of grammar helps writers express ideas more effectively, even in the early stages of writing. Ehrenworth and Vinton (2005) assert that understanding language even contributes to voice in writing and, thus, should be considered not just at the end of the writing process:

> If, as we believe, grammar is linked to voice, students need to be thinking about grammar far earlier in the writing process. We cannot teach grammar in lasting ways if we teach it as a way to *fix* students' writing, especially writing they view as already complete. Students need to construct knowledge of grammar by practicing it as part of what it means to write, particularly in how it helps create a voice that engages the reader on the page. (p. 10)

Burke (2001), in his discussion of Textual Intelligence, sees the connection between language and writing from an even broader perspective. For him, language knowledge develops an understanding of how texts work—and influences many decisions writers make, even before they begin to put words on paper: "The more a student understands [how language works], the more options he or she has when starting to write" (p. 57). His argument, that students' understanding of how language creates responses in readers can be useful to their writing, supports the notion of teaching grammar integrated with writing but suggests that such integration is much broader than what is used only during editing and is not just for "fixing" the inevitable mistakes.

Did we do our students a disservice when we thought we were doing better by connecting grammar to writing? If we have made the connection only as a remediation strategy, it's not surprising that students still see grammar as an unfamiliar, unpleasant aspect of writing. Instead, if grammar is taught as part of the entire writing process, it can seem integral to expression, not a separate element added later to satisfy some picky reader or grader.

All of this talk of integrating grammar with writing assumes an understanding of the conversation about grammar instruction over the last few decades. As I mentioned earlier, the controversy over grammar instruction arose largely over the failure of traditional instruction to have an impact on student writing. In fact, all the statements about that failure were couched in terms related to writing. The consequence of that research

---

EXTENDING YOUR KNOWLEDGE

Burke (2001) lists the following ways understanding language can help a writer prior to editing:

- Choosing a genre
- Choosing sentence types
- Creating a tone
- Selecting effective formats (lists or paragraphs, for example)
- Finding the right word (p. 57)

All of these writerly decisions come early in the writing process. Because language informs them all, we can help students see that grammar will aid them as writers through the entire writing process.

has been an outpouring of published materials about teaching grammar with the purpose of improving writing, about teaching grammar in the context of writing. And that makes sense: As Weaver (1996b) claims, "teaching 'grammar' in the context of writing works better than teaching grammar as a formal system, if our aim is for students to *use* grammar more effectively and conventionally in their writing" (p. 23). Poth (2006) explains the reason grammar in isolation doesn't work: Grammar exercises are often simpler than real language, and, if students can complete the exercises, they feel that they "know" grammar—but they can't transfer what they know into their writing.

Poth (2006), working on transfer in learning, also identifies additional reasons why traditional grammar hasn't worked—but her ideas show us why we need to be careful when we integrate grammar, too. In order for students to apply their learning to new situations, we need to deliver instruction in ways that can "easily be retrieved," that are "logically organized," and that can be easily used: "When students learn a grammar principle, they should learn all the ways that it should be applied" (p. 11). Teaching grammar with writing does appear to improve writing. Recent research confirms that "teaching students to focus on the function and practical application of grammar within the context of writing...produced strong and positive effects on students' writing" (Graham & Perin, 2007, p. 21). An understanding of grammar can improve student writing, but it should be taught in a way that also makes sense to the learners and seems useful to them so that they can transfer their learning to other situations.

Traditional Grammar

Creating Cinquain Poems

Poetry is an effective way to build students' understanding of traditional grammar through writing. Many poetic forms require students to use specific parts of speech, but all poetry focuses on language—its denotative and connotative meanings as well as its metaphorical and symbolic uses. The enlarged perspective of language that students can gain from writing poetry is beneficial in numerous ways to their growing understanding of language.

1. Begin by teaching students the form of the poem. *Cinquain* poems are poems with five lines that allow students to write poetry at the same time as they use their knowledge of parts of speech. In this form, the first line is a noun that announces the subject (and title) of the poem. The second line consists of two adjectives that describe the noun. Line three consists of three verbs in the *-ing* form. Line four differentiates between phrases and clauses by requiring a phrase that represents a feeling, image, or metaphor about the subject. Line five is a single noun, a synonym for the first line or subject of the poem.

2. To complete the poems, students need to know the ideas of the parts of speech and the idea of phrases and clauses—even if they can't define them or explain them in traditional grammar terms. Seeing models helps my students, who otherwise would be confused, to know what I mean by the terms I use to explain the directions. There are many models available on the Internet (just type in "cinquain"). Show students models and discuss them until students understand the expectations for the poem. Then have them write their own poems and share them. Following is my example:

Alaska
Enormous, Empty
Freezing, Flowing, Quaking
Land of the Midnight Sun
Home

Alternative Suggestion: Other poetic forms can also help students learn about traditional grammar concepts—if not the terms themselves. *Diamante* poems work like cinquains except that they have two more lines (duplicating parts but not content of the second and third line after the phrase line). Weaver uses "I Am" poems to help students learn participial phrases (1996a, pp. 214–217). The poems begin with a metaphor in the first line, with each subsequent line describing how the metaphor works and beginning with a participial phrase, an *-ing* verb form. Most poems have three or four such lines after the first one. I show students models of the poetic form and discuss with them what they see and what they understand about the poems and the form. They see from the examples that some of these poems are pretty concrete; others are more abstract, as shown in this example from Weaver's book:

I am a strong lasting tool.
Nailing friends together
Pounding kindness into the world
Sawing through problems
Sanding rough edges in life. (p. 216)

Students write these "I Am" poems about themselves, about characters in books they are reading, or about concepts they are studying. A preservice teacher, Tonya Hamill, adapted the concept to a lesson on metaphors and similes by having her students identify the metaphors in art by Vladimir Kush and then explain those metaphors in poems built with participial phrases. In Tonya's lesson, students were learning a literary concept, using writing to explore their ideas and thinking, and learning about grammar—all at once.

Other poetic forms that can help students to learn traditional grammar concepts or terms include the following (all explained very nicely with examples in *R Is for Rhyme: A Poetry Alphabet*, Young, 2005):

- *Doublets* are poems built around a word ladder—words in a list, each word one letter different from the word before. The form encourages creativity with and sensitivity to words.
- *Haiku* poems require sensitivity to imagery and language. Examples from *If Not for the Cat* (Prelutsky, 2004) can help students see how adjectives and adverbs can be used in this poetic form.
- *Rap poetry* encourages students to play with language and rhythm in ways that help them learn about grammar as they try to make meaning in rhythmic language.

Writing From Different Perspectives

Another way I use writing to help students learn traditional grammar concepts is when I have them rewrite a scene or story, but from different perspectives.

1. Begin by retelling familiar childhood stories such as The Three Bears or The Three Pigs from the perspectives of different characters in the stories. In these oral retellings, students practice shifts in stance that they can apply when they write their own experience from different perspectives. This gives them practice with using first person (I/we/me) and third person (They/he/she/them).

2. Have students choose an event that they attended with at least a few other people: a football game, a concert, a movie, and so forth. Initially, have them write a first-person account, as this allows them to review the event in what (for my students at least) is the most comfortable perspective to retell an event. I tell them this means that they use *I*, *we*, and *me*.

3. After they complete the first-person draft, have them rewrite the event in the third person. Discuss what this means orally first so that students understand that not only do we shift pronouns, but we also have to consider other aspects of the event— what would others see and experience that I might not have? What would others not experience that I did? Then have students write the second version of the event.

4. When students have finished their two versions, have them compare and contrast them in small- or whole-class discussion. What differences do they notice? Students discover that shifting perspective changes the information selected and the stance toward that information. More than that, though, they should see that the different stance creates a different tone—first person is more immediate and personal while third person is more distant and impersonal.

5. With this foundation about the effects of pronoun choice laid, have students investigate different genres that are traditionally written in first or third person.

Newspaper articles, for instance, are written in third person, as are traditional research papers. Letters, however, are written in first person. Even business letters, which are more formal than personal letters, aren't as objective and distant as news articles or research articles. Students should discover that the genres use the different perspectives for a reason—those perspectives are part of each genre's situation and purpose.

6. Next, have students rewrite selected genres from a different perspective. This will teach them about writing and genre while they learn about language. For instance, when they rewrite a news article from a first-person perspective, they can see what is lost and what is gained. Personal letters written from a third-person stance (this is tricky) lose something that makes a letter meaningful. After students write these genres from alternate stances, lead them in a discussion about how stance is related to the genre and the situation in which the genre is acting. Although there are variations in genres, students can build awareness of traditional grammar (pronouns) not only as parts of speech but also as related to the effects they create in writing different genres.

Alternative Suggestion: In a similar application, Burke (2001) suggests having students rewrite text passages—either published ones or their own—in a different verb tense to see the resulting effect. As he notes, "Such exercises help students to understand how language functions to orient the reader in time, and to create different perspectives on the same story or subject" (p. 59). Ehrenworth and Vinton (2005) agree and suggest reading literature by authors such as Sandra Cisneros for things like examples of shifts in verb tense to see how Cisneros creates voice and point of view. As they note, "It is hopeless to ask students to memorize verb forms, especially irregular verb endings, until they see the choice of verb tense as a meaningful one" (p. 69). Again, the shift in grammar creates resultant shifts in tone and position that readers should notice and writers can emulate when necessary.

Editing

Punctuating for Meaning

In *Image Grammar: Using Grammatical Structures to Teach Writing*, Noden (1999) remarks that for "most authors, meaning takes precedence over rules" when it comes to punctuation (p. 98). Iyer (2000) represents this idea in his description of punctuation as guides, not as rules:

> Punctuation marks are the road signs placed along the highway of our communication—to control speeds, provide directions, and prevent head-on collisions. A period has the unblinking finality of a red light; the comma is a flashing yellow light that asks us only to slow down; and the semicolon is a Stop sign that tells us to ease gradually to a halt, before gradually start-

ing up again. By establishing the relations between words, punctuation establishes the relations between the people using words. (pp. 93–94)

Helping students see punctuation as road signs, as meaning making, benefits them as readers and writers—and, in the long run, helps students understand how their own choices as writers can benefit readers, or make it harder for readers to understand what they are trying to communicate.

> **EXTENDING YOUR KNOWLEDGE**
>
> Romano (2004), an advocate of alternate style and personal voice, recognizes the value of conventional correctness: "I also want [students] to realize that if their writing is a mechanical disaster, their natural voice might be dismissed by others, regardless of how authentic, colorful, and pointed it is" (p. 73).

1. Begin by reading with students the following passage from a short story by Adam Schwartz, shared by Randy Bomer (2006). Help students develop their understanding of how punctuation can assist readers by having them imagine the phrasing created by the commas in the sentence. Here's the original text:

    I told her I knew she might be disappointed, but I wasn't rejecting her; I only wanted to spend more time with my father, to know and love him as well as I knew her. (p. 528)

2. In his rewriting of the passage, Bomer punctuates the sentence to show that "to figure out what sentences are saying, we have to hear the words (in our mind's ear) together in the appropriate phrasing" (p. 529). What follows is Bomer's repunctuated version that, interestingly, doesn't get flagged by the grammar check on my computer. Read it aloud to contrast it with the original sentence:

    I told her. I knew she might. Be disappointed. But I wasn't rejecting. Her I only wanted to spend. More time with my father to know? And love him as well as I knew her. (p. 529)

    Ask students what they notice. How does the repunctuation make communication harder? Students will see the obvious—punctuation can make a big difference in communicating effectively. It isn't only about "right" and "wrong."

3. Next, speak sentences or passages you have prepared and have students punctuate them so that another person reading the printed text would read it as we said it. For example, how might a writer punctuate this sentence so that a sense of frustration (or even a threat) is evident in the written text? "I haven't gotten to you (pause) yet." Students could write it this way: "I haven't gotten to you yet." But that doesn't suggest the pause at all. They could write, "I haven't gotten to you, but I will eventually." Different words—but the message is closer to our intent. What about this version? "I haven't gotten to you—yet." Better. How is this version different? "I

haven't gotten to you. Yet." Is this more threatening? Have students discuss how they can use punctuation to make meaning clear. Find sentences in conversations or in movies, and take them to class to use in explorations like this one. This activity helps students get practice in making editing choices that guide readers and that make punctuation a contributor to meaning, not just an application of rules.

Using Models to Help Students Infer Reader Expectations for Punctuation

When my students have trouble with conventions that interfere with my reading of their writing—and these problems are not a result of trying to make meaning but more a result of failing to consider reader expectations—I find sentences that exemplify the conventions I want my students to edit for, sentences that help them know that readers read punctuation like road signs. If writers put up a stop sign when they want the reader only to slow down, that's a problem.

1. Find examples of the punctuation challenges students are having in texts you read. For example, I had noticed that my students' writing had distracted me because of their use (or, rather, the lack of use) of commas with long introductory elements and in compound sentences. When I read the book *Sitting Ducks* (Bedard, 1998), I realized it could help my students learn reader expectations for commas in these constructions. I read the book to them and used sentences from the text for a minilesson. I gave students three sets of sentences and asked them to tell me what they could learn about comma use from the examples. The following is an abbreviated sample set.

    But one day, an egg came through the incubation chamber unhatched.
    Dazed by this rude introduction into the world, a little duck emerged and surveyed his strange surroundings.

    He just had to sneak away and explore the streets below.
    He rushed in and hopped up onto a stool.

    At first, the alligator was bewildered by this weird welcome, but soon he joined in the crazy dance.
    They even tried going out together, but it proved to be very awkward. (n.p.)

    The students infer, correctly, that they should use commas after introductory elements and between independent clauses (although they didn't use those terms) but not if the second part of the sentence wasn't a "whole sentence."

2. Next, have students return to their writing and implement what they have learned about punctuating for reader expectation. Encourage students to pay attention to punctuation when they read so that they become familiar with reader expectations about punctuation. There is only one caution—and that is that some writers don't always follow the "rules." Sometimes the reason is because expectations change over time, and an author's punctuation may have been appropriate for the time period in which the text was written but isn't now. Sometimes different genres have differing expectations for punctuation. It's good to teach students that punctuation rules change through time and among genres—a helpful and useful thing to know. But some alternate use of punctuation goes back to meaning: Sometimes writers use unexpected punctuation to draw attention to an idea. By not doing what's expected, readers have to slow down, pay attention, interpret. For example, using the following paragraph from Wiesel's (2007) essay "Why I Write: Making No Become Yes" draw students' attention to the three compound sentences listed below the paragraph, each of which is punctuated differently.

Where was I to discover a fresh vocabulary, a primeval language? The language of night was not human, it was primitive, almost animal—hoarse shouting, screams, muffled moaning, savage howling, the sound of beating. A brute strikes out wildly, a body falls. An officer raises his arm and a whole community walks toward a common grave. A soldier shrugs his shoulders, and a thousand families are torn apart, to be reunited only by death. This was the concentration camp language. (2007, p. 23)

- A brute strikes out wildly, a body falls.
- An officer raises his arm and a whole community walks toward a common grave.
- A soldier shrugs his shoulders, and a thousand families are torn apart, to be reunited only by death.

After reading the paragraph and paying specific attention to these three sentences, ask students why Wiesel might have used commas in both expected and unexpected ways: Meaning is enhanced by punctuation. My students' answers astound me with their insight. With regard to unexpected punctuation use, students should also realize, however, that being a student writer and being a published writer are two different things. Sometimes readers have different expectations of each type of writer. It's not fair, necessarily; it just is how things are.

Usage

Writing Letters to Different Audiences

In working with children of migrant workers in his classroom, Shafer (2001) found that traditional lessons on usage and language didn't engage his students. He learned that language lessons needed to be a part of "authentic language experiences that directly touched the lives" of his students (p. 38). Interestingly, instead of simply teaching usage as a standard, which is how some teachers might approach such a situation—even if teaching grammar in the context of writing—he taught language as flexible, as responsive to situation. Dunn and Lindblom (2003) argue that a flexible approach is more effective:

To combat these barriers to upward mobility, students do not need to know "the rules" for writing successfully. What they need is the ability to communicate effectively with people in all kinds of contexts for all kinds of purposes.... Pretending that grammar rules provide a smooth, toll-free road to economic success is a harmful myth. (p. 45)

For Shafer, teaching effective communication meant that "each assignment, then, would probe the worthiness of the language used and the reason why it was successful" (2001, p. 39). This lesson idea follows Shafer's experience somewhat.

1. Have students start by writing a short letter to a friend or relative, one that they will read in class but that is a legitimate letter—one they will actually give or send to the person. After they have written their letters, have students share them as a way to begin to understand how language responds to situation. Have students look for usage that is unique to the relationship—for example, shortcuts of language or signal words that might not mean the same thing outside of the relationship. Students should definitely note the informal usage that is more like speech that often pervades letters to friends or family.

2. Next, have students write a letter to a prospective employer. I have also had students write to businesses to complain or compliment products or services (Dean, 2000). Either way, students first need to analyze the situation and consider the audience: How is this audience different from the one they had previously written to? What do those differences entail in terms of language? As students work through the writing process on these letters, they explore the answers to these questions.

When they realized the different levels of usage that were expected in the different situations, Shafer (2001) explains that his students "discussed the place of power and the way it tends to define what is 'standard' or 'correct'" (p. 40). Dunn and Lindblom (2005), referring to Lippi-Green's research, assert that "the advice to use 'appropriate' language for each situation, while better than 'proper' or 'correct,' continues to give students the message that their home language is not 'good' enough to be used in academic or formal situations" (p. 193). Although there is a risk that teachers' talk of appropriate usage could alienate some students, the reality often is that certain situations place expectations on language use. Power is a factor in U.S. society. For better or worse, the way people use language in certain situations plays into power relationships. To be accepted, to have our ideas matter, to have people pay attention to our requests—all of these require some conformity of language to situational expectations. And that applies to both formal and informal situations. That conformity can have some flexibility, though. It isn't completely rigid.

Students seem to move instinctively to more formal language in some situations, even if they don't know all about correctness. For example, when they write to a business person they don't know and want something from, they automatically make some adjustments with language. As Shafer notes, and as I also observed, when writing these letters students pay more attention to issues of correctness. We should help students note this attention and the shifts in usage they make as they write for different purposes to different audiences, and we should build on their instinctive shifts, creating an authentic purpose for learning more about usage issues. Students come to an important understanding about language as they work through writing experiences that use different levels of usage and pay attention to the language differences.

Analyzing Grammar Rants

Grammar rants are found all around us. They are writers' observations and opinions about language, usually focusing on some aspect the writer finds interesting or bothersome. The recent bestseller *Eats, Shoots & Leaves: Why, Commas Do Make a Difference!* (Truss, 2006) might be considered a lengthy grammar rant—the introduction definitely is one. Dunn and Lindblom (2005) explain an idea for analyzing grammar rants that helps students learn about usage issues and develop into what they call "savvy writers" (p. 192). Their rationale for these analyses is one I endorse: "If we continue to teach students that there is such a thing as a single, correct English, we continue to perpetuate a myth that is harmful to students and their potential as writers" (p. 193). To Dunn and Lindblom's idea of analyzing grammar rants orally, I add a writing component to encourage reflection and longer lasting learning. Here's how I teach their idea.

1. To prepare students for the world of grammar rants, share with them the satirical rant "What Is and Ain't Grammatical" (Barry, 1993). In this essay, Barry raises (in a humorous way) some of the issues underlying grammar rants. I use the essay to start a discussion about attitudes toward grammar so that the rants students read later have some context.

2. Next, provide students with some grammar rants. Have students work in pairs and read the rants. These rants can be found in newspapers or magazines. Many local papers have a language column that could be used for this activity, or teachers could

search online for "grammar columns" or "grammar rants." As students read, ask them to look for the following points:

- The "problem(s)" about which the writer is ranting
- What the writer sees as the problem with the "problem"
- Why the writer is so unhappy about the "problem"

As students read and discuss their articles, encourage them to place the rants in a larger, cultural context. What does it say about language and people that there are writers who write about these issues? When students share their findings with the whole class, help them see that usage issues (most often the subject of the rants) have moral overtones as well as implications about power and relationships.

3. Next, using Schuster's (2003) proposal of analyzing the way language is actually used, have students hunt for examples of published writing that violates the "rules" that were the subject of the rants. When they have some evidence (and it's all around us), have them work in their same partnerships to write a rebuttal to the rant. In this rebuttal, they can cite the places and authors that "break the rule" to show that usage expectations are situational or that they change with time. I agree with Dunn and Lindblom (2005) that analyzing grammar rants (and researching the subject of the rant so that students can respond to the charges) can "make both teachers and students more sensitive to the particular pet peeves of professional and amateur grammar guardians everywhere, making students more careful shapers of language for each rhetorical situation" (p. 203). When students respond to the rants with "rants" of their own, they develop as critical thinkers about language.

Writing Stories to Develop Language Sensitivity

Usage often relies on students' hearing. We can aid students in acquiring an "ear" for standard usage with their own talk in the classroom by calling attention to the differences between informal and formal usages in the texts that are read aloud in class. One way to generate texts for students to practice different varieties of usage with is to have them write the stories of wordless picture books. Table 2 contains some titles that work for this practice.

1. Have students work in pairs first to "read" the pictures and develop the general plot of the book they have selected, using talk before writing to create the basics of the storyline. Fravel (2005) believes that talking "plays a crucial role and impacts the writing of all students regardless of their native language because language acquisition depends on social interaction" (p. 74). I agree. Talk also prepares students

TABLE 2. Wordless Picture Books for Developing Language Sensitivity

Armstrong, J. (2006). *Once upon a banana*. New York: Simon & Schuster.
Blake, Q. (1995). *Clown*. New York: Henry Holt.
Briggs, R. (1978). *The Snowman*. New York: Random House.
Collington, P. (1995). *The tooth fairy*. New York: Knopf.
Day, A. (1989). *Carl goes shopping*. New York: HarperCollins.
Ludy, M. (2005). *The flower man*. Windsor, CO: Green Pastures.
Macaulay, D. (2005). *Black and white*. New York: Walter Lorraine Books.
MacGregor, M. (1988). *On top*. New York: William Morrow.
Melling, D. (2004). *The ghost library*. Hauppauge, NY: Barrons.
Nygren, T. (1987). *The red thread*. New York: R & S Books.
Panek, D. (1979). *Catastrophe cat at the zoo*. Scarsdale, NY: Bradbury Press.
Prater, J. (1986). *The gift*. New York: Viking Penguin.
Priceman, M. (2005). *Hot air: The (mostly) true story of the first hot-air balloon ride*. New York: Atheneum.
Rogers, G. (2004). *The boy, the bear, the baron, the bard*. Brookfield, CT: Roaring Brook Press.
Rohman, E. (1994). *Time flies*. New York: Crown.
Weisner, D. (1988). *Free fall*. New York: HarperTrophy.
Weisner, D. (1991). *Tuesday*. New York: Clarion Books.
Weisner, D. (1999). *Sector 7*. New York: Clarion Books.
Weisner, D. (2006). *Flotsam*. New York: Houghton Mifflin.
Weitzman, J.P., & Glasser, R.P. (1998). *You can't take a balloon into the Metropolitan Museum*. New York: Dial Books for Young Readers.
Weitzman, J.P., & Glasser, R.P. (2002). *You can't take a balloon into the National Gallery*. New York: Penguin.

with ideas to write. The wordless picture books provide a frame for the story—but no two finished stories are ever exactly the same—which allows students a chance to focus more on the telling of the story than on developing a plot. As such, they are able to focus on language.

2. Consider requiring students to include both informal and formal language in the story, perhaps using characters' dialogue in informal, speech-like language and narration in more formal usage. In this way, students get to practice a variety of language levels in writing as they tell their stories. They can use novels and picture books as mentor texts if they need help with this dual use of language in the same text.

3. After the stories are written, have students share them in small and large groups. Discussion about the stories should focus on how language was used effectively to tell the stories. Have students reflect on the kinds of usages that are easier for them to write, on how the different levels of usage worked to accomplish different purposes in their stories, and on how they knew to adjust for the different purposes. From this reflection, have students consider other writing situations that have expectations for certain levels of usage, and discuss how they know the expectations and what they can do to achieve them.

Language Change

Writing Advertisements

When students listen to advertisements, they may not be attentive to the language being used to influence them or connect to them. When they have to write their own ads, though, they become much more sensitive to language used to connect or to change perceptions and behavior.

1. Begin by having students analyze the language of oral advertisements. I start with oral ads so that students will focus on language more than the visual appeals that play into ads on television, the Internet, or in print. Have students bring in the texts of ads they hear on the radio or the words from television ads without the accompanying visuals. Encourage students to find advertisements that don't mention price directly, that are more subtle in their use of language. Strongly worded promotional ads don't always use the most effective language, relying instead on price or economics as the sales tool: "Call now and we'll throw in a second _____ absolutely free!" Some soundtracks for ads can be obtained from the Internet. For example, www.beefitswhatsfordinner.com/ads/radio.asp is a site with ads from the Beef Industry that may be familiar to students. I favor these advertisements because they are not the typical promotional ads with which students are more familiar. The language of these ads is used to connect with consumers and to encourage positive feelings toward the product, not necessarily to sell it. This more subtle use of language can help students see how effective language can be used to make connections between consumers and products—and has nothing to do with economics, which is the aspect of advertising language our students are more familiar with.

2. When students have their scripts for the ads, guide them as they investigate the language, specifically looking for the way language is used to persuade listeners. They might want to look at the imagery in word choice, the level of formality, the use of pronouns, or the use of sentence types (imperative, interrogatory, exclamatory, or declarative) as well as the way the words are spoken to see how the writers of the ads appeal to their selected audiences. Considering the audience should be a major part of this exploration and analysis.

    In the ads on the site just mentioned, for example, the script for one of the ads is as follows:

Twilight lingers over your backyard. The charcoals turn from black, to red, to white. It's time. Four perfect steaks hit the grill, making a sizzling sound that says "Summer is here." The cicadas hit their crescendo. They're saying, "Welcome back, friend. We missed you." The feeling is mutual. Beef. It's what's for dinner.
Courtesy of the Beef Checkoff Program.

The ad uses declarative sentences to describe a scene that writers hope will appeal to listeners. The variety of sentence lengths seems more like spoken language, like a friend is talking to us. With students, discuss how the word choice creates an emotion—nostalgia, longing—that makes the product appealing, even if the listeners might not ever have grilled steaks in their backyards at twilight to a cicada serenade. The use of imagined dialogue between "friends" draws us in even more.

The words create an ideal image, maybe borrowed from movies or television, which connects the audience emotionally to the product being advertised, without ever mentioning a price. This is the hard part for students. They are more used to direct persuasion, the kind that says, "All of this for only $39.95!" To help them see the difference, have students compare ads like the Beef Industry ad to the ones with which they are more familiar, especially because those exclamation point-filled texts tend to be the kind students write when *they* want to be persuasive. After exploring several ads and analyzing the way writers use different varieties of language, including how the speaker in the beef ads sometimes drops his g's (to sound more friendly than sophisticated), students come to see how advertisers use varieties of language—formal and informal, descriptive and commanding, personal and impersonal—to create appeal for the product in the target audience.

3. After analyzing several ads and how they use language to persuade, have students write an ad. To begin, modifying an idea by Fuchs (1991), I have my students create a product from six items I give them: a piece of tag board, a paper clip, a rubber band, a popsicle stick, a brass fastener, and a piece of felt. They can add decorations and one other item of choice to the provided items to create their products.

After students have a creation, they should name it. Perrin (2007) offers ideas for teaching language through product names. Having students work through his short lesson will give them ways to use "the power of language" in naming their own products (p. 36). When they have made the product and named it, have them write a short ad to persuade their classmates to *use* the product. I encourage them to avoid trying to "sell" the product because then they get into cost wars, worrying about prices without paying attention to persuasive aspects of language. If students have analyzed a variety of ads effectively, they usually have several appropriate strategies they can use to write the ads for their products.

4. Finally, have them present their ads to the class. As they read their ads and show the product, have the class analyze the techniques of language employed and determine the effectiveness of the choices. The analysis, the writing, and the evaluation of peer ads all work to develop sensitivity to language. And the benefit to the students, as consumers who are more knowledgeable of the techniques used to entice them, will be significant.

Writing Dialogue

Although we teach students about ethos in persuasive writing, Napoli (2005) asserts that even in fiction, writers need to be believed. Some of what makes a story believable—what makes the storyteller trustworthy—is the language used by the characters. And it's hard, even for more experienced writers, to make the language of characters sound natural, in part because of the difference between speech and writing. When students are writing creatively, they need to understand how to add credibility to their stories by creating effective dialogue.

1. According to Napoli (2005), some of the aspects of speech that are difficult to imitate in writing are as follows:

   • Pitch

   • Intensity

   • Duration of sounds

   • The way individuals pronounce the same word differently

   • The way several people may speak at once or overlap

   • The syntax of dialects

Help students look for how writers represent these aspects effectively by identifying and analyzing a variety of texts. For instance, reading aloud the beginning pages of *The Great Gatsby* (Fitzgerald, 1925) allows students to hear a particular kind of speech—more formal than today's speech, perhaps, but still more like a variety of spoken language than written. That specific speech-like quality is partly a function of word choice (*rather*, *indeed*), punctuation (lots of dashes and commas), and syntax (lots of appositives and long sentences): "It was on that slender riotous island which extends itself due east of New York—and where there are, among other natural curiosities, two unusual formations of land" (p. 10). As students read texts, help them notice the characteristics of written language that translate into sounds for oral language. Another book—a picture book—that helps students develop a sense of how oral language can be represented in print is *Kibitzers and Fools* (Taback, 2005). In one of the stories in the book, we can hear the Jewish intonations in the printed word:

> **EXTENDING YOUR KNOWLEDGE**
>
> In writing about creating dialogue, Napoli (2005) acknowledges that "there are many things that happen in spoken language that cannot happen in the same manner on the page. The job is not to reproduce spoken language faithfully, but to play the game so well that no one notices the gulf between the written word and the spoken word" (p. 211). Having students listen to language, try to replicate it in writing, and then notice how authors do it will help them as writers at the same time as it generates interest and curiosity in language—both written and spoken.

"So...I'm here!" said the waiter.

"Taste this soup!" said the customer.

"Twenty-five years we have been making chicken soup," answered the waiter. "Nobody has ever complained—"

Students can see that punctuation (ellipses for pauses and exclamation points for emphasis) as well as syntax (putting "Twenty-five years" first instead of last) help to create the sound of real voices on paper. As students study novels and stories to see how the authors they read use spelling and punctuation to help readers "hear" the voices on the page, they will gain more ideas for writing their own dialogue—and develop sensitivity to the diverse ways individuals use language all around them every day.

2. Next, students need to have conversations they can practice translating into written texts. Taping conversations might create legal problems, so simply have students pay attention to conversations around them in public places and then jot down snippets of what they hear to work with more carefully in class. Crowe told me that in his preparation for writing *Mississippi Trial, 1955* (2002) he visited the South. He said he walked around the town, listening to the language as it surrounded him. Then he would write down some of the phrases and sentences he heard, trying to replicate the sounds and rhythms of speech that would be true to the place (C. Crowe, personal communication, April 26, 2005).

   Because students can't travel, using movie clips allows them to hear different patterns of speech they might be able to use for characters. Have them listen to clips of actors from old movies and hear the drawl of John Wayne; or the more formal, crisp speech of Vincent Price; or the lilting speech of Cary Grant. Then have students compare them with clips of more current speech patterns of actors like Brad Pitt or Hugh Jackman to see other speech qualities they can try to replicate in writing. Paying attention to the ways different speakers speak develops students' sensitivity to language.

3. As a class, practice how to replicate some of those different qualities to develop that sensitivity even more—and also develop students' understanding of how written and oral language differ and how written language can be used to (partially) represent speech. Have students play around with using punctuation (ellipses to show pauses, for example) or spelling (repeating letters to show duration of sounds, as in *Wha-a-a-at?*). Have them "hear" the difference between *Pleeeeease* and *Puh-lease*. Napoli (2005) also suggests using "a dash between words" or italics, to indicate stress (pp. 212–213). After practicing as a class, have students practice individually to create "voices" that they can have peers read and identify.

4. Also teach students about using dialogue tags to overcome some of the challenges of creating effective voices in written text. Many students (at least among my classes) depend so heavily on the tags or misuse them that they diminish the credibility of the writer rather than aid in revealing the characters in the story. Napoli (2005)

encourages writers to use tags that reveal the "intensity of the overall utterance," using words such as *yell*, *whisper*, *murmur*, and so on (p. 214). She rejects using tags that don't give information about intonation (such as *giggled*, which is an act that occurs, usually, before or after the comment). Tags that give information evident from the text (*asked*, *repeated*, *replied*) aren't useful. Giving students some hints about these overall intonation cues can help them write dialogue more effectively.

Rhetorical Grammar

Using Sentence Structures to Reflect Meaning

Reading aloud helps students learn about the ways sentence structures contribute to meaning—and music can help students understand rhythms of sentences.

1. When introducing students to the 1920s as a background to *The Great Gatsby* (Fitzgerald, 1925), include music of the era, namely, jazz. Students need to hear some jazz, particularly if they are unfamiliar with it. *Jazz: My Music, My People* (Monceaux, 1994) can provide background information to this listening activity, as it introduces the artists whose music influenced the time period of the novel. Be sure to have students listen to music by Duke Ellington as part of this sensory introduction so that the writing that follows will connect.

2. When students have some experience with jazz, read aloud *Duke Ellington* (Pinkney, 1998). This book provides interesting information at the same time as it allows you to teach about how the technical aspects of language—sentence structure and its effect on rhythm—can enhance our reading experience. After reading, ask students what they notice about the sound of the language. Because the book is carefully crafted so that the rhythm of the sentences sounds like jazz, students should recognize that musical element. When they do, show them some selected sentences, such as those I've included, to indicate how Pinkney created the sound through her use of punctuation. Early in the book, we don't hear the jazzy rhythm because Duke was encouraged to play traditional piano by his parents:

But his piano playing wasn't always as breezy as his stride. When Duke's mother, Daisy, and his father, J.E., enrolled him in piano lessons, Duke didn't want to go. Baseball was Duke's idea of fun. But his parents had other notions for their child. (n.p.)

Contrast that rhythm with later in the book when we hear the jazz in full swing:

Yeah, those solos were kickin'. Hot-buttered bop, with lots of sassy-cool tunes. When the band did their thing, the Cotton Club performers danced the Black Bottom, the Fish-Tail, and the Suzy Q. (n.p.)

Although word choice plays a part in the rhythm (something students should note), they should also see that the sentences vary greatly in length, lending themselves to the rhythm that is reminiscent of the jazz music they have been listening to.

3. Be sure to consider with students why these choices might have been made. In fact, contrasting the book *Duke Ellington* with the page about him in *Jazz: My Music, My People* (Monceaux, 1994) will encourage students to see the difference. The writing by Monceaux is lovely, but it isn't jazzy: "Growling, muted brass instruments, liquid clarinets, and smooth saxophones all had a place in his band, and were blended together with skill and subtlety. He used his piano to drive the rhythm of the piece and provide harmonies" (p. 27). Have students compare the different rhythms and determine how they are created to understand how sentence structure contributes to fluency.

> **EXTENDING YOUR KNOWLEDGE**
>
> Micciche (2004) quotes Didion about the power of sentences: "All I know about grammar is its infinite power. To shift the structure of a sentence alters the meaning of that sentence, as definitely and inflexibly as the position of a camera alters the meaning of the object photographed" (p. 721). This feeling of the ability of sentences to shape perception is exactly what I hope students gain from working with sentences in my class.

4. Next, have students apply this concept to their own writing by choosing to write about a topic and matching the sentence lengths and rhythm to the subject—long and slow to write about a drive through the country or a walk in the park (for example), or quick and jumpy to describe the last minutes of a riveting basketball game or a wild ride at the amusement park. If students still need examples of sentences and rhythm, have them find text passages or picture books that use sentence rhythms effectively and imitate them. One book they could use is *Come on, Rain!* (Hesse, 1999). Students can contrast the heavy, slow sentences that portray the hot weather before the rain with the faster (relieved!) sentences that appear after the refreshing rain comes. I also use the passage in *To Kill a Mockingbird* (Lee, 1960) where Jem is creeping onto the Radley's porch to look in the window. The sentences where he is creeping up have a rhythm that follows his slow, careful movements. The sentences where he runs back, though, read much faster (p. 53). Have students look at the word choices and sentence constructions to see how Lee makes the rhythm match the content so that they can use similar strategies in their own writing.

Alternative Suggestion: Students may have questions about the sentences Pinkney uses that are not traditional, complete sentences. As I mentioned in chapter 2, teachers should be prepared to address the issue of "minor sentences" (Weaver, 1996a, p. 252) as a stylistic choice that creates an effect. Too many writers use fragments effectively for us to tell students that they are always wrong (Schuster, 2006). Fragments or minor sentences might be inappropriate in some genres, or ineffective, or not serve a rhetorical purpose, but fragments aren't simply an issue of right and wrong. I agree with Schuster, who urges that "we must not forever exclude this writerly choice from students' revision tool kits" (p. 83).

Growing Sentences

In a recent report published by the Alliance for Excellent Education, Graham and Perin (2007) conclude that 11 practices are effective in helping students improve writing. One of those is sentence combining; in fact, they explain that sentence combining can "provide an effective alternative to traditional grammar instruction, as this approach improves students' writing quality while at the same time enhancing syntactic skills" (p. 21). Sentence combining is an activity that encourages students to combine ideas into complex syntactic structures, through one of two methods: open-ended or cued.

Open-ended combining asks students to use any method they can to combine kernel sentences into longer, more syntactically complex sentences. The advantage of this method is that students can use many options in how they combine the ideas; the disadvantage is that students are often limited to the options they know. Cued combining, conversely, is designed to give students clues so that they can combine sentences into certain constructions. The advantage is that students can be directed to build constructions they wouldn't ordinarily construct; the disadvantage is that the cues constrain (to a certain degree) the options available, which is not true of real writing. That is, when we write, we don't have cues directing us to combine our sentences in certain ways. On the other hand, once I learn about creating participial phrases or absolutes through cued sentence combining, I might then use them when I write my own sentences.

1. Begin by using open-ended combining, giving students sets of kernel sentences and asking them to combine them *in more than one way*. This is important. If they combine them only one way, they don't learn that sentences are flexible—and they might get the false idea that this is a right-and-wrong kind of activity. That is not what they should learn from sentence combining. After they've written different versions, have them make a star beside the one they like best. Then have students share their favorites and discuss the reasons they like some sentences better than others. Discussion of the sentences and the reasons why some constructions are favored over others is essential for students to gain the benefits that can accrue from work with sentence combining. These discussions develop students' sensitivity to sentences and how sentence construction can enhance meaning. These discussions also enlarge students' understanding of rhetorical effectiveness. When students are sensitive to the rhetorical effect of sentences, when they understand why some constructions appeal more than others or why some are better suited than others, they are really on the road to becoming effective writers.

2. As students continue to combine sentences, they need to have new options that extend their existing repertoires. This is the best time to introduce cued combining, selecting sentences that help students develop constructions they don't regularly use. Use the same procedures with cued combining as with open-ended: Have students combine sentences in more than one way, mark a star by the one they like best, and discuss the reason for their choices with others. The practice with cued

combining, alternating with opportunities for open-ended combining allows students to build syntactic awareness and skill. Students may not be able to name the structures they are constructing, but they can use them in their writing beyond the practice with sentences they do in the class, especially if teachers encourage such use by expecting the constructions in polished writing.

Open-ended sentences can be found in a number of sources, but I prefer to make my own out of sentences my students will read in class materials. I take a sentence I think has an interesting construction that my students can practice or learn, and I break it down into its kernel sentences. I deconstruct or "de-combine" it. Sometimes I have students do this, too, so that they begin to see how many ideas can be embedded in a sentence—and sometimes they do a better job of de-combining than I do. As an example of my own de-combining, following are some kernel sentences I used with my students (shown with their original sentences, from *An Interview With Harry the Tarantula*, Tyson, 2003):

I looked up out of the bottle.
I looked up when she opened the lid.
I looked up with my eight eyes.
I saw a huge face.
The face was staring right at me.
Original: When she opened the lid, I looked up out of the bottle with my eight eyes and saw a huge face staring right at me. (n.p.)

I can paralyze a cricket.
I can do it in one bite.
The poison will turn the cricket into something.
It will turn it into a morsel
The morsel is very juicy.
Original: In one bite I can paralyze a cricket, and the poison will turn it into a very juicy morsel. (n.p.)

For cued combining, I use some examples from books, but I have also created my own as needed. Examples of cued combining follow. The directions are to eliminate the words in italics and use the cues in parentheses to combine:

The construction crew worked steadily. *They* stopped only for a quick break. (Use -*ing*.)
Alexander the Great was king of Macedonia. *He was* one of the greatest generals in history. (Use commas.)
(*McDougal, Littell English*, 1989, p. 148)

Ray (1999) provides a series of steps for students to follow as they find structures in published writing that they might want to use in their own writing:

1. *Notice* something about the craft of a text.

2. *Talk* about it and *make a theory* about why a writer might use this craft.

3. Give the craft a *name*.

4. Think of *other texts* you know. Have you seen this craft before?

5. Try and *envision* using this craft in your own writing. (p. 120)

Teaching students to notice and imitate effective structures in published writing can help them develop understanding about language effectiveness as it also helps them gain confidence and improve as writers.

Students are more likely to create specific constructions through this method than they are with open-ended combining. However, if they don't already have the desired constructions in their sentence repertoire, then they will gain new ways of writing from this approach. After working over a period of time with both kinds of sentence combining and being expected to apply their learning to their writing, students' writing does improve its syntactic effectiveness.

Using Mentor Sentences

Imitation has a long tradition in writing instruction. I suggest it here as a method that helps students consider language in ways that benefit them as writers. With this long tradition, it will be obvious that I am not the only person to recommend the methods that follow. Many educators today—including Ray (2006), Ehrenworth and Vinton (2005), and Angelillo (2002)—advocate imitation of mentor texts as a way for students to gain understanding about language that improves their effectiveness as writers.

1.   Introduce the concept of imitation by sharing good writing with students and asking them to notice sentences. When they do, ask them why they are drawn to a particular sentence. When I use mentor texts with the whole class, I have ideas of particular sentences that I hope they will see, but I try to let the experience be one that allows students to explore language, finding structures that fit their needs and appeal to them as writers. To that end, students need to know how to look for sentences and structures, so we practice in class and then they work on their own. I have found the text from *Scarecrow* (Rylant, 1998) an effective way to begin. The first few pages of the book contain these sentences:

His hat is borrowed, his suit is borrowed, his hands are borrowed, even his head is borrowed.

And his eyes probably came out of someone's drawer.

But a scarecrow's life is all his own. (n.p.)

By reading the text a few times and then looking at the way the sentences are structured, students notice many things (even from these beginning lines) that they can use in their own writing. They don't know the "names" for what they observe, but they identify the repetition of ending elements (epistrophe) and the use of a different phrasing to emphasize an idea. They don't always notice the lack of conjunction in the first series of joined clauses (asyndeton), but sometimes they do. In later sentences in the book, they will notice the repetition of initial words (anaphora), the elimination of that initial repetition (ellipsis), and lists. After students find structures that they like, discuss the effects of the different structures. It's important that this isn't seen as just "find and copy." Discussion of the effect of the choice is essential to students' growth as writers.

2. When students understand how the structures work and what they do for the writing, have them find places in their own writing where they can experiment with those structures. Growth as writers doesn't happen all at once, but, eventually, students' sensitivity to language manifests itself in their writing as they implement the structures they've imitated from published writers who use language in interesting ways.

Alternative Suggestion: Imitation can extend beyond the sentence level, too, as students develop their abilities to recognize, consider, and use textual structures and elements that are effective. For example, in *Mississippi Trial, 1955*, Crowe (2002) uses language effectively to describe a place:

> Coffee. When I was at Gramma and Granpa's house, I woke up every morning to the smell of coffee. The nutty aroma floated up the back stairs and into my room through the transom window above my door. Once I was awake, I tried to separate the other aromas of my grandparents' house: Some mornings the meaty, spicy scent of sausage came up the stairs; other days the sweet fragrance of fresh muffins. Behind those morning smells lingered the mellow scent of mildew, wood, and Ivory soap. To this day, if you dropped me blindfolded at my grandparents' home, I'd know I was there as soon as you opened the door. (p. 9)

When we reread the passage, we can see the effective use of adjectives, as well as alliteration and specific details. I help students prepare to write a descriptive passage that imitates this one using these steps:

- Think of a place you have good memories of. Write down where it is.
- Put yourself in that place. Look around. Now smell. Brainstorm all the smells you associate with the place.
- Choose the most significant smell. What is it? Write down the word, just the word. Now explain why that smell is significant. Then talk about the other important smells with this beginning: *Other times....* Then list the least noticeable smells with this start: *Behind those smells....* Finally, end with this sentence and complete as appropriate for your place: *To this day, if I were taken blindfolded to _____, I'd know I was there as soon as I _____.*

Here's the way I completed the imitation—and I share it to show how the imitation allowed me to use effective language to explore a memory that I hadn't thought about for years but that is significant to me.

> Cinnamon. That was first when we opened the door from the cold into Grandma's oven-warm kitchen. It blew in steamy gusts that accompanied us as we entered. After we unbundled ourselves, leaving coats and boots and hats and scarves and mittens in a pile by the door, I would notice the other smells: coffee first, then grandpa's cigars. Behind those, especially when I'd spend the night, I would notice the lemon polish and the musty smell of wet wool from our snowy boots soaking the rugs. To this day, if I were taken blindfolded to my grandparents' house, I'd know I was there as soon as I smelled cinnamon.

QUESTIONS FOR REFLECTION

1. What writing assignments do you currently give students that could be adjusted to include a component that enhances your students' language learning?

2. How can you make writing and grammar more integrated in your classroom?

3. Where in other places of the writing process, besides editing, can you include language lessons that will benefit your students as writers?

CHAPTER 4

Challenges With Teaching Language: Working With English–Language Learners and Preparing Students for Testing

"Language is the tool of my trade.
And I use them all—all the Englishes I grew up with."

—AMY TAN

BACK IN THE CLASSROOM...

T:	OK, let's try parallel structure with our own ideas. We wrote about predicting the jury's response to Atticus's final speech. Let's say we're going to try to persuade someone else about our prediction. We really want to convince them that our prediction is correct, so we'll give them at least two reasons and we'll put the reasons in parallel structure. For example, I might write [Writing on overhead]: "The jury will believe Atticus because he put himself in the jury's shoes by taking off his coat and tie and emphasized Mayella's guilt and the lies of racism." Where are the parallel parts? What are the two things he did?
Trent:	"Put himself in the jury's shoes" and "emphasized Mayella's guilt and the lies of racism." But I have a question about your first try. Can you add more stuff onto one part of the parallel structure like that? Make one part really long while the other's short?
Jon:	And is that right to say two things in one section? I mean, your sentence also says he emphasizes two things, so it's like doubling up.
T:	Sure, you can say more in one part of the parallel pieces. If you keep all the parts of the structure exactly the same in length, you create a special effect with rhythm that's called *isocolon*. Now, hardly anyone knows this term, but it's kind of cool to know. What it means is that each part of the

parallel structure is exactly the same in length on top of being the same in structure. So "I came, I saw, I conquered" would be an example of isocolon. But lots of times we can't stay exactly the same in length because we need to add more information to one part of the structure, so we just make sure the main parts are parallel. I thought he emphasized two things, so I had to add them. Does that make sense?

Trent: There are lots of *ands*. Is that OK? I mean, it's kind of confusing.

T: Good point, Trent. To us, the sentence makes sense because I read it a certain way. To a reader, it might be confusing. How can I revise it to reduce potential confusion?

Trent: "The jury will believe Atticus because by taking off his coat and tie he put himself in their shoes and...." I want to say "he emphasized" but now it seems like he emphasized guilt and lies because he took off his coat. That won't work.

T: But it's a good try. Sometimes it takes a few tries. Any other suggestions?

Leslie: Can you say, "The jury will believe Atticus because after he put himself in their shoes by taking off his coat and tie, he emphasized Mayella's guilt and the lies of racism"? Then the parallel part is short—only the two things he emphasized.

T: What do the rest of you think? It's parallel, but it's different. Does it say what we mean?

Several: Yeah. It's easier to understand without all the *ands* in a row.

T: Thanks, Leslie. I like it better because it also allows the emphasis to be on those two things he emphasized instead of making it equal to taking off his coat. Good work. Now all of you take a few minutes to write your parallel sentences and be ready to share them.

T: [After several minutes] OK, first, I want you to share your responses with the person next to you. See if you can identify the parallel parts and help make sure the sentences work in parallel structure. Then we'll share some. [After some time has passed] Who'll share first? Matt? Thanks.

Matt:	"The jury will be convinced because Atticus went over the evidence and reminded them of their duty." I had it different in my first sentence, but Angie helped me change it.
T:	Is it parallel?
Several:	Yeah.
T:	What did you have different, Matt?
Matt:	Well, I wanted to say more about their duty, but it made it so it wasn't parallel. My first sentence was "Atticus went over the evidence and made them think about the duty they had to make sure the court was fair."
T:	Actually, Matt, that is still parallel because you have two verb phrases— "went over the evidence" and "made them think about the duty..." so both would work. Everyone look at the bottom of page 205. I want you to see the next-to-the-last sentence Atticus uses. It starts "I am confident...." Do you see it? Atticus wants the jury to do three things. What are those three things?
Tiffany:	"Review without passion the evidence you have heard, come to a decision, and restore this defendant to his family."
T:	Yes. *Review*, *come*, and *restore*. Those are all the same kinds of verbs, so the sentence is parallel. But do you see that what comes after them is of different lengths? That doesn't make it unparallel; it just makes it not iso-colon, which is OK. So, both your sentences worked, Matt. Who else?
Tanner:	"Even though Atticus gave a good speech, the jury won't be convinced because they come from a prejudiced town and they are worried that people will come after them if they say he's innocent." Does that work?
T:	What do the rest of you think?
Jon:	"They" and "they." That's the parallel part, right?
T:	I think we need to go a little more into the sentence than that, just to be sure. Remember it's not just that the same words are repeated.

Angie:	What if he just said, "They won't be convinced because they are prejudiced and afraid"?
T:	Tanner, does that say what you want it to say? It's parallel and it's economical, but does it say what you meant?
Tanner:	It would if I could add "afraid of what other people in town will do to them." Would that still be parallel?
T:	What do you think?
Tanner:	Yeah, because I'm still keeping the two first parts, "prejudiced" and "afraid." Yeah, I like it better.
T:	Anyone else?
Sara:	I'm not sure this works, but I wanted to try something else. "Atticus convinced the jury by reviewing the evidence, making himself an equal, and reminding the jury that the courts should be different than the town." I have all the parts starting with -ing words, but they are different after that. Is it right?
T:	Let's have you read it again, and everyone listen to see if the parts are parallel.
Sara:	"Atticus convinced the jury by reviewing the evidence, making himself an equal, and reminding the jury that the courts should be different than the town."
Several:	Yeah.
T:	I think it works. Nice try at extending the idea.

For about five months during my junior year of college, I attended school in Paris, France. Prior to that semester, I had had several years of high school French and two years of college French. When I first arrived in Paris, thinking I knew something of the language, I was rudely awakened: I could barely make myself understood—and I could rarely understand anyone else. By the time I left, though, things were different. I felt confident that I could understand and speak French adequately, if not well. I could ask directions, find my way, communicate with clerks and waitresses and gendarmes. I had met several French students of my age and we socialized. I went to French movies and plays. I could visit with the concierge in my building and felt comfortable wherever I went knowing that if I didn't speak the language well, I could at least do what I needed to do.

I recently returned to Paris many years after my schooling there. My French was rusty, to put it nicely. At first, it took me a long time to formulate the questions I needed to ask or the requests I wanted to make. I could only vaguely understand the responses I received. But I found my understanding and ability with the language coming back rather quickly. After 10 days, I was dreaming in French again! Both times, though, my experience as a second-language learner made me realize some things about learning another language that help me understand something about English-language learners (ELLs) in the classroom. I liked people to correct me sometimes, but I liked them to do it helpfully, not rudely. I didn't like them to treat me as though I was unintelligent just because I couldn't remember the gender of a particular noun or the appropriate conjugation of a verb. I found that when I asked for something incorrectly in a shop and the clerk repeated the request correctly but as a question, I learned without feeling judged. And I appreciated when people waited while I formed sentences and questions, showing appreciation that I was trying to speak their language.

The number of ELLs in U.S. schools is increasing. NCTE reports that between 1996 and 2006 the population has grown 65% (2006, ¶2). Cruz (2004) estimates that "close to 7 percent of all secondary students are categorized as having limited English proficiency" (p. 14). Andrews (2006) suggests that the numbers might be even higher, noting that "the percentage of limited English proficient students enrolled in kindergarten through 12th grade nationwide from the 1991–1992 through the 2001–2002 school years increased 95%.... During that same decade, the overall school-age population increased by 12%" (pp. 316–317). Even without statistical evidence, teachers in many classrooms already know the challenge of teaching English classes with increasing percentages of ELLs. At a conference a few years ago, I sat next to a teacher from Indianapolis. She told me that in the past 10 years, her classes had gone from having one or two English as a second language (ESL) students to being the reverse: In her current class, 90% of the students had English as a second language. This was in the Midwest—not in border or coastal states that have traditionally had higher numbers of second-language learners. The pressure on schools and teachers who have not historically faced the concerns of teaching English to ELLs is great. The related issues can no longer be considered a regional or local concern.

At the same time, public concerns for accountability have raised pressures to measure student achievement in language, both written and spoken. As a result, most states have tests in place that are supposed to measure this achievement. Consequently, not only are ELLs on the spot, but so are native English speakers who may use dialects or vernacular language that doesn't conform to the kind of language being measured in the tests. We also have to concern ourselves with teaching a dialect of English to native speakers: formal or academic English. In this way, the

> **EXTENDING YOUR KNOWLEDGE**
>
> Teachers who find their classes increasingly populated with students for whom English is not their first language sometimes panic, wondering what practices they should use to help these students learn. Andrews (2006) assures us that "Certified ELL teachers are not wizards of the arcane; they do not employ academic alchemy. They modify successful, proven practices in order to meet the needs of their students" (p. 325). We can do that.

concerns about preparing students for tests and helping ELLs gain proficiency with the language overlap. Both require classrooms where the best practices for thinking about, learning, and using language are employed.

English–Language Learners

Because of the growing numbers of ELLs in classes across the United States, more and more information is available to teachers about how we can help our classrooms become places that value those students' home languages at the same time as we help them acquire English-language skills that will bring them success. Haussamen (2003) suggests that teachers first need to have a sense of the differences among languages. In *Grammar Alive!* he provides an accessible overview of some of the most common languages we meet with students in our classrooms. In summary, Haussamen (2003) provides the following list of ways that those languages may diverge from English:

> **EXTENDING YOUR KNOWLEDGE**
>
> I am reassured by the following sentence from *Grammar Alive!* because, as a teacher, I often feel I can't learn enough fast enough to be the best teacher to my ELLs: "The first and best way to differentiate instruction for your ESL students is to be a gracious host to them in the classroom" (Haussamen, 2003, p. 51). *That I can do.*

1. The nouns might take gender.

2. Other languages may use articles differently, or no articles at all.

3. Plurals may be formed by adding words or syllables to the sentence, or by giving context clues in the sentence.

4. The word order may not follow the familiar subject-verb-object pattern.

5. The pronoun may not have to agree in gender or number with its antecedent.

6. Other languages may have fewer prepositions, making it confusing for the novice to know which preposition to use in English. Also, the preposition may not precede its object.

7. There are differences in inflection and pacing.

8. There are differences in written conventions, such as punctuation and capitalization.

9. Nonverbal communications, such as gesture, eye contact, silences, and what people do to indicate that they understand, differ from culture to culture. (p. 55)

By knowing these basic differences, I am better able to understand why ELLs in my classroom use the constructions they do in their writing. As a result, I am better able to help them learn. In addition to learning about the differences among languages, Lee (2005) urges teachers to know something about the students and their first languages: "Only after teachers recognize what communicative resources students bring with them, can they begin to successfully help them acquire the language rules of the classroom" (p. 19). Research suggests that students' understanding of their first language may have some impact on their acquisition of the second language (Harmon & Wilson, 2006; Heck, 1999). And teachers who know something about the students, about their background and their interests, can select instruction and activities that will most benefit those students' acquisition of language in the classroom.

Besides teachers who care about them and learn something about them, what else do ELLs need to gain language skills in our classrooms? One big thing is time. We need to remember that language acquisition is a lengthy process and that there might be backsliding and uneven development before any significant progress is recognized. The *NCTE Position Paper on the Role of English Teachers in Educating English Language Learners (ELLs)* (2006) asserts the importance of providing time for these students, encouraging teachers to remember that learning a second language "is a gradual developmental process" and to build "on students' knowledge and skill in their native language" (¶14).

We also need to have ELLs do "immediate things" with language in order to help them gain language facility (Andrews, 2006, p. 322). Christy (2005) refers to these activities as "everyday" uses of language—students reading newspapers or listening to news reports and then talking about what they've read or heard. She also suggests pairing students, a native English speaker with an English-learning student, and having them make short, informal presentations to the class about idioms or colloquialisms that may be confusing to the ELLs but necessary to their communication skills. I know that when I was in Paris I would hear phrases that didn't seem to make sense (they say it's "raining ropes" or "raining frogs" instead of "raining cats and dogs," as Americans do, to describe heavy rain). When I heard these phrases or terms, I would write them down and take them to a French friend who spoke some English and who lived upstairs from us. He would explain the meaning so that I was able to learn more about the everyday uses of French than I learned in my classes. By spending a few minutes of class time explaining idioms and expressions, teachers not only help develop ELLs' understanding of English, but they also help native speakers learn something about their own language that will develop their sensitivity to it.

Besides reading everyday texts such as newspapers, websites, and magazines, we can use literature to help ELLs learn more about English. Kooy and Chiu (1998) assert that "literature—a place where language and culture meet—offers a significant source" for what they call a "broader vision" for helping ELLs gain fluency with language (p. 79). "Literature," they continue, "merits its own place in ESL teaching and learning—not only for its intrinsic worth, but as an integral part of a language-learning program" (p. 79). We should choose literature that will help students learn about language as well as about the context in which that language occurs.

Literature—both traditional as well as picture books—should be read aloud to students, at least some of the time. That way, students can hear the way language in literature sounds. Reading aloud can help students understand more than they do when reading silently because teachers' inflections and the connections to illustrations (in picture books) can help students understand more than their language level would normally allow. And keeping the learning about literature social, through discussions, also helps develop students' facility with language. Such discussions, in small and large groups, help students understand what Fagan (2003) urges as important to all students, not just ELLs, "that the words on the page should be *thought* about and not just decoded" (p. 38). Kooy and Chiu (1998) recommend a variety of activities when teachers implement literature as a way to help students engage with and develop language: not only sharing insights through whole-class readings but also through book clubs and reading logs. As they note, "texts alone do not change ESL classes or mystically improve language. *How the texts are read and shared* brings language to life and life to the literature" (p. 82, emphasis added). When teachers read aloud and then encourage a variety of language-rich activities as ways to respond to literature, all students learn language more effectively.

Frequent writing in a variety of genres also helps students develop their language skills. By writing informally, students are able to express themselves without worrying about every aspect of written language—thus developing fluency and the ability to convey thoughts through writing. Using models helps students extend the range of options they see available to them as writers. Teachers' comments on more formal writing should be explicit and clear to help students understand where their use of written language doesn't communicate as well as it could. In terms of correcting, though, repeated studies show that grammar correction does not necessarily result in improved use of the corrected concepts in further writing (Gray, 2004; Loewen, 1998). Gray's research shows that the use of teachers' time in correcting multiple errors was neither a good use of time nor beneficial to the student in the long run. Gray lists several possible reasons for what Sjolie (2006) calls the "incomprehensible" corrections not being helpful. Those reasons include teachers and students not communicating well—teachers misunderstanding student writing and students finding teachers' comments "vague, confusing, and contradictory" (Gray, 2004, ¶9). Despite the research, teachers often feel compelled to "correct" writing for ELLs, and students often believe that is the role the teacher should play in helping them with writing (Gray, 2004). Loewen (1998) reports that many of his students had this opinion, although "more than half could not identify the type of correction used on their essays" (¶34).

Clearly, writing is essential to students' development with English, but correcting many errors in that writing may not achieve what teachers hope it will. It might be more effective to give students lots of opportunities to write for different purposes and audiences—purposes and audiences that expect different levels of correctness with language. Students can use informal writing situations to take risks. With formal writing, teachers might focus on a specific aspect to work on improving, instead of feeling that every misuse of language should be addressed.

Besides being given the opportunity to use writing to develop their language skills, ELLs also need to know the language of academics—but that is something all our students need. As Hagemann (2003a) observes, "For language minority students and for nonreaders, learning 'school talk' is a monumental task" (p. 73). In fact, many researchers (e.g., Heck, 1999; Horning, 1987) suggest that what may be the best way for all students—ELLs, speakers of a vernacular form of English, or students who haven't had much exposure to print text—to learn academic language is to approach it as a second language or, as Hagemann calls it, a "second dialect" (p. 73). All students need to learn the meaning of terms such as *analyze* and *synthesize*, and they all need to learn the structures of sentences used in academic writing.

Much of the research literature suggests that good instruction for ELLs is also good instruction for native English-speaking students (Andrews, 2006; Burke, 2004; Harmon & Wilson, 2006). If we are aware of the differences in the languages their students come to class with—whether that is another language or a dialect of English—and if teachers come to know their students, their choices of effective practice will benefit all students as they develop facility with and awareness of multiple levels of language use.

> **EXTENDING YOUR KNOWLEDGE**
>
> Hagemann (2003a) notes that "given what we know about how languages/dialects are learned, pedagogical approaches that encourage language minority students—indeed *all* students—to notice, understand, compare, test out, and integrate new formal features into their writing facilitate their overall success in learning 'school talk'" (p. 76). Providing these opportunities is an important part of effective pedagogy for teaching all students about academic language.

Preparing for Tests

Because tests differ on what they expect students to know, it's important for teachers to know what their own state's test will assess students on. Some states are more traditional and others less so in their approaches to what they see as achievement in language. States may test a variety of aspects of language such as usage, punctuation, spelling, syntax, levels of formality, even structures of paragraphs and essays. Some states ask students to identify parts of speech (nouns, adjectives, or prepositions) or parts of sentences (subjects and predicates) on tests, while others ask students to select the "correct" sentence from a list of options. If a test asks for parts of speech, students will need to know those, and—despite how we might feel about teaching traditional definitions—we do students a disservice if we fail to help them learn what they need to succeed on the tests. We can and should work to make changes in those tests, to help those who make the tests or who mandate them understand best practice. In the meantime, though, we should also use best practice when we prepare students for tests. For me, that means not spending all of class time on test preparation and, instead, helping my students put what they need to know to succeed on the test in perspective with the other things they should be learning that will extend past the test and into their lives beyond school, as I show in the dialogue that begins this chapter and the next. There, I address concepts students will need for large-scale tests—but not as test prep.

If a state's test asks students to identify parts of speech, it would be important, first, for teachers in that state to understand that words aren't only one part of speech—the part of speech is determined partly by the function of the word in the sentence. *Grammar Alive! A Guide for Teachers* (Haussamen, 2003) gives a good, brief explanation of form, function, and frame to help teachers appropriately address traditional grammar for tests—at the same time as it gives students a useful foundation for moving beyond definitions. Simply teaching the definitions of parts of speech doesn't accomplish what we want, as they are mostly "definitions that do not define" (Schuster, 2003, p. 19). Meyer (2003) compares words to pieces of a chess game; the part of speech (or the use of the pawn) isn't always the same—it depends on "the way it fits into the system" (p. 40). Helping students learn that concept will prepare them for the test and will also move them beyond simply thinking of words as belonging to one category or another, unconnected to use. Beyond the fact that the definitions of parts of speech rarely help students identify, much less use, words correctly, Meyer (2003) argues that tests that require students to consider definitions as essential to parts of speech do a disservice to students' understanding of English as a whole because they "[reinforce] the idea that the structure of English is already completely known and is no longer subject to increased understanding or insight. What is being tested here is knowledge, not of serious study of English grammar, but of tradition" (p. 38). Helping students understand how to answer the questions on the test about parts of speech is important; helping them understand how that knowledge is only the beginning of understanding the dynamic nature of English is the rest of the story, the big part of the iceberg that is under the water. We don't want to leave students unaware of the immense part of language that is there for them to discover.

Some tests ask students to identify the correct or "best" sentence from a variety of options. These sentences may have issues with punctuation or with grammar or usage (such as pronoun or subject–verb agreement). The ability to select the "correct" sentence from the choices is often seen as evidence of the students' ability to write well. I know—that doesn't make sense. How can choosing a sentence be the same as writing one? But that is what we have. To help students prepare for these tests, then, students need to think about and play around with sentences—ones they write and ones they read. We may need to have students take an effective sentence and mix it up, make it part of a test question for the rest of the students in the class, so that they can practice moving from the "correct" to the "incorrect." Will students know how to do this? Probably not at first, but they can learn. And it makes more sense to me that they work with good sentences, sentences that do what they are supposed to do, more than with seeing "problem" sentences in three out of every four examples.

As teachers, we need to develop students' sensitivity to sentences. We can do this, at least in part, by reading aloud to students and commenting on sentences that work well so that students become aware of how effective sentences work. Such practices encourage students to begin to notice effective sentences themselves. Even if they don't write them, the practice will help them on tests that ask them to simply pick the most effective sentence—not write one. Developing that sensitivity will help them when sentences like the following are among their choices:

> I see the park going to school every day.
>
> **Which is the best way to write this sentence?**
>
> A. Every day I see the park going to school.
>
> B. I see the park on the way to school every day.
>
> C. Every day I see the park on my way to school.
>
> D. I see the park every day going to school.
>
> (*California Standards Test Grade 9*, California Department of Education, 2005, p. 35)

Students would first need to note that the question asks them about *writing* the sentence and not speaking it, because in speech we would all be able to know exactly what the speaker meant. Not many students are going to read the sentence in its original form and really think the park is going to school. The best way to help students with questions like this is to have them hear, read, and think about good sentences—about how they work and the way they convey meaning. In that way, students will develop the sensitivity they need to prepare for not only the tests but also their own needs as readers and writers.

Do the methods of teaching writing that we use to help students grow as writers work in preparing students for tests of writing that don't ask students to write? Do they even help prepare them for tests that do require writing? Warne (2006) speaks to those questions when she addresses Romano's approach to teaching conventions. Romano (2004) asserts, "I want students to steadily improve their skills in language and in producing written texts that reflect the norms of standard edited English (and to break those norms when they can do so meaningfully)" (p. 74). When Warne argues that Romano "advocates rule breaking for valid communication or artistic purposes—but he was not preparing students for a high-stakes test" (Warne, 2006, p. 24), she makes a good point. How do we help students think about writing as they should—adapting it according to their purposes, audiences, situations, and genres, when what will really matter (at least in the short term) is their ability to correct sentences like the following on a test?

> It is easily the best place in the city <u>for: sports,</u> picnics, concerts, walking, and enjoying nature.
>
> **How should the underlined part of the sentence be written?**
>
> A. for—sports,
>
> B. for: sports,
>
> C. for sports,
>
> D. for: sports
>
> (*California Standards Test Grade 9*, California Department of Education, 2005, p. 35)

As Weaver (2007) shows in her analysis of American College Testing (ACT) language questions, many test questions are complex, measuring multiple areas of knowledge about language. Whether or not tests ask for grammatical terms, we need to be aware that a broad exposure to written language with an eye toward noticing what happens in the craft of writing is probably a solid preparation for tests of language. And it benefits students as writers, too.

From experiences described by Smoot (2001) and Gold (2006), it's clear that parents and administrators—even students—often want class material to focus directly on the test. Gold (2006) describes having parents upset that his teaching, based on research into best practice, didn't seem to be preparing their children to succeed on standardized tests. He acknowledges that "to a parent fearful that his or her child will do poorly on the SAT [Scholastic Aptitude Test], no amount of citing educational research is going to allay that fear; we need to make a personal connection" (p. 46). By having parents read their children's writing and see improvement over time, Gold was able to show that his teaching could accomplish both purposes: prepare students for tests and help them improve as writers. Smoot's (2001) experience was a little different, perhaps partly because he worked in a different situation. In his school, students also resisted the teaching of grammar integrated into reading and writing, but mostly because they wanted a unit on grammar to have a definite beginning and end.

> ### EXTENDING YOUR KNOWLEDGE
>
> Poth (2006) cites research to support Smoot's conclusions: "Students should learn information in the specific way that they are to recall it in order for the transfer of that learning" (p. 11). Still, that doesn't mean all the time we spend helping students prepare for tests must be in formats exactly like the test. Nor does it mean that we need to spend a lot of time practicing for the tests. If students have good instruction that prepares them for multiple situations, limited test practice will be sufficient to prepare students for tests because it will build on that solid instruction.

In addition, Smoot found that having students do well on the standardized tests "meant working at least some of the time within that traditional framework" (2001, p. 39). In other words, the teaching had to match (at least some of the time) the assessment. Even though students' writing and reading abilities improve through effective integrated instruction, testing means we have to think about the test and work at least partly with the goals and principles the tests value and measure. Weaver (2007) gives the following advice to teachers about how to approach language instruction in times of testing:

1. Don't abandon best practice in the teaching of writing.
2. Make the most of the overlap between revision and editing skills needed for your state's test.
3. Reserve for test preparation those items that are important for your students, not only for the test but as writers.
4. Use practice test items with students.
5. Teach students to write like published authors and then teach the standardized test's "rules" as part of test preparation. (pp. 64–65)

I support the suggestions. Students need to know what's expected on the tests—but they also need to know that tests are only one measure of writing ability. If they know that language shifts for different situations—and they know the language needed in the different situations—they should be able to make the adjustment between testing and using language in other, more authentic, situations.

In the lesson ideas that follow, I have tried to consider the needs of ELLs as well as the needs of all students who must adjust language for different situations, including those of testing. I am comforted by the comments of many of the teachers whose writing I've read as I've tried to determine the best approaches for my students who do not have English as their first language or academic English as a dialect. As Burke (2004) explains,

> ESL students have unique needs, to be sure, but in many respects, good teaching for one group of students is good for all students, so long as the teacher uses the techniques that move everyone forward regardless of their current ability. (p. 42)

The ideas that follow take into account the general philosophy of language this book promotes as well as what Burke urges. I hope they help every student grow with regard to language understanding and use, especially in high-stakes situations.

Traditional Grammar

Writing a Story Collaboratively

Using the children's book *Fortunately* (Charlip, 1964) as a prompt helps students generate sentences and connect them to previous sentences, and it teaches them about adverbs and agreement of pronouns and subjects and verbs. At the same time, students are having fun in a collaborative writing project.

1. Begin by reading the book aloud to the students. It is a story about a boy whose life is punctuated by alternating fortunate and unfortunate events. The events are linked by the two adverbs (*fortunately* and *unfortunately*), and students quickly see the pattern the book establishes.

2. After briefly discussing the book's pattern, have each student write the opening sentence to a story at the top of a piece of paper—a sentence that sounds as if it will bode well for the character mentioned in it and begins "Fortunately." It's important for teachers to know (and to share with students) that this book was published in 1964. Since then, the expectations for comma use after an introductory adverb have shifted. According to current grammar handbooks, every one of the sentences should have a comma after the adverb, but the text does not have them. If you show the sentences to students, you might want to make clear the changed expectations so that students will know them for tests and other situations where it will matter. Certainly, you should make students aware of the current expectation so that they can practice it when they write the sentences for their stories.

3. When all the students have written a beginning sentence, have them pass their paper to another student. This student writes the next sentence that begins "Unfortunately" and complicates the story by showing a negative, unanticipated outcome. Continue this process for several sentences, with each student reading the sequence of sentences on the new page he or she is handed and continuing the pattern of fortunate and unfortunate events. After several passes, have students start writing sentences that seem to circle around to (potentially) resolving the story. The final person should write the last two or three sentences to finish the story. Give the papers back to the original writers and have them share them in small groups.

4. As students read the stories aloud or share them with their groups, they can check for appropriate grammar conventions (punctuation of initial adverbs, subject–verb and pronoun agreement) as well as vote for which story to read to the whole class. Students tend to feel less worried about sharing because the story is a result of group effort. Any "errors" that might exist are fairly anonymous, so you and your students can discuss them without worrying about putting a single person on the spot. By generating the writing that is used for the instruction, students are more invested in their learning about the grammar involved.

Identifying Adjectives and Using Them in Writing

One task some state tests ask students to do is identify adjectives in sentences. Although such a task doesn't have much application outside of a testing situation, students' ability to use adjectives effectively—to communicate clearly and to set a mood—is one that can benefit all student writers. Haussamen (2003) also recommends the practice for ELLs.

1. Begin by reading the book *Where the Wild Things Are* (Sendak, 1991). At the page where the wild things first appear, stop and have students visualize their own "wild things." Then, have them draw their vision—but the head only—on a piece of 9 in. × 12 in. tag board. Where the mouth of the monster is, have students cut two horizontal slits, at least a ½ in. apart and 2 in. long.

2. Next, have students brainstorm words that describe. Talk about the questions adjectives answer—questions about what kind, which one, how many, or what color. You can also help students to understand the forms of the words: They can end in -ed (such as *iced*) or -y (such as *silly*) or -ing (such as *bleeding*) or -ous (such as *enormous*).

3. After the class brainstorms, have students individually list possible adjectives for their wild things, using words that describe either the appearance or the character. When they have the start of a list, have them work with a partner to generate more word possibilities. After students have a number of possibilities, they should identify the best 10 and write them on a strip of paper (just under 2 in. wide and about

10 in. long). The words should be listed just a little more than a ½ in. apart. When students are done, have them thread the paper through the two slits on the mouth of the monster so that one adjective at a time shows in the mouth. Have students share their wild things and the words they've selected to describe them with each other and with the class.

4. Finally, have students use the adjectives to write a description of their wild things. At this point, I address structures that they can use as alternates to "My monster is *big*," repeated in various forms. We discuss using prepositional phrases ("*enormous*" could become "with an *enormous* mouth"), changing adjectives to adverbs ("*wild*" could become "swinging his arms *wildly* about his head"), or using adjectives out of order ("*green, hairy* monster" could be written as "*green* and *hairy*, the monster..."), in sentences like these that I wrote as an example: "Shockingly green and hairy, the enormous monster frightened the penguins who had never seen such a furry beast—nor one so colorful. The screeching monster gestured wildly with his four arms while his three long ears bounced like bunnies around his square head." By isolating the adjectives first and then using them in a variety of ways in their writing, students can begin to see how adjectives work in writing so that if they need to identify them for a test, they have some idea of the places adjectives live in sentences.

> **EXTENDING YOUR KNOWLEDGE**
>
> Some parents or observers might question the appropriateness of this activity for secondary students. Weaver (2007) notes that "for some—perhaps many—classes at all grade levels, focusing on sensory detail and the use of precise nouns, verbs, adjectives, and adverbs may be an important prelude to playing around with more sophisticated modifying constructions" (p. 58). She continues by saying that "activities appropriate for elementary students are often equally appropriate for students at higher levels" (p. 58). It has certainly been my experience that many secondary students need the activities that we think belong only in elementary school in order to gain the learning they still need as older students.

Alternative Suggestion: Burke (2001) recommends another way to have students use their knowledge of grammar terminology: to annotate directions on tests and assignments. Students underline the verbs in the prompt to make sure they respond appropriately. He explains that "such work up front not only helps students manage the assignment, but reinforces for them that words have a function and that function informs" (p. 58). After annotating prompts a few times, have students write their own directions for an assignment and then trade them with a classmate who annotates the student-generated version to give feedback on verbs.

Editing

Becoming Observant About Punctuation

One of the most obvious ways to help students learn editing skills needed for tests or for formal, academic writing is to have them study punctuation in the texts they read. To see it and notice it and talk about it would be the best preparation they could have.

A student teacher I observed had her students stand and use what she called the "Victor Borge" method of punctuating. Following Borge's lively and exaggerated movements when playing the piano, students made large gestures in the air to emphasize quotation marks, commas, periods, even colons. It was great to watch; students really got into it. Best of all, students really knew their editing and paid more attention to punctuation when they read and wrote.

1. First, help students become observers of punctuation by drawing their attention to it as you read texts together. Doing so will be more meaningful and generally provides better learning than instruction with "rules." For example, looking at sentences from *Long Night Moon* (Rylant, 2004) can help students inductively learn the "rule" about commas with coordinating and cumulative adjectives that I find in *The Brief Penguin Handbook* (Faigley, 2006):

   You can recognize coordinate adjectives by reversing their order; if their meaning remains the same, the adjectives are coordinate and must be linked by *and* or separated by a comma.... Commas are not used between cumulative adjectives...two or more adjectives that work together to modify a noun. (p. 479)

   Following are some sentences from *Long Night Moon*:

   In June the Strawberry Moon shimmers on succulent buds,...on <u>quiet, grateful rabbits</u>.
   In July the Thunder Moon trembles, shudders, and disappears in a <u>thick black sky</u>. (Rylant, 2004, n.p.)

   Is it easier to see the "rule" with these sentences than it is with the explanation in the rule book? For me, it is. I think for some students it will be also. You can find additional sentences in the book that also teach the concept—and some that teach other concepts about commas and adjectives.

   Teachers with whom I work do this kind of "observant reading" with all kinds of texts they read as a class, sometimes extending their observations about a particular use of punctuation across several readings. Their work in this way effectively develops students' abilities to understand punctuation's uses.

2. But our work doesn't have to stop at only noticing punctuation in our reading—and some students might need more direction. To prepare students for tests, you might also want to periodically present a question from the test that might provide more direct practice. Although I wouldn't recommend such decontextualized practice all the time (that would be akin to the worksheets that we know didn't work in the past), seeing the type of questions asked in the test and articulating the required responses might benefit some students, especially if students can attach their answers to the observations they've made during reading. And using the test questions doesn't have to limit my explanation of language in my classroom to simple right

or wrong. For instance, I might put up the following test question one day for discussion, just so students will know the kind of multifaceted questions they will be asked:

Dear Mayor Lewis:

How should this be written?

A. Dear mayor Lewis

B. Dear Mayor Lewis—

C. My Dear Mayor Lewis,

D. Leave as is.

(*California Standards Test Grade 9*, California Department of Education, 2005, p. 35)

Note that the question requires students to consider punctuation, capitalization, and tone—all in reference to a particular genre, a business letter. Discussing this question can help my students prepare for the test, but it also allows me to talk about how the choice might change if we change the situation—so I get to use the test prep in ways that fit with my overall goals of teaching language for life outside the classroom and not simply of language as right or wrong.

Using Pattern Books to Teach About Sentence Structures and Punctuation

Many teachers of ELLs suggest the use of pattern books to help students learn the patterns of English; the strategy can work for native speakers as well because it also helps them practice editing skills as they write.

1. Begin by reading *That's Good! That's Bad!* (Cuyler, 1991) to the class and discussing the pattern. In that book, the story starts with something that looks like it will be a good thing, but then it's not—and a pattern is established that reverses itself throughout the story: "That's good! No, that's bad!" As is obvious, students will practice using apostrophes in contractions and commas after introductory words. In the rest of the sentences, they can practice other forms of punctuation as well.

2. Have students work on this story pattern by instructing them to start the story and then pass the partially completed story around the room until it's completed, as in the activity described in the previous section using the book *Fortunately* (Charlip, 1964), or by having students write their own complete story following the pattern. Either way, the emphasis should be on the way punctuation is used to help the story language match the emotion of the story's swings of fortune and misfortune. Have students work in groups and put their stories on an overhead transparency so that the rest of the class can read along and also so that students can work on the punctuation to make sure that it does what it should. Students learn punctuation—and a lot of other things about language—in the context of talking and writing.

Usage

Teaching Tone Through Analogy

One thing many tests measure is the appropriate tone for a piece of writing. Questions may ask students to choose the best way for something to be written, but they are really asking about tone, as in the following question:

In paragraph 2, sentence 5 begins with the word <u>Kids</u>. How should this be written?

A. Small children, because it is more formal

B. Tykes, because it's friendlier

C. Kids, because that's how people talk

D. Little kids, because it's more descriptive

(*California Standards Test Grade 9*, California Department of Education, 2005, p. 35)

Students will need to make a choice based on the idea of whether the word is an appropriate level of formality for the rest of the writing. It's important for them to understand that the answer isn't simple: Writers don't always choose the most formal option; nor do they always choose the friendlier, more descriptive or familiar forms. They must fit choice to situation. We can help students understand more about language by contrasting their informal usages with more formal usages. Wheeler and Swords, whose book *Code-Switching: Teaching Standard English in Urban Classrooms* (2006) provides an effective way to teach this aspect of language, note that "'Proper English' is not always proper" when they teach students about adapting usage to situation (p. 72).

> ### EXTENDING YOUR KNOWLEDGE
>
> In teaching levels of formality, we help students develop language skills that will benefit them throughout their lives. Haussamen (2003) suggests that
>
> one of the goals of education should be to make every high school graduate bidialectical. What this means is that everyone should have two language varieties, the informal, more private speech they use with family and friends, and the public, formal language of the business world and formal occasions. (p. 61)

1. Bring in different kinds of clothing to have ready for the lesson. I bring in casual clothes and more formal wear, as well as sports clothes (even a swimsuit). Have students name situations where they have to be appropriately attired. I usually begin by naming an after-school dance. Which clothes would they pick from the displayed clothing—and why? For each activity that students name, discuss why some of the choices of clothing are appropriate and some are not.

2. Next, make the connection to language: Do students know different situations where different expectations of language would be anticipated? In the discussion, be sure that students are specific: What is the situation? What specifics of language would be appropriate, and what usages might have social or economic consequences? Students (at least mine) are savvier than I realized. When I have this discussion, although students might not have thought of it before—and although they sometimes resent the expectations of different situations—they find they are al-

ready language shifters, adjusting their language to situation. As long as they have the appropriate options. When students realize the need for knowing those options, they are ready to learn some options that they don't yet have for situations they might face.

Wheeler and Swords (2006) suggest something like this activity in their book. Although they acknowledge that language and clothing have differences, the comparison works on several levels and helps students think about language in terms of appropriateness more than in terms of simple correctness. When awareness of levels of formality is more developed, Wheeler and Swords recommend having students build contrastive charts of particular usage patterns that are specific to the needs of the students. On one side of the chart, students collect examples of an informal pattern; on the other side, they collect examples of formal patterns that match in intention. By examining multiple examples and contrasting the levels of formality, students build an understanding of the "rules" that govern both—and they gain an understanding of the way that language shifts for different situations.

Wheeler and Swords (2006) also provide a "shopping list" that students use to keep track of the evidences of code-switching they see in their writing. In this way, students can review formal writing with specific usages in mind if the situation calls for formal language. Although Wheeler and Swords list the patterns they discuss in their book on their shopping list, you could adapt the idea to the usages you have addressed with your own students.

Pragmatics

Another aspect of language variety we can address with our students comes from the field of linguistics, particularly pragmatics. Hagemann (2003b) explains pragmatics as "a person's understanding of the various linguistic demands of various social contexts" (p. 116), in other words, how we adjust our language for different social situations. Because I'm not a linguist, I can speak only as a novice who finds the topic interesting. But the work on how language shifts for politeness as a reflection of differing relationships, using "various linguistic strategies such as indirectness, hedges, or politeness markers to strategically avoid conflict" (Lee, 2005, pp. 21–22), for example, is another way to raise students' awareness of language, in general, and usage, in particular.

1. Begin by explaining to students the idea of politeness as a language concept. Conduct a short discussion about how students ask friends for things as opposed to how they ask a figure of authority—say a principal or police officer. Most students already understand that we make some requests differently, depending on whom we are asking. Expand their understanding by sharing some of the reasons for these differences as explained by Lee (2005):

Each speech community develops politeness principles from which they derive certain linguistic strategies. The decisions about which strategy is used within a culture depend on how the culture assesses the following three factors: the relative power relationship between speaker and hearer...; the social distance between speaker and hearer; and the individual ranking of the particular imposition in the social context in which it is used. (p. 23)

2. Next, use an exercise suggested by Wolfram (1998) to consider the idea in more depth. Have students rank the following sentences in order of politeness, generally. Have them work individually first, and then in small groups before the whole class discusses the rankings.

   • Pass me the butter!
   • Can you pass me the butter?
   • I would like you to pass the butter.
   • You need to pass the butter.
   • Would you mind passing the butter?
   • Are you using the butter?
   • These potatoes could use some butter. (p. 105)

   There isn't a particular order to this ranking, so it's important to ask students why they made the rankings they did as a way to discuss language and its varieties in different situations.

3. Next, following Wolfram's suggestion, have students generate a list of ways to ask for something else, such as asking someone to open a door or window. By creating their own lists and ranking them, students learn more about language use, how we often create difficulties because of inattention to principles of politeness, and how these principles reflect cultural expectations. Some of these cultural expectations are related to gender, age, or relationship. I sometimes use Calvin and Hobbes comics to help students see how effective communication is a function of relationships. It seems that Calvin sometimes has trouble communicating with his parents—and understanding them. Using examples such as these or ones students bring in can solidify the point about language use. When a class is reading a piece of literature, you can reinforce this discussion by asking students to consider a request made by one character to another. How does the way the request is made show the relationship of the characters? In what other ways could the character have made the request? Why didn't he or she use another form of request? In *To Kill a Mockingbird* (Lee, 1960), for example, when Atticus is cross-examining Mayella Ewell, she is offended by his language (see pp. 181–182). It turns out she thinks Atticus's use of terms of respect such as *Ma'am* and *Miss* are mocking her. What in their relationship or in her experience would lead her to think this? Students connect this incident very well with

issues of politeness as they relate to communication and language. In this way, students learn about language variation as they learn about literature and writing.

Understanding Language Through Metaphors

Dong (2004) writes about the use of metaphors in English and how they enhance and pervade the language. To most people, metaphors are poetic devices, used mostly in descriptive writing. They are figures of speech we use consciously when we want to sound poetic or musical or, even, smart. Most of us do not realize how, as Dong asserts, metaphors have "become a part of everyday English" (p. 30). Citing Pollio's research she shows how prevalent they are: "It is almost impossible to avoid metaphors in daily life.... An average native English speaker uses about 5 metaphors per minute, 300 per hour, and more than 1,000 metaphors per day at the rate of a 4-hour speaking day" (p. 30). Nilsen and Nilsen (2004) note that the use of metaphor is

> universal because human minds all work much the same, and all speakers live in the same real world and so are likely to talk about such things as the *head* of a company and the *teeth* of a comb, a rake, or a saw. However, the details may differ because metaphors highlight only a single feature of a comparison, so the speakers of one language might choose to focus on the shape of something, while the speakers of another language might focus on an action. (p. 27)

Because many metaphors in English have parallels in other languages, the study of metaphors not only benefits ELLs' acquisition of English but also gives them opportunities to share aspects of their language with native English speakers. All students benefit as they learn more about language.

1. To begin, students may need a refresher on metaphors. In the most basic sense, they are implied comparisons—one item associated with another. They are distinguished from similes by the fact that similes make a direct comparison through words such as *like* or *as*. Metaphors can be stated somewhat directly, usually using a "be" verb: That man *is* a snake. They can also be implied—and these implied metaphors are trickier for students. Murfin and Ray (2003) explain it this way: The thing being represented by the metaphor is the *tenor* (in the previous example, the man), and the thing used to compare is the *vehicle* (in the previous example, the snake). In implied metaphors they become one thing, as in this example, "Last night I plowed through a book" because the act of reading is inferred by the metaphor of "plowing through" (p. 260). Because metaphors have this implied aspect, they are often abstract and embedded in language.

2. Share the following example with students to begin the discussion of how pervasive metaphors are in life as well as how they work through time and develop from numerous sources:

> If you say someone was *sacked* (fired), you are using a term that originated from the practice of handing workmen their tool sacks upon discharging them (Rosenthal & Dardess, 1987). If you *sack* the quarterback by tackling him (or her) behind the line of scrimmage, you're relying on a different metaphorical origin. It comes from the *sack* that means to loot and pillage, presumably because it was in sacks that one carried away the loot. And if you "hit the *sack*," you are using a World War II expression for going to bed, which for a soldier was often a bedroll or sleeping bag—a "sack." (as cited in Pugh et al., 1997, p. 13)

Even if students (or teachers) don't know the origin of the metaphors people commonly use—a blanket of snow or bending someone's ear—metaphors pervade the English language, and discussing this passage is a good way to begin to consider how they are used in English.

3. Have students listen carefully for several days for metaphors they hear around them. To get them started, make some suggestions of terms to listen for. Dong (2004) provides her students with a list of many uses for the word *bread* as literal, bread, but also as other ideas, as in these common sayings: knowing which side your *bread's* buttered on; taking *bread* out of someone's mouth, and *bread* as money. Have students keep notes on what they find until the class discussion; at that time, list all they found on the board.

4. Then have students select one metaphor they want to listen for in particular—the use of a specific term such as *table* or *bread*, or transportation or sports terms used as metaphors. They should follow their selected metaphor's use through several days (or longer), noting whenever they hear the metaphor and how it was used: by whom and in what situation. After they have several encounters with the metaphor, have them report to the class about the use of the metaphor—its frequency and any variations in meaning or situation they found. They also might find that certain metaphors are ineffective in some situations, perhaps even inappropriate for some situations. By seeing metaphors used in real-life contexts, students learn about language development and its layers as well as how to more effectively use it. Dong (2004) notes that "research has shown that class discussion of metaphorical language can cultivate critical and creative thinking and language skills" (p. 33). Investigating and reporting the metaphors they find in everyday language will benefit all students' development of language understanding.

Acquiring Academic Language

Carroll and Hasson (2004) note that some ELLs have become so proficient with the English they use in social situations that teachers may assume they have the language skills necessary to write effectively with academic language, even though the two are separate dialects. Learning to use academic language is not only a necessity for ELLs—it may also be a necessity for native English speakers, many of whom do not have the vocabulary or syntax expected for academic writing in their linguistic tool box. It's highly possible that all students will need some understanding of the dialect that is academic language for tests.

> ### EXTENDING YOUR KNOWLEDGE
>
> Heck (1999) explains that many native English speakers, when learning academic language, exhibit aspects of second-language learners. In the same way that ELLs might use vocabulary or syntax from their native language in acquiring the new language, inexperienced native speakers often transfer aspects of speech to their writing. Hagemann (2001), also seeing similarities between learning a second language and acquiring the dialect of academic English, makes this assertion: "Whether students acquire two languages or two dialects, their success depends on their ability to develop a different mental representation for each system" (p. 76). We can help all students do that.

1. Begin by collecting pieces of academic writing appropriate for your students' level to read together in class. I find that if the piece is too long, my students become overwhelmed, so in those cases I use passages (introductions, bodies, conclusions—at different times) instead of whole texts. As students read the academic pieces, ask them to mark differences they see between what they are reading and what they might say if they were retelling the same information. Discuss what they found and make some lists of differences. Students should notice specifics that correspond to these generalities: word choice (more formal); sentence structures (more complex) and sentence length variety (less variety than in speech); and, of course, differences in content and larger structures such as paragraphs and so on. Have students consider why those choices might be appropriate for the situation; that is, why does academic writing often contain these characteristics? This investigation is important because it helps students understand that the language and structures of this kind of writing are useful in certain situations, but it doesn't set up academic writing as the only way to write or the only correct way to write. It's a kind of writing that fits a situation, just as informal writing fits other situations.

2. Next, ask students to notice what they already know how to do with regards to the traits of academic writing. Do they know the sentence structures they've observed? The vocabulary? The larger structures, such as topic sentences and thesis statements and integrating others' words into our own? When students first notice the differences and then compare those differences to what they know, they are ready to learn the traits that will move them closer to the kind of writing that is accepted in academic situations.

3. Finally, help students begin to acquire the features of academic writing through practice in the classroom. Cruz (2004) suggests providing a scaffolded approach to

learning academic English, using the language and structures of academic language orally first. Have students work together to gather information about a topic of interest to the class and then present their findings in academic language. By using more formal, academic language orally first, students prepare themselves for the writing that will follow. Cruz suggests giving students sentence patterns to use in oral presentations, patterns that will transfer into writing. Her suggestions include the following:

According to (source), (state your argument...)

As noted by (state the occupation and name of source), (state your argument...)

Opponents believe that...; however.... (p. 16)

The book *They Say/I Say: The Moves That Matter in Academic Writing* (Graff & Birkenstein, 2006) provides similar help that I have found beneficial for my students. It contains words that help students integrate others' words into their own writing, in the style of academic writing, as well as sentence patterns, like those from Cruz (2004), that help students make the moves expected in academic writing. By practicing these as a class and then individually, students begin to acquire the language patterns they need to be successful with academic language.

Language Change

Discovering Different Terms for Similar Ideas

Sometimes even native speakers are unaware that other native speakers use different terms to refer to the same item or action. I enjoy my husband's use of "tricky bars" to refer to the "jungle gym" of my childhood playground—the metal climbing bars found in many school yards. As we have traveled around the United States, we have noticed the prevalence of "pop" or "soda" differs when people refer to carbonated drinks.

1. Begin the lesson by asking students to share the words they have for different items or activities. Some questions I ask to get students started include the following:

    • What do you call the things we often eat for breakfast that are a batter poured on a hot pan and then turned over and served with butter and something sweet, often syrup?

    • What do you call the pan those things are cooked on?

    • What do you call the long piece of furniture people sit on in the main social room of the house?

    • What do you call that room?

    • What do you call it when the sun appears? When it disappears?

2. When students have discussed their various answers to the questions, discuss other terms they may use that differ. For instance, many people call their grandparents by family names, rather than traditional ones. There are other regionalisms and words that change through time, too. People from older generations may have used different words for something that was in style (Groovy, Hot, Cool, and so forth). Have students think of as many examples as they can. Then have students pick an idea they find interesting and conduct informal surveys about people's use of the terms for that idea. For example, they could do a study about what people call a certain thing, such as what they call carbonated drinks.

3. Next, have students report their findings and conclusions to the class: Do people from certain places use similar terms, or is the usage more often a reflection of age or gender? What are students' feelings about what they learned? Helping students conduct a kind of ethnographic study of these terms can expand their understanding of English as well as contribute to a sense of the way language develops in different areas and among different groups.

Alternative Suggestion: As an additional look at how terms are used differently, students can research the use of different language patterns by gender (the assumption that girls use more color words, for example), or students could write a paper about a conceptual word and how it is used in different sources (see, for example, Dean, 2006, pp. 44–51).

Learning Common Words in Different Languages

One aspect of language I find interesting is the way universals are represented in different languages. I still remember a friend in elementary school who had emigrated from Sweden with her family and whose words for animal sounds were different from mine. I remember being fascinated to learn that what I thought should have been the same sound—after all, animals don't have different languages—was different for people who speak different languages. A few years ago, I watched a Public Broadcasting Service (PBS) television special about the developing brain. In the segment on babies' brains, the researchers found that all children are born with the ability to make all the sounds of all languages. By 11 months, however, their brains are wired to make the sounds of their own language. I assume, then, that we translate animal sounds into our own range of sounds.

1. Begin class by reading two picture books that deal with common sounds or words in different languages. The book *Cock-a-Doodle Doo! What Does It Sound Like to You?* (Robinson, 1993) tells how common sounds—sneezes and animal noises, for example—sound in different languages as an introduction to this idea in class. The book *Yum! Yuck!* (Park & Durango, 2005) tells of common exclamations in a variety of languages. Reading these with students gets them thinking about language diversity.

2. Discuss with the class the way different languages express common ideas or thoughts. Some students will know other languages and can share common expressions. If you have students with native languages other than English who are willing to share with the class, have them teach the class common expressions. For instance, they can share greetings (Hello, Good Morning, Goodbye), felicitations (Happy Birthday, Happy New Year, and so forth), ways to show appreciation (Cool! Thanks!), ways to show dismay or disapproval (Oh no, Take a hike, and so forth), or slang terms that might correspond to some that native English speakers use. This exploration of common usages in different languages can help students understand more about language in general and can generate curiosity and wonder about English in particular. Why do we express ideas the way we do?

Rhetorical Grammar

Generating Sentences With Patterns

As I mentioned earlier, learning sentence patterns can help students—both ELLs and native speakers—expand their range of expressions for different situations. Specific to this is the use of academic sentence patterns described earlier, but the concept can apply as well to other situations and other sentence types. I have a few different sentence patterns I use with students to help them generate writing at the same time as they learn some sentence patterns that may be of use to them in a variety of situations.

The first set of patterns comes from the book *I Want to Be* (Moss, 1993). In the book, a girl's response to the question about what she wants to be when she grows up isn't a traditional one (a lawyer, a teacher, a firefighter); instead, she describes characteristics in sentences that follow two different patterns.

1. Read the book to students first, so they can see the concept of the book and become familiar with the patterns. Then explain the patterns and have them use them to write their own "I want to be..." sentences, encouraging them to use vivid verbs and imagery for the nouns and adjectives. The first pattern is exemplified in the following sentences from the book:

I want to be green but not so green that I can't also be purple.

I want to be fast but not so fast that lightning seems slow. (n.p.)

With this pattern, I encourage students to see that the completer is not a thing, but a describer—an adjective. Following the initial assertion "I want to be *something*," students complete the pattern with the starter "but not so *something* that...." Although this particular pattern is used to describe, the general pattern of assertion followed by limitation is one that students can use in many situations, including academic ones. After students share the sentences they've written in this pattern, discuss those other possible situations as a class. For example, students could consider a sentence such as this one: Hamlet is indecisive, but not so indecisive that he fails to do something.

2. The second pattern is exemplified by the following examples:

    I want to be a language, a way to share thoughts.
    I want to be a new kind of earthquake, rocking the world as if it's a baby in a cradle. (n.p.)

    With this pattern, students complete the starter with a *something*, although it's not something people usually *are*. People are doctors and clerks and business owners, not languages or earthquakes. The assertion, then, is followed by an elaboration— either a restatement (appositive) or an elaboration beginning with certain kinds of words: *-ing* words (participial phrases) or subordinate conjunctions (modeled by other sentences in the book). With this little explanation, students are amazingly ingenious in elaborating their own sentiments and learning new patterns for sentences they can use in multiple situations. Again, follow this writing with discussion of how, although students used the pattern for a particular purpose, the pattern can work in other situations when students want to explain more about an idea in an efficient manner—not in another whole sentence. An example of this pattern for an academic essay could be the following: Romeo in love was an optimist, believing that feuds would fail in the face of such love.

3. Two other books can serve as models for other patterns, particularly for how to add ideas to a core sentence: *Here Is the African Savanna* (2006a) and *Here Is the Tropical Rain Forest* (2006b), both by Madeleine Dunphy (examples used by permission of the publisher, Web of Life Children's Books). In these books, Dunphy shows sentences that grow incrementally longer as the observer looks more and more closely at a scene, which is the title and first sentence of the book. Dunphy begins with an obvious feature of the place (rain or grass, in these two books) and establishes a base sentence from which all other sentences in the book grow. As the reader moves through the book, not only do the sentences grow longer with dependent clauses, but the subject of the sentence focuses on different aspects of the scene, subordinating the previous idea, until the last sentence returns to the subject of the first sentence. For example, the first sentence in *Here Is the African Savanna* reads, "Here is the grass that grows on the plain which turns green or brown depending on rain: Here is the African savanna." The next page offers this sentence: "Here are the zebras who eat the grass that grows on the plain which turns green or

brown depending on rain: Here is the African savanna." After identifying lions, giraffe, trees, baboons, impalas, birds, hippos, and the river (among other items), the last sentence returns to the grass. To show the idea of the cumulative effect, here is the last sentence of *Here Is the Tropical Rain Forest*:

Here is the rain that fills the river, which is home to the caiman that fights the jaguar who stalks the peccaries that eat the figs, which are dropped by the monkeys that flee from the eagle who hunts the sloth that hangs from the tree, which holds the bromeliad that shelters the frog who bathes in the rain that drizzles and pours and may fall every day in this lush and wet world: Here is the tropical rain forest. (n.p.)

This process of building a long sentence full of dependent clauses works best if the class practices together first. Have students think of a foundation sentence, about the classroom perhaps. As a class, build on that sentence with dependent clauses (students don't have to know the name of the construction, but they can get the idea from the model). As the class works together, be sure to discuss what it is they are doing and why some suggestions work better than others for the sense of the sentence. Then, have students start with their own idea and build their sentences by adding new subjects and subordinating previous ideas. In this way, students learn about subordination at the same time as they develop sentence sense by seeing how ideas can combine effectively.

4.   A last sentence pattern I use is from *The Important Book* (Brown, 1949). In this book, Brown uses a pattern to describe several items that are familiar to young readers. The pattern identifies what the important thing is about the item and then notes several other aspects of the item before concluding with a repeat of the initial assertion about the important thing, as in this example:

The important thing about the sky is that it is always there. It is true that it is blue, and high, and full of clouds, and made of air. But the important thing about the sky is that it is always there. (n.p.)

After you read the book to students, have them articulate the pattern and then use it for writing. I use the pattern with any number of topics, sometimes having students use it to write a summary for a concept I have taught or for a particular reading the students have completed. To me, the "important" thing isn't one particular aspect (a "right answer" so to speak) as much as it is that each student is able to identify what is important about the topic or article to him or her and use ideas in a pattern that might serve him or her well in other situations.

Following is the example I wrote:

The important thing about sentence patterns is that they help students develop their sentence sense. They can also help students learn punctuation or practice language that is unfamiliar to them. They can be a place to take risks and generate writing. But the important thing about sentence patterns is that they help students develop their sentence sense.

Combining to Add Detail and Interest

All students can benefit from work with sentences—and sentence combining can be used to teach them a variety of structures that are useful in all the writing they do: in school, on tests, and for life. In fact, the more automatic some structures are, the better help they are to students who are writing in the constrained circumstances of tests. In the following lesson, which uses sentence combining to create appositives, students learn how to identify, punctuate, and generate appositives—all of which can be helpful preparation for large-scale tests.

1. Have students look at sets of model sentences with the appositive structure underlined. These sentences can be pulled from the reading the class is doing (that's the best idea) or from a set you collect ahead of time, but they should represent as wide a range of appositives as your students are prepared to handle. For example, although one of my textbooks notes that any phrase that can fill a noun position (gerunds and infinitives) can act as an appositive, I usually don't include those at first as they can confuse my students. The following sentences are an example of a short sample set:

    All we had was Simon Finch, <u>a fur-trapping apothecary from Cornwall whose piety was exceeded only by his stinginess</u>. (Lee, 1960, p. 3)

    The ruler of Florence, <u>Lorenzo de' Medici</u>, asked him to deliver it as a gift to the duke of Milan. (Fritz, 2001, n.p.)

    <u>A balding, smooth-faced man</u>, he could have been anywhere between forty and sixty. (Lee, 1960, p. 166)

    An oppressive odor met us when we crossed the threshold, <u>an odor I had met many times in rain-rotted gray houses where there are coal-oil lamps, water dippers, and unbleached domestic sheets</u>. (Lee, 1960, p. 106)

    He collected 58,000 pounds of metal—<u>tin and copper</u>—which would be heated until it was fluid. (Fritz, 2001, n.p.)

    Have students examine the sample sentences, describing what they see and, in small groups, working out a definition of the underlined structures. Although, technically, the definition of an appositive is a noun phrase that adds information or detail, students can define it in whatever words work for them; adherence to a textbook definition isn't as important as gaining an idea of the concept. Students should notice that appositives can contain a lot more than a noun, as shown in these samples.

2. When students have an idea of what appositives do, they should also notice where they can be placed in sentences: the most common place is what some textbooks refer to as the subject–verb split—that is, after the initial noun in the sentence. Other placements are after any noun, at the end of the sentence, or at the beginning (probably the least common, although very interesting to construct). Have students work in pairs to investigate texts in the classroom—either ones they are reading or ones you bring in for them to use (picture books work, but so do magazines and newspapers)—to find more examples of sentences with appositives. By working together and discussing possible examples, students refine their understanding of the concept. In this collection process, be prepared for students to be incorrect, that is, to gather more than appositives and to gather some of the sort I mentioned (infinitives and gerunds). Don't worry about that—the fact that students are looking for language constructions in a variety of texts outweighs an emphasis on correctness, especially at this stage of their learning. From the examples students find, select ones you will use for class work from this point on.

3. Using sentences from the examples they have collected, have students discuss the rhetorical effects of an appositive, including the effect of where it is placed: What effect does it have on the subject to interrupt the sentence and add information about it? What is the different effect of having an appositive at the beginning of a sentence rather than at the end? Do those kinds of appositives have a different effect than the ones in the middle of a sentence? Kolln (2003) explains the rhetorical effects of placement, noting that the end of the sentence is the main point of focus, but that the opening appositive can emphasize the subject. Tufte (2006) discusses different purposes for appositives that you can review with students: repeating a noun and then adding information in order to emphasize the noun; listing a number of specific examples of a general term; or using a synonym in order to explain the meaning of a term or add information about it. Students might have other ideas of their own.

4. Next, again using some of the sample sentences you or your students have gathered, have students de-combine sentences that contain appositives—that is, break the sentence with the appositive construction into two or more kernel sentences. For example, using one of the previous examples, I would de-combine in the following way.

<u>A balding, smooth-faced man</u>, he could have been anywhere between forty and sixty. (Lee, 1960, p. 166)

He was a balding man.

He had a smooth face.

He could have been anywhere between forty and sixty.

Again, there isn't a single right answer to this practice; my students often get more kernel sentences than I do from de-combining. The point is that they begin to see how ideas from individual sentences combine into a single sentence with an appositive.

5.   After students have de-combined sentences, have them trade the kernel sentences with someone who isn't familiar with the sentence and ask that student to recombine the sentences in more than one way. One sentence might be similar to the original, but the other should be different. For example, recombining the previous sentence, students might write this: "With his smooth face, the balding man could have been anywhere between forty and sixty." Requiring students to combine in at least two ways pushes them to consider other constructions and allows for class discussion on the rhetorical effects of appositives—as compared with other choices writers have. Discuss the following questions: Which sentences do students like better? Why? Why should a writer choose an appositive over another construction? When might it be better to choose another construction (compound constructions or dependent clauses, for example)?

6.   Students need to know something about options for punctuating appositives before they begin to write their own. Use model sentences to help students consider their punctuation options and the effects of choosing one option over another. Using examples like the following, show students that they have three punctuation choices: commas, colons, and dashes. Although these examples all show appositives at the end of a sentence, the option still exists for other placements: Appositives in the middle of a sentence can use a pair of commas or a pair of dashes while those at the beginning almost always use a dash but sometimes use a comma as well, if the comma isn't too confusing for the reader.

For a man who liked to ask questions, Leonardo da Vinci was born at the right time—April 15, 1452. (Fritz, 2001, n.p.)

Everywhere there was confusion and noise: grinding gears of overheated cars and the frightening drone of German scout planes. (Borden, 2005, p. 47)

I thought of myself as hanging in the store, a mote imprisoned on a shaft of sunlight. (Angelou, 1969, p. 113)

Show students plenty of examples. After examining them, have students discuss the differing rhetorical effects of the three options: How does the dash differ from the colon in the tone it seems to suggest? Are there genres where the expectation is for one kind of punctuation more than another? Why would punctuation of appositives be related to genre expectations?

7.   Students need to have practice writing appositives of their own. If they need more scaffolding, have them practice first by combining cued sentences from a book. Such

sentences can be found in most textbooks, from books by Killgallon (e.g., 1997; see also Appendix A for annotations of works by this author), or (with older students) from Kolln (2003). When students are ready to write their own sentences with appositives, have them write two to four sentences with the same subject, something the class has been studying (a character in a novel) or something they know well. When they have the sentences written, have them combine them into one sentence that includes an appositive. Then have them write the sentence again, moving the appositive to a different place in the sentence, if possible, to see how such a move creates a different effect. For example, the following sentences generated about Atticus from *To Kill a Mockingbird* (Lee, 1960) can be combined in the two ways that follow the kernel sentences.

Atticus was a lawyer.

Atticus defended Tom Robinson in a case he knew he couldn't win.

Atticus was a courageous man.

Atticus had strong principles.

Example #1: A courageous lawyer with strong principles, Atticus actively defended Tom Robinson in a case he knew he couldn't win.

Example #2: Atticus, a courageous lawyer with strong principles, actively defended Tom Robinson in a case he knew he couldn't win.

8. After writing sentences with appositives over a period of time and sharing the sentences with small groups and as a class to discuss their effectiveness, have students discuss and write reflectively on how using appositives benefits their writing.

9. Reinforce the lessons about appositives: When students have a longer piece of writing drafted, ask them to highlight nouns in the piece of writing, particularly fairly general nouns (like *students*, *music*, *messy room*, and so forth) or terms that readers might need to know more about (such as technical terms or jargon). Then, have students add appositives that provide more information about the nouns. Getting into this habit of thinking of what will help the reader and of adding information—and of using appositives to do both tasks—will help students build habits of sentence construction that will help them in tests and beyond.

QUESTIONS FOR REFLECTION

1. What are the language concerns for the tests your students have to pass? How can you address these concerns in the context of the reading and writing your students already do?

2. For the aspects of the test that can't be addressed or that aren't already in your instruction, how can you address those items in ways that connect to purposes other

than practicing for the test? How can you teach language in a way that allows your students to pass the test at the same time as it opens their eyes to broader language issues and teaches them language knowledge they can use outside of the test?

3. What do you know about the ELLs in your classes? How can you learn to know them and their languages better? How can you implement just one or two ideas from this chapter that will benefit the ELLs as well as the native speakers in your classes?

CHAPTER 5

Putting It All Together: Building a Language-Rich Classroom

"Grammar bridges the world of the living to the world of writing, reading, and speaking."

—HARRY NODEN

BACK IN THE CLASSROOM...

T: Now, let's try one more thing for the last few minutes of class. I want you to look at another sentence Atticus uses in this speech; one I also think is very effective. It's toward the bottom of page 204: "You know the truth, and the truth is this: some Negroes lie, some Negroes are immoral, some Negro men are not to be trusted around women—black or white."

Several: I put a sticky note by that sentence.

Brady: Hey, it's parallel!

T: Did you? You're right, Brady. It's a powerful sentence especially because it sets up the emphasis on "some" with that repetition in the parallel structure—and then the next sentence goes on to show how this is true of all people, not just a single group. But I want you to look at the use of the colon. What effect does it make to say "The truth is this:" when Harper Lee could have written it this way: "The truth is that some Negroes lie," and so on?

Vanessa: I think it is more like "pay attention to this" or "something is coming."

Emily: Yeah. In the colon one, you really see what comes after. In the other one, it was just like going on with the sentence.

Trent: Kinda like what you said earlier about where certain words get emphasized. You know, at the end and after commas and stuff. This kinda sets that up.

T: Sure it does. And it's especially effective because it sets up a parallel structure that also has the same word at the beginning of each part of the parallelism, so it's even stronger. What I'd like you to do is try it with your sentence. See if you can use a colon to set up your reasons so they stand out more, sound more impressive. Here is my sentence so you can see an example [Writing on board]: "The jury will believe Atticus because after he put himself in their shoes by taking off his coat and tie, he emphasized two things: Mayella's guilt and the lies of racism." Now I want you to notice that I had to do something to my sentence; I couldn't just stick in a colon. What did I do? Shelby?

Shelby: You added "two things."

T: Yes, I did. And there's a reason for it. Look at the sentence in the book. Atticus didn't say "The truth is" *colon*. He said, "The truth is this" *colon*. I didn't write, "He emphasized" *colon*. I wrote, "He emphasized two things" *colon*. What is the difference? Look at them and listen to the difference. What is it?

Maria: It's like a whole sentence in the correct way, a whole sentence before the colon.

T: You're absolutely right. Do the rest of you hear that? That's one of the things about using a colon. It can kind of say, "Hey, stop, pay attention to what I'm going to say next." But it works best for those purposes when it comes after a complete thought. We can't really just plop it in; we have to do a little rewriting to make it work.

Jon: So it doesn't come after *because* or *is*?

> **THOUGHTS FROM THE CLASSROOM**
>
> This is a hard choice to make as a teacher: I can give a rule or I can explain the punctuation as part of meaning. Because I want students to understand punctuation not only as a system of rules but also—and more significantly—as "an active, meaning-making system" (Cordeiro, 1998, p. 54), I need to make sure they understand that even if they see colons used in other ways, we are attaching its use in this instance to meaning. Over time, students seem to remember these aspects of punctuation better. It doesn't mean that they don't make mistakes. In fact, many students get so excited about learning punctuation this way that they overuse what they learn. But that's part of learning, too.

T: That's a good rule of thumb. I've seen it in a few places where it's different—and I think its use might be changing—but because we're talking about it as a way to increase emphasis for what comes after, I think it's important that there's a whole sentence before the colon. Both of those words—*is* and *because*—suggest that something else is coming right after, so nothing should come in between. But we can say "is this" or "because of these reasons" or something along those lines. Does that make sense? OK, take a minute and rewrite your sentence with parallel structure and a colon on a note card. We'll share a few. [After a few minutes] OK, let's hear one or two of the new sentences. Volunteers?

Beth: "Even though there is prejudice in Maycomb, the jury will be convinced for these reasons: Atticus went over the evidence to show Tom was

	innocent, he reminded them of their duty, and he said he had confidence in them." I didn't know how to add that because Atticus was such a good example his confidence would matter. Is it parallel?
T:	What do the rest of you think? Come up here and write it on the board, Beth, so we see it.
Beth:	[Reading what she wrote] "Even though there is prejudice in Maycomb, the jury will be convinced for these reasons: Atticus went over the evidence to show Tom was innocent, he reminded them of their duty, and he said he had confidence in them."
Emily:	Yeah, it works. Could you make it shorter by starting this way: "Even though there is prejudice in Maycomb, the jury will be convinced by three things Atticus did: reviewed the evidence...." Well, maybe that doesn't do the same thing.
T:	It is parallel, but that's a good thing to explore, Emily. We should always try to combine parallel structure with economy, what you mean by "being shorter." We don't want to make our sentences too wordy. But at the same time, we want the ideas to be clear. Someone else?
Sara:	I'll share mine: "Atticus convinced the jury three ways: by reviewing the evidence, by making himself an equal, and by reminding the jury that the courts should be different than the town."
T:	Good job. What do you think is different between your two sentences— the one without and the one with the colon?
Sara:	I think it's that the one with the colon sets apart the reasons more than the one without.
T:	Do you like one better than the other?
Sara:	Yeah, the one with the colon.
T:	Why?
Sara:	I don't know. I guess it just sounds cooler, more impressive. It makes the reasons stand out more, I guess, so it's more convincing?
T:	What about the rest of you? Which do you like best? [Mixed responses] Why?
Matt:	I like the one with the colon most, too, I guess for the same reason Sara said. It just seems to make my reasons be more important.
Angie:	Me, too.

Tanner:	I like the first one better. It's shorter—and I like shorter. I don't like that I had to add words.
Emily:	I like the one with the colon the best. I just like how it sounds. I think when it sounds good it's more persuasive.
T:	Why do you think so, Emily?
Emily:	I don't know. It just seems to sound smarter, like whoever says this has got to be smart so it'd be good to believe them, I guess.
T:	OK. Before we're done here, write your thinking about your sentence work today on the back of your card—which sentence did you like best, why, and when could you use these ideas of parallel structure and a colon for emphasis in other writing—and be sure your name is on your card. Then, when the bell rings, drop it in the basket on your way out. I'll see you tomorrow, and we'll find out if you're right with your predictions.

THOUGHTS FROM THE CLASSROOM

More and more is being written about the importance of reflection as part of making learning meaningful. For my own part, making sure students have a chance to think about the learning that's occurred and how it can be used beyond the current class is essential, especially their learning about language. Strong (2001) acknowledges that "experiential learning probably remains less than complete unless we have opportunities to make sense of it" (p. 31). Since I've implemented more reflection in my classes, I've found that students retain what they learn better and use their learning more in other situations than they previously did. I'm convinced of the value—and the necessity—of reflection.

Seeing grammar all around us—and seeing multiple ways to bring it into our students' lives—can provide opportunities for learning that exceed expectations. Students become engaged in learning about language without even knowing it. Integrating language—the heart of what we are about—into our classrooms makes learning in the classroom meaningful to all of life. At the same time, this approach is not without challenges. In the first place, just changing from what we've done in the past can be hard. It can be scary, wondering if we know enough, if we have the energy and the time to rethink what we have done for years, wondering what will happen if we try something that might not work at first. Besides those worries, what will our colleagues think? Administrators? Parents?

There are challenges, without a doubt. Beyond the fear of change, one challenge is that this approach doesn't lend itself easily to a scope and sequence. A comprehensive, integrated approach isn't easily planned out—adjectives and adverbs in seventh grade, phrases and clauses in eighth

EXTENDING YOUR KNOWLEDGE

"Grammar teaching seems to be on the way back after a period of absence, but we must make sure that it is free of the fatal weaknesses that almost killed it" (Hudson, 1999, p. 109). A return to the teaching of grammar needs to be different than what we did in the past—even if it's a little more work.

grade. But what we've done in the past when we did have a scope and sequence didn't work. How many of us wondered why students came to us in ninth grade without understanding the least bit about subjects and verbs and complete sentences? Even when I taught students in subsequent years in junior high, during the time period when we were required to teach traditional terminology, students would claim they had never "had" the information before—and I was certain I had taught it to them the year before! Even with an integrated approach, though, it's possible to frame a flexible scope and sequence. Berger (2006) suggests such a plan when she describes a different sentence construction each month of the school year. With such a plan, we can be aware of and point out to students the sentence-variation-of-the-month in their reading, conduct minilessons on writing them, and expect to see them used in polished writing. This approach could help those of us who want a little more structure to our instruction, but it shouldn't limit what we do. If I'm focused on using participial phrases but I see great examples of language variation or use of appositives, I wouldn't keep silent. A plan should still allow flexibility to address the needs of the students and the content of the class.

Without a strong scope and sequence, some teachers have told me that they worry about an integrated approach allowing them to address everything they need to cover. It's true. It's hard to be sure that we will. Sorenson (1996) addresses this concern, describing some teachers' feelings that an integrated approach is "just too hit or miss" (p. T5). It might be that, but what I believe, and what I tell teachers, somewhat addresses that: If we are *all* doing this, if we are *all* considering the needs of our students and finding ways to integrate language learning in the literature we study and the writing we have them work on, students will eventually get everything they need. They might not get it in a sequential way, perhaps; and they may not get it all at once. But they will get it from immersion in thinking about language as they read and write and discuss and think. If we are *all* doing this, they will learn. Even if all the teachers in your school or district aren't integrating grammar, aren't making language a central part of their classes, students will still benefit from what you do. Hudson (1999), after reviewing research on literacy instruction that includes grammar study, concludes that the positive results mean that teachers "can achieve something even by studying one small area of grammar" (p. 106). Little bits add up. Research supports integration: What we do in our classes will accrue and benefit students' learning about language.

Because the nature of teaching grammar in the context of other work of the classrooms, in connection with the reading and writing students do, is different, we have a different preparation. We have to make language instruction match *our* class and *our* students and *our* content. And there isn't really a program we can buy or borrow that will do the work of planning that for us. A few years ago I attended a conference with teachers interested in teaching grammar. They were all informed by research and seemed supportive of the presentations that talked about the nature of teaching grammar effectively—in context and according to student need and development. But when a speaker presented a prepackaged program for a sentence a week, with different tasks for the sentence on each day of the week, the teachers became ecstatic. The energy was amazing: These teachers wanted a short cut. They hoped they could avoid some of the hard work associated with this approach. Teaching according to the needs of students and the kinds of texts they read and write can be challenging. Preparation can be a little more time-consuming. Integrating language instruction is, however, more effective. So, even if it is a little more work at the start, it's worth it.

One of the most threatening aspects of teaching grammar in context is that it requires knowing something about grammar. I know that some of the teachers I work with worry that they don't know enough about grammar, that they won't have all the answers. As a result, they don't want to address anything about language or grammar for fear a question will come up that they don't know an answer to—or if they address language at all, they want a textbook with an answer key right there. I understand the desire for security, for keeping our ethos as teachers intact, but I also don't think it matters if we know all the answers. As I do, Donna (1999) envisions an effective language arts classroom as

> a classroom where teachers will be delighted to have questions they cannot answer, for these teachers will be trying to convey to their students, from the start, the secret linguists have been sitting on for at least four decades: that language is teasingly infinite and infinitely delightful, both in its mysteries and in the hints it allows us to ferret out in trying to solve them. (p. 71)

We don't have to know everything to begin. Just being curious about language is a good place to start.

In fact, not knowing all the answers may be a better place to be with our students. In addressing teaching inquiry to students, a key feature in current education, Townsend (2005) observes that we don't model inquiry when we have all the answers, that "teachers rarely ask genuine questions of real, personal uncertainty" (p. 113). If we don't often ask questions we don't already know the answers to, we don't model true inquiry effectively for our students. He explains inquiry as "a kind of dance: Inquirers turn to others, asking for help in moving beyond their present understandings" (p. 112). If we have all the answers, how can we speculate or wonder with our students about language and its functions? How can we effectively model for them curiosity about the possibilities that exist for answers about language? Asking students to help find answers to their questions can be an important part of learning for our students. They learn about language—and about learning.

To start, though, we don't have to know a lot. We can begin by learning a little and bringing that little bit into the classroom. We don't have to learn everything all at once, or in one year totally revise all our lessons. Learning to integrate grammar into the language arts is a process, and we should allow ourselves to work through the process. Part of my comfort in knowing I don't have to know everything to begin lies in questions Strong (2001) poses:

If exercising language is the work of lifetime [*sic*]...do most of us routinely encourage middle school and high school learners to pursue language inquiries—simple at first, then more complex—focused on questions that genuinely interest them? And do we regularly use our own language learnings, whatever they may be, as authentic live demonstrations? (p. 8)

If using language is "the work of a lifetime," certainly learning about it is, too.

Like our students, we start with what we know (simple at first, perhaps) and add to that as we learn more—and we don't stop being intrigued and (I hope) fascinated by language. It's all around us. There's so much to find and to find interesting! Then, when we bring our interest into the classroom along with what we're also learning as we go along, we encourage students to become interested in language, in grammar. I'll admit, sometimes students have said my enthusiasm for a well-crafted sentence or an interesting use of language or a new word is "weird," but they also grow to enjoy it and to bring me examples they think I'll appreciate. When they do that, I know they are paying attention to language in the world around them. That's a start.

As teachers, we can begin with learning a little more about language than we knew last year and then apply what we learn as we learn it. I suggest starting with one unit of study and integrating language learning into that unit first. Or find one way to talk about language and integrate that. Then, the next year or semester, as you learn a little more, revise another unit or add another piece—and so on, until language learning is a part of everything you teach. Until grammar is all around you and your students in the classroom.

Finding Grammar in Our World

To get grammar to surround us in the classroom, we need to find language curiosities all around us and bring them to class. I receive e-mails all the time—as I assume other teachers do—about unique aspects of the English language. Just recently a friend sent me a list of sentences for "word lovers." Some of the sentences are these:

- A bicycle can't stand alone; it is two tired.
- Time flies like an arrow; fruit flies like a banana.
- A will is a dead giveaway.
- A calendar's days are numbered.

Bringing these sentences into class and discussing why they are humorous enough to get passed around the Internet, even if we don't mention the reasons (such as the difference between *like* as a verb and *like* as a preposition), can help students become curious about language, curious enough to wonder, to ask questions, and to develop sensitivity to the ways language can work for them. I don't have to know the terms for why these sentences create their effects to talk about them, but if my students brought up the questions I would be so thrilled that they were interested enough to notice and ask that I would go learn the reasons. The point isn't just my knowing answers. The point is students increasing their awareness and curiosity about language and how it works and how it works for them.

Whenever I find something interesting about language, I collect it. Eventually, I bring it to class, and I wonder about what I found with my students. Although these "language adventures" may not always be strictly connected to content (although many of them could be), they are useful because they tell students that my class is a place where we talk about language and wonder about how it works and what people do with it. A clever satire on grammar published by *The Onion* (www.theonion.com/content/node/29949) is funny enough that it gets students interested in why the English language works the way it does, and it can develop in them interest in language's structures. Because the satirical article "announces" a governmental change in syntax and because the article follows that change, teachers and students can discuss parts of sentences as well as patterns of language (grammar!) and how these patterns help us communicate. Dave Barry writes columns as "Mr. Language Person" that introduce, in humorous ways, many issues related to all aspects of language: punctuation, spelling, word change, usage, and so forth. Many of these columns are available online, and they encourage conversations about the importance of usage in relation to the content and situation.

Grammar is all around us. Every day we are surrounded by it. *Puns* are a "generic name for those figures which make a play on words" (Corbett & Connors, 1999, p. 399). A specific kind of word play traditionally called *paronomasia*, or more currently called a *paragram*, changes one or more letters of a word or expression to create humor or irony or, Collins (2004) suggests, to achieve "dramatic, critical—or bathetic—effect" (p. 129). Thus, *Swan Lake* becomes *Swine Lake* in a Marshall book (1999) about pigs performing a ballet; a chapter on grammar in electronic communication in *Woe Is I* (O'Conner, 2003) is titled "E-mail Intuition"; and Lars Anderson (2005) uses a paragram in the title of a *Sports Illustrated* article about exercise programs for NASCAR pit crews with "Making a Fit Stop." Once they're aware of paragrams (and other ways to play with words), students will find them everywhere—in newspapers and ads and store names and on T-shirts. Having students collect what they find and share them shows, once more, how much language—grammar!—is all around us. And when students need what Collins (2004) refers to as "attention-catching language" (p. 125) for titles or other writing, they have one more device they can try.

Even our everyday experiences with language can lead to language discussions—and learning. When my son and his friends taped "Scott is a pimp" on the top of their mortarboards at graduation, I asked them about the word choice. My son assured me that the word doesn't mean the same to them as it means to me. When I asked my students what they thought about it, we had a good discussion about language change and how different people react to those changes. I went to the online version of the Oxford English Dictionary to show them the definition I was familiar with—"someone who makes money from arranging for others to perform sexual acts" (n.p.). Students told me that the word meant "cool" or "fresh." The online Urban Dictionary (www.urban dictionary.com) also lists these words as possible definitions. Since my son's graduation, the word has taken on even new meanings with the television show, "Pimp My Ride." So, now the word also means to make something fancy, decorate it, or make it cool. I don't know if I'll ever feel totally comfortable with the new uses of this word, but with my students I could at least discuss how situation might make a difference in what language options we choose to use. The important thing is that if students see that our awareness of language around us brings topics of language to class, they will also develop awareness of and interest in the grammar that is all around them, too.

Although eventually teachers should develop their own collection of language ideas and activities that connect to the specifics of their courses and students, we all need a place to begin. A number of books and articles provide options for teachers to start to incorporate language exploration and discussion in their classrooms. Hudson (1999), in trying to show what he calls the "range of things that can be done in the name of grammar," provides a list of ideas. I include a few of them to give an idea of the possibilities teachers could implement to help students see language all around them.

- Gather examples of the use of passives in different kinds of texts and have students develop theories for the use of passives. As Hudson notes, "The immediate point is to deepen the students' understanding of grammatical conventions, but such activities also relate to general topics such as genre differences and probably help children's own use" (p. 108).

- Look at ambiguity in jokes and consider the issue of ambiguity in other language situations. I often bring in Far Side cartoons to use to talk about language; that is a way to also address humor and how language works to create it.

- Look at teen magazines and consider why they "wrap information up in so many words" (p. 108). Hudson suggests reworking short passages into more direct language and then allowing students to explore what is gained and what is lost as a way to understand language used to create interest, excitement, and so on.

Another source of possible classroom activities to engage language can be found in books by Richard Lederer. I use *Adventures of a Verbivore* (1994), but his other books are also interesting, providing engaging examples of language to use as a basis for discussion. In *Adventures of a Verbivore*, chapters on slang and puns reside next to chapters on prep school language and grammar. There are several quizzes and teasers that I have used (in pieces) with my students, not for a grade but as a way to get them thinking about language and what it does and how it works and all its mysteries. One activity my students like involves sentences that can be punctuated differently to take on new meanings.

Take the following sentence, for example: "A clever dog knows its master" (p. 247). With an apostrophe added, the meaning is totally different: "A clever dog knows it's master" (p. 263). Letting students play with language this way helps to create an interest in language. Also, using Truss's picture book, *Eats, Shoots & Leaves: Why, Commas Really Do Make a Difference!* (2006), is a way to bring pictures and language together to instigate discussion and curiosity about punctuation's relationship to meaning.

Language Exploration and Awareness (Andrews, 2006) provides numerous activities that allow students to explore language use and speculate about the meaning of their discoveries. In one exploration, students read a few articles in a tabloid newspaper and then answer questions that allow them to see how the language use makes unsuspecting readers believe the stories are 100% true. In other explorations, students create apologies for different people or review a number of ways to agree with someone and then consider when each is appropriate or inappropriate. These activities, and others like them, can be connected to the literature discussions the class is having or the writing students are working on. Through activities like these, students increase their awareness of language and its adaptations for different situations. After they consider these variations of language, not only are they more aware of shifting language for their own speaking and writing purposes, but they also become more sensitive to such shifts in the texts they read.

ReadWriteThink.org, a website cosponsored by IRA and NCTE, provides lesson plans that can also help teachers begin to build a collection of activities to bring grammar instruction into their classrooms. Table 3 shows a sample of the lessons that teachers might use. As the examples show, there are many ways to bring language into the classroom to help students see that grammar—in all its shapes—is all around us and is interesting to consider. As teachers, when we've become comfortable with some of these ideas and the possibilities they represent, we should begin to find examples of our own with which to build classroom explorations or to begin class discussions. And our example of curiosity about language can encourage students to do the same and bring their own wonderings and observations to the class for exploration.

Finding Grammar in Reading

As I mentioned, integrating grammar means there isn't a traditional scope and sequence. But integrating grammar shouldn't be totally without a plan, either. We can and should make some plans—and then also allow for flexibility as questions and needs arise. Figure 4 (see p. 142) is an overview of what aspects of language could be taught, chapter by chapter, with *To Kill a Mockingbird* (Lee, 1960). An outline like this could be designed for each piece of literature we teach. Creating this outline is not so different from the way we already plan for teaching literature—by taking notes on themes or characterization or literary devices that could be addressed throughout a text. Just as we do not address every literary element in a text when we study it with students, we may not address all aspects of language that are possible, either. But knowing that they are there, that they

TABLE 3. Sample of Lessons for Integrating Grammar Instruction

Traditional Grammar

Manipulating Sentences to Reinforce Grammar Skills
www.readwritethink.org/lessons/lesson_view.asp?id=248

   In this lesson, students use knowledge of grammar to investigate and rewrite sentences they find
   in famous quotations and in their own reading.

When I Was Young in...A Literature to Language Experience
www.readwritethink.org/lessons/lesson_view.asp?id=911

   In this lesson, students write of a childhood experience by following the model of *When I Was
   Young in the Mountains* by Cynthia Rylant. In doing so, students (especially ELLs) focus on using
   past tense verbs correctly.

Playing With Prepositions Through Poetry
www.readwritethink.org/lessons/lesson_view.asp?id=34

   Through writing poetry, students experiencing this lesson learn about and use prepositions.

Action Is Character: Exploring Character Traits With Adjectives
www.readwritethink.org/lessons/lesson_view.asp?id=175

   This lesson helps students learn about effective description through listing actions and their
   corresponding traits (adjectives) for the characters in novels they are reading.

Editing

Every Punctuation Mark Matters: A Minilesson on Semicolons
www.readwritethink.org/lessons/lesson_view.asp?id=260

   As the title indicates, this lesson teaches about semicolons by using Martin Luther King Jr.'s
   "Letter From Birmingham Jail."

Usage

What Did They Say? Dialect in *The Color Purple*
www.readwritethink.org/lessons/lesson_view.asp?id=790

   This lesson provides excellent strategies for introducing the concept of dialects. Students engage
   with recordings to explore attitudes about dialects. Although this lesson is connected to a specific
   novel, it can easily be adapted for any novel in which characters speak in dialects.

Exploring Language and Identity: Amy Tan's "Mother Tongue" and Beyond
www.readwritethink.org/lessons/lesson_view.asp?id=910

   With this lesson, students consider implications of Amy Tan's essay in relation to their own
   language use—and then write essays about their individual language experiences.

What's My Subject? A Subject–Verb Agreement Minilesson
www.readwritethink.org/lessons/lesson_view.asp?id=950

   Although this lesson teaches rules about subject–verb agreement, it also asks students to look at
   song lyrics where the "rules" are broken as a way to explore different usages in formal and
   informal situations.

Language Change

Introducing Shakespeare: The Bard's English
www.readwritethink.org/lessons/lesson_view.asp?id=1031

   This lesson works as a thorough introduction to Shakespearean language by setting it in the
   larger frame of language change. Students explore old and new words before focusing on
   Elizabethan language and writing cartoons using what they've learned.

(continued)

TABLE 3. Sample of Lessons for Integrating Grammar Instruction (continued)

Rhetorical Grammar

Choosing the Best Verb: An Active and Passive Voice Minilesson
www.readwritethink.org/lessons/lesson_view.asp?id=280
> After encouraging students to explore how different genres use active and passive voice, this lesson enables them to revise their own writing for appropriate voice for the genre.

Style: Defining and Exploring an Author's Stylistic Choices
www.readwritethink.org/lessons/lesson_view.asp?id=209
> Although this lesson analyzes the style of Hurston's (1998) *Their Eyes Were Watching God* and stays at the analysis level, it could be used with other books, and teachers could extend the analysis into writing.

could be addressed, will raise awareness of options. And when we are aware of options, we can bring them in to aid in understanding the literature as well as to help students engage with language learning. In addition, it should be noted that some of the items listed in the overview are pretty brief. The study of language with reading doesn't need to take up a lot of time, so we shouldn't look at these aspects as taking away time from the study of literary elements (character, plot, themes, and so forth). In many ways, talking about language with reading enhances the reading experience—at the same time as it builds students' knowledge and curiosity about language.

Finding Grammar in Writing

As with reading, when we make plans to have students write specific genres, we should consider what aspects of language are characteristic of the genre and its situation—and have students think about those language characteristics as part of the writing. Certainly editing, usage, and rhetorical aspects of language are closely aligned with writing genres proficiently because genres function within social groups and respond to the social purposes of the situation. However, considering traditional grammar might also be a part of thinking about writing, and language change is an element that could relate to genres' situations and audiences.

In a manner similar to the outline made for teaching a novel, teachers can outline which aspects of language they could address with a specific writing assignment. Figure 5 shows two sample outlines. Although some of the suggestions relate to the specific characteristics of the genre, we each know our own students' needs better and, thus, could make a more appropriate outline for our classes on the more generic aspects. For instance, if students are writing movie reviews, the first outline might be aspects of language we could consider addressing as we help students work through the writing

Chapter 1
Rhetorical Grammar: Linked independent clauses, repeated verb phrases
Editing: Use of commas

Chapter 2
Usage: Compare teacher talk to students' talk; "tough talk" of boys in school

Chapter 3
Usage: "Ain't"; "last-will-and-testament diction" (p. 31) (What does Atticus's use of language suggest about roles and relationships?)

Chapter 4
Usage: Chants and superstitions; "nigger-talk" (p. 37)
Rhetorical Grammar: Develop descriptive writing ("Summer was our best season....")

Chapter 5
Rhetorical Grammar: Shift from dialogue to narration creating different tones

Chapter 6
Rhetorical Grammar: Analyze sentence structure and word choice (pp. 53–54) to see how pacing differs, slow and fast to match content

Chapter 7
Traditional Grammar: "Delete the adjectives" (p. 59)

Chapter 8
Language change: "Morphodite"

Chapter 9
Usage: Name-calling and bad language (Is bad language a stage? Why do we call people names?)

Chapter 10
Rhetorical Grammar: Sentence construction and word choice to set mood

Chapter 11
Language Change: Definitions of words (*courage*)

Chapter 12
Usage: Cal's code-switching at church

Chapter 13
Editing: Use of semicolons

Chapter 14
Editing: Use of colons

Chapter 15
Language Change: "Shinnied up"
Usage: Pragmatics—turn-taking in conversations (Why did Scout's verbal actions work when Atticus's did not?)

Chapter 16
Traditional Grammar: Adjectives out of order
Editing: Use of colons and dashes

Chapter 17
Traditional Grammar: Subject after verb; repeated prepositional phrases
Editing: Punctuating dialogue
Usage: Mr. Ewell's responses; consider how they are inappropriate for situation ("Cap'n")

Chapter 18
Usage: Pragmatics (Why does Mayella think Atticus is mocking her? What in his roles and his manner does she interpret this way?); contrast Atticus's language with Mayella's: educated and not
Language Change: "Chiffarobe"

Chapter 19
Usage: How is Tom's language different from Ewell's?
Usage: Euphemisms ("Lying" vs. "mistaken in her mind")
Language Change: Words some groups can use that others cannot (*Sorry*)

Chapter 20
Traditional Grammar: Use of pronouns and lack of names in court scene
Editing: Effective use of colons
Usage: Informal and formal language as representative of character
Rhetorical Grammar: Syntax to show emphasis

(continued)

Chapter 21
Language Change: Regionalisms—"giving her precious Jem down the country" and "If Mr. Finch don't wear you out"

Chapter 22
Traditional Grammar: Multiple antecedents for *it* (pp. 212–213)

Chapter 23
Usage (p. 221): Atticus says women on jury would interrupt all the time, but research says "men interrupt more frequently than women, and men's interruptions often assert control of the conversation; women's interruptions more often support or encourage the speaker through minimal responses and cues" (Harmon & Wilson, 2006, pp. 128–129)—as a class, discuss perceptions of who talks more, when, and why. (Are perceptions accurate or are they stereotyping?)
Usage: *Gave* vs. *given, hung* vs. *hanged*
Editing: Dialogue, using quotation marks, commas, periods, and colons

Chapter 24
Editing: Use of colons and semicolons
Rhetorical: Effect of repetition of initial phrases
Language Change: Different levels of meaning for a word (*lady*)

Chapter 25
Rhetorical Grammar: Use of pronoun with unclear antecedent to create an effect—"set him out" (p. 238)
Usage: Whose voice is using hate-speech on page 241? How do we know?

Chapter 26
Editing: Use of colons and semicolons

Chapter 27
Traditional Grammar: Appositives

Chapter 28
Rhetorical Grammar: Using syntax and word choice to slow reading (p. 263) or to speed it up (p. 262)

FIGURE 5. Sample Outlines of Topics to Address With Two Different Writing Assignments

Outline #1: Writing a Movie Review
　　Traditional Grammar: Using active verbs and adjectives effectively
　　Editing: Punctuating titles and proper nouns correctly
　　Usage: Determining the level of formality and how it's represented in the text
　　Language Change: Determining the jargon appropriate for the audience and movie
　　Rhetorical Grammar: Using appositives to condense and combine details; using subordination to show relationship between ideas

Outline #2: Writing a Literary Analysis Essay
　　Traditional Grammar: Ensuring subjects and verbs agree
　　Editing: Punctuating and citing quoted material correctly
　　Usage: Identifying how academic language differs from other writing (i.e., distance, nominalizations, and so forth)
　　Language Change: Considering the connotations or denotations of words used in the text being analyzed as well as in the analysis
　　Rhetorical Grammar: Imitating sentence styles to blend others' ideas with the author's

process. If students are writing a more traditional school paper, such as a literary analysis essay, the outline could look like the second example.

Assessing Grammar Learning

Some teachers worry about assessing grammar instruction when grammar is integrated with reading and writing instead of in separate units that can be assessed directly. How can we measure learning when it isn't a separate unit, when it's mixed in with everything else we do, and when some of what we're teaching is more abstract than concrete? Certainly the effect of teaching grammar with writing can be assessed through the students' writing: We can see if students are applying what they learn through the quality of

TABLE 4. Sample Statements to Use for Student Attitude Surveys

- Language change is a process of decay.
- Some dialects are "better" than others.
- Writing and speech are essentially the same thing.
- Language is an interesting subject to learn about.
- Understanding sentences and how they are constructed benefits me as a reader.
- Understanding sentences and how they are constructed benefits me as a writer.
- Knowing about punctuation helps me read better.
- Knowing about punctuation helps me write better.
- I pay attention to how language changes with situations.
- I talk the same way wherever I go.
- People who speak with an accent are probably less intelligent.
- Knowing and using good grammar is a sign of intelligence.
- People shouldn't change the way they talk at home or school.
- Different ways of speaking are still grammatical.
- Language has power to hurt people.
- People use language to manipulate ideas and emotions.
- I am influenced by others' use of language.
- Words mean exactly what their definitions say.
- I speak a dialect.
- The characters in books that use slang or dialects are not like real people.
- I don't like to read books with characters that use "bad grammar."
- Bad grammar is a reflection of a person's goodness.
- Grammar matters in my home.
- Grammar matters only at school or when we get a job.
- Grammar applies only to writing.
- When words change, language is weakened.
- We should add new words to the dictionary every year.
- Everyone in the world should be able to speak English.
- Older people have a right to get upset at how younger people change the language.
- English is made up of words from many languages.
- It's good for English to change over time.
- I like to learn about language.

their writing. Its effect on reading can be somewhat measured by students' improved reading comprehension and analysis abilities. Beyond that, however, it is also possible to assess grammar learning through attitude surveys given at the beginning and end of a course. The statements that appear in Table 4, placed on continuums that range from "totally disagree" or "not at all" to "totally agree" or "very much" and administered at the beginning and end of the course, will allow us to measure students' attitude changes. The first three statements are from Hazen (2005, pp. 182–183), the rest are my own. We can select pertinent statements from the list to use with our own classes. That selection will depend on what we will be addressing over the course of the year.

Blending and Extending

In addition to planning aspects of language that could be addressed with the content of their classes, teachers also need to consider what else contributes to the effectiveness of an integrated language approach. The first has to do with class talk.

As is evident in the classroom dialogues through this book, learning occurs as students and teachers talk about the language that is part of their reading and writing. That means that students need to feel comfortable expressing ideas in classrooms and to respect ideas that may differ from their own. The classroom community should encourage curiosity and tolerance so that students feel confident that they can question and wonder about language. We need to help students develop the ability to tolerate ambiguity and consider ideas that may be different from their own or what they are used to. When students don't agree with others' perspectives, they should have the ability to respect the difference and maintain appropriate responses even with those differences.

> ### EXTENDING YOUR KNOWLEDGE
> I found that teaching grammar this way requires something different from me. As Nunan (2005) states, "Before teachers of grammar can teach grammar differently, they must think differently and approach the subject analytically and pragmatically" (p. 74). So, one of the first ways we implement an integrated approach is to adjust our own thinking in regard to teaching.

We also need to be examples of curiosity and models of what it means to inquire. Our example of the kind of inquiring mind and questioning attitude that helps us learn more about language will develop students' abilities to wonder and inquire. The kinds of questions teachers pose in class will, in a large measure, determine the kinds of questions students will learn to ask—and the level of curiosity they will bring to their own language experiences outside of school. Questions should be open-ended, encouraging analysis and theorizing rather than "rightness." I recently wondered why signs on stores say "open" and "closed" instead of "opened" and "closed," which would make more sense. I theorized that English speakers must shorten some past participles. I had read that "ice cream" used to be "iced cream," and I saw a box in the grocery store that said "mash potatoes" instead of "mashed potatoes"—so I had some other examples to bring to my theorizing. At a luncheon, I happened to be seated at a table with a linguist, so I asked about my theory. I found out that I was partly right: English speakers do shorten past participles used this way, usually when the –*ed* is unheard or hard to hear (that's the part I hadn't considered). I also learned that such shortening is true of other languages as well. That's the kind of observation and questioning we should encourage in students. And, in case you don't get to have lunch with a linguist, the LINGUIST List website (www.linguistlist.org/) allows people to ask questions of linguists—so you and your students can get answers to your own questions.

Because an important part of teaching grammar as part of content means that there will be a lot of talk in the classroom, we need to teach students how to discuss effectively. Roberts and Langer's research (2000) shows that class discussions where the teacher is the questioner and students answer back—in a kind of recitation format—isn't really a discussion. Instead, students should respond to comments made by other students and to questions posed by other students so that their engagement is real and not only a response to our questions. Discussions—the quality of classroom talk—are essential to language learning, partly because they encourage inquiry that extends beyond the classroom and partly because students are using the very substance of that inquiry: language.

Learning about language through an integrated approach requires us to be aware of different kinds of knowledge: declarative, procedural, and conditional. If we know about these categories, we can structure classes to allow students not only to get some information from us or from books (declarative knowledge) but also to learn how to work through problems and questions to gain procedural knowledge about language and inquiry. We know that students need to have some knowledge of how language works and how they can talk about it. However, we also need to give students time to reflect and develop conditional knowledge about language: Under what conditions do the characteristics of language take effect and how do those effects change with situation? This question, and the reflection associated with it, could be attached to any language exploration or activity students participate in. And giving students the opportunity to think conditionally will help them transfer their learning to their lives beyond the classroom.

A Final Word—or Two

A friend standing with me in the line at a wedding reception asked what I was currently writing. I told him it was a book on teaching grammar. He made a face (a grimace, actually) and then told me the story of his school experience, especially of one junior high English teacher who taught diagramming of sentences. Although he was a reader and he generally liked English, he just didn't "get" diagramming and, consequently, did poorly in the class. "As a result," he said, "I thought I was stupid—at least in English." As I listened and thought about his story, I wondered how many other students not only miss the exciting aspect of learning about language (something they use every day and should be curious about) but also end up thinking they are stupid because they don't "get" grammar. The idea makes me sad. Language is just so fascinating!

In the end, even with a good idea like bringing language into all we do in our classrooms, success with our students isn't so much with the pedagogy as it is with us. It is, after all, our passion, our interest, and our energy that make the difference in teaching. Strong (2001) observes that "creating active learning environments resides not so much in instructional materials or in tasks themselves but rather in coaches who help students understand what they are learning, why the learning is useful, and how it might be approached" (p. 193). As teachers, we can learn what we don't know yet—and we can answer, together and with our students, questions that arise in the context of a classroom that truly integrates grammar into the rest of the content. We can help students understand why the study of grammar matters. It just makes sense: Language is part of life. How can it not be part of everything we do in an English language arts classroom?

QUESTIONS FOR REFLECTION

1. Who can you anticipate might have trouble with your using an integrated approach to grammar in your classroom? What might be their concerns? How might you help them allay those concerns?

2. What will be the first unit or area where you will integrate ideas about language into your classes? What do you need to do to plan for that integration? How will you begin to collect language items and activities that you could use?

3. In reflecting on the classroom dialogue through this book, what are some ways that the teacher could have integrated other aspects of language and grammar into this lesson? It's obvious that time has to be a consideration—we can't teach everything there is or we'd never finish a novel and we'd lose the students. What are some other considerations for what to choose to address in a classroom? How will you choose?

APPENDIX A

Annotated Resources

I n my own growth as a learner and teacher of language, I have had many mentors—most of them authors of books and articles. When teachers ask me to recommend only one or two books to get them started, it's hard to limit myself. I have so many I could suggest—and what one teacher needs may differ from what another would find useful.

So that readers of this text might have a little more guidance than the references in this book (which is a good overall list, I think), in this appendix I offer some titles that I've annotated to give you enough information to help you make judicious selections. The titles are grouped to match the contents of the chapters of this book, to give additional places to go if the ideas of a specific chapter are of more interest to you than other chapters. Some of the titles are also found in my references; some are not. If I don't have a book noted in this appendix, that doesn't mean it might not help some of you. Instead, I had to be selective; these are the ones I use most often. The others in my reference list, though, are also recommended. I hope you will find the annotations useful in helping you find the resources that will best help you meet your individual needs.

Resources for Chapter 1

Traditional Grammar

For information on traditional grammar that extends beyond traditional terms and exercises, I recommend the following sources:

Haussamen, B. (with Benjamin, A., Kolln, M., & Wheeler, R.S.). (2003). *Grammar alive! A guide for teachers.* Urbana, IL: National Council of Teachers of English.
  This is a short book (about 100 pages of text) that provides 12 vignettes from classrooms to show how the ideas discussed in the chapters would look in practice. All but one of the vignettes address the different ideas of the chapters, so the book is teacher friendly, with an interesting (and understandable) approach to grammar terms.

Hale, C. (1999). *Sin and syntax: How to craft wickedly effective prose.* New York: Broadway.
  I like this book, as I mentioned in chapter 1, because of the descriptive way Hale approaches grammar terms. Plus, the author uses actual writing to show the aspects

of parts of speech and parts of sentences, so the work feels real to me, not contrived like a textbook. And an even bigger plus is the playful approach: Reading this book is just plain fun.

Editing

For work with editing, I recommend these sources:

Ehrenworth, M., & Vinton, V. (2005). *The power of grammar: Unconventional approaches to the conventions of language.* Portsmouth, NH: Heinemann.

> In this book, the authors show a lesson (pp. 46–48) and later in the book describe a unit with enough detail that readers can see what the teaching looked like (pp. 106–126). The rest of the book is very interesting reading and has some classroom experiences interspersed. The emphasis, however, is on grammar (especially punctuation) integrated with writing. The authors make an effective argument for the use of mentor texts for grammar instruction, but their focus is on improving writing, not necessarily improving reading (although I could see that as a consequence of their work).

Anderson, J. (2005). *Mechanically inclined: Building grammar, usage, and style into writer's workshop.* Portland, ME: Stenhouse.

> This is a teacher-friendly book that provides examples of Anderson's work with students throughout the text. Although it focuses on punctuation, other aspects of grammar are also addressed in the context of writer's workshop. The author explains how to find examples in the texts students are reading to use as minilessons for writing.

Angelillo, J. (2002). *A fresh approach to teaching punctuation: Helping young writers use conventions with precision and purpose.* New York: Scholastic.

> This is another readable book about punctuation that goes beyond punctuation work with writing to include punctuation with reading, too. It provides suggestions for helping students see punctuation as a response to rhetorical effectiveness more than as rules. Students are encouraged to use mentor texts as they imitate and practice effective editing and punctuation skills. I like the author's suggestion of "accountability slips" (p. 94) and "assistance slips" (p. 97). Although Angelillo addresses issues from an elementary school perspective, I know some of my secondary students still had trouble with aspects of punctuation that the author gives ideas for how to teach in a more contextualized way. The ideas are adaptable.

Usage and Language Change

To learn more about usage, I suggest first finding a good usage book, one that addresses issues regarding usage as well as the prescriptions. For ideas on usage and language change, I've found a number of sources, but I like ones that also address teaching these issues as well as providing some background information. These three sources have been the most helpful:

Denham, K., & Lobeck, A. (Eds.). (2005). *Language in the schools: Integrating linguistic knowledge into K–12 teaching*. Mahwah, NJ: Erlbaum.
> The first half of this book is about the kinds of linguistic knowledge that are useful in applying linguistic principles to teaching. The second half of the book is about application, with chapters providing specific classroom ideas for the principles addressed in the first half. The ideas address all levels of instruction K–12, but most are also adaptable to other grade levels.

Simmons, J.S., & Baines, L. (Eds.). (1998). *Language study in middle school, high school, and beyond: Views on enhancing the study of language*. Newark, DE: International Reading Association.
> Of the three recommended books here, this one has the most applications to teaching, with overview chapters on adolescents' study of language and contextualizing language study as well as sections on studying language through literature, using writing and speaking to study language, language use in content areas beyond language arts, and emerging trends in language study, including one chapter on film.

Wheeler, R.S. (Ed.). (1999). *Language alive in the classroom*. Westport, CT: Praeger.
> Another book based on linguistic principles, this one has five sections. The first addresses the issues related to grammar instruction (particularly traditional instruction), while the second one has chapters on various linguistic applications in classrooms. The third and fourth sections deal with teaching language with writing and literature, while the last one is about dictionaries and online sources for grammar. Like the other two books, the ideas are interesting and applicable to a wide range of classrooms.

Rhetorical Grammar

Books that address rhetorical grammar are more plentiful (see chapter 3 for more ideas). For an overview, though, I'd suggest these two sources:

Kolln, M. (2003). *Rhetorical grammar: Grammatical choices, rhetorical effects* (4th ed.). New York: Longman.
> This book gives a good overview of the idea of rhetorical grammar. Although there's a lot of grammar here, the text is not hard to follow, and the emphasis on the effects of grammatical choices is part of the application of grammar through the whole book.

Schuster, E.H. (2003). *Breaking the rules: Liberating writers through innovative grammar instruction*. Portsmouth, NH: Heinemann.

>I really enjoy this book. The writing is engaging, and the ideas are applicable to the classroom. Although Schuster doesn't provide scenarios for how the lesson ideas play out, once teachers have a vision of what integrated grammar instruction looks like and an idea of what lessons can be found in this book, they shouldn't have any trouble adapting the ideas to the needs of their students.

Resources for Chapter 2

I haven't found any books that specifically address using grammar or language as a way to improve students' reading. But there are some articles—and more are being published all the time now. From what I've found, I would recommend the following:

English Journal, May 2006.

>In this issue of *English Journal*, there are several articles that discuss using language as a way to improve students' reading at the same time as they develop facility with and knowledge about language. Specifically, I recommend articles by the following authors: Bonnie Warne, Eileen Simmons, and Barbara Stanford (all found in the references). These articles contain additional practices that can help teachers use language to build reading proficiency.

Reid, L. (2005). Teaching grammar in contexts *for* writing. In F. Claggett (Ed.), *Teaching writing: Craft, art, genre* (pp. 136–151). Urbana, IL: National Council of Teachers of English.

>After a brief rationale for teaching grammar in the context of reading, Reid provides several suggestions for activities that include sentence combining, writing found poems, or adding adjectives with texts students are reading. The author ends the chapter with an overview of research about teaching grammar and writing. This chapter echoes the ideas presented in this book.

Burke, J. (2001). Developing students' textual intelligence through grammar. *Voices From the Middle, 8*(3), 56–61.

>This article explains some strategies for helping students understand how texts work—through grammar. Although there are references to writing and test preparation, some of the ideas also apply to reading more effectively.

Resources for Chapter 3

I could have a long list for this section; however, to be efficient, I include here three that I found particularly helpful.

Killgallon, D. (1997). *Sentence composing for middle school*. Portsmouth, NH: Heinemann.

This book (and its companions, *Sentence Composing for High School*, 1998, and *Sentence Composing for College*, 1998) offers teachers sentences to work with for combining as well as imitating and generating. Although I use the sentences sometimes when I am too pressed for time to make up or find my own, I have had to be selective. Sometimes the exercises are pretty challenging. I do them first myself—just to make sure they are appropriate for my students (despite the title of "Middle School") and to make sure they help me accomplish the goals I want for my students. In other words—this can be a great resource, but it isn't one that teachers should use without thinking first.

Johnson, T.R. (2003). *A rhetoric of pleasure: Prose style and today's composition classroom*. Portsmouth, NH: Boynton/Cook.

In this book, Johnson provides a rationale for teaching style—rhetorical grammar—to students as a way to communicate effectively and appropriately. At the same time, Johnson hopes students come to look on using language this way as pleasurable, not painful. In an appendix, Johnson provides one of the most concise summaries of rhetorical devices I've found; they're very helpful for me in learning on my own as I find structures I don't know the names for.

Strong, W. (2001). *Coaching writing: The power of guided practice*. Portsmouth, NH: Heinemann.

This book has examples of sentence combining—as should be expected because Strong is a well-known proponent of the approach. But the book also frames sentence combining and other writing practices in a bigger picture of a coaching approach to writing instruction. In the book, Strong gives examples of using sentence combining for various language purposes, including improving usage and voice. Although teachers will need to go beyond the book for sentences to use for practice (and Strong has those books, too), this one is excellent in the rationale it provides for using sentence combining in a multitude of ways.

Resources for Chapter 4

There are a number of resources that address issues of preparing students for tests and teaching English-language learners—but they don't focus on language. These sources do more than others.

Weaver, C. (2007). *The grammar plan book: A guide to smart teaching*. Portsmouth, NH: Heinemann.

This book provides insight on principles that teachers can use to follow good instructional practice even as they prepare students for standardized tests that include questions about language. Weaver includes a short overview of the language concepts tested in the ACT—an overview that teachers could use as a model to draw their own analyses of the tests their students take.

Warne, B.M. (2006). Teaching conventions in a state-mandated testing context. *English Journal*, 95(5), 22–27.

> This article explains how a teacher used literature to help her students improve their writing *and* prepare for state tests—not an easy task. Warne addresses challenges as well as successes—and I really appreciate the thoroughness. Although the author uses examples from *To Kill a Mockingbird*, the application can easily work with any novel students read.

Wheeler, R.S., & Swords, R. (2006). *Code-switching: Teaching Standard English in urban classrooms.* Urbana, IL: National Council of Teachers of English.

> This book provides a good plan for a constructivist approach to develop an understanding of how language use involves considering situation. Students investigate language themselves—their own usages and those they see and hear around them—to develop their understanding. At the same time as they learn, they gain appreciation for and new perspectives about language.

National Council of Teachers of English. Secondary English Language Learners www.ncte.org/collections/secell

> This site contains links to articles, books, and lesson plans that teachers can use to design instructional practice appropriate for ELLs in their classes.

Resources for Chapter 5

For ideas about finding grammar—language—all around you and for integrating it smoothly into your curriculum, these are the sources I recommend.

Patterson, N., & Pipkin, G. (2001). Grammar in the labyrinth: Resources on the World Wide Web. *Voices From the Middle*, 8(3), 63–67.

> This article lists a number of online sources that teachers could use to bring grammar into the classroom. The sites contain articles about teaching grammar as well as sites that help teachers learn about traditional grammar, usage, and style.

Andrews, L. (2006). *Language exploration and awareness: A resource book for teachers* (3rd ed.). Mahwah, NJ: Erlbaum.

> This book presents numerous interesting activities (what Andrews calls "explorations") that develop in students an interest, knowledge, and curiosity about language. For example, one activity asks students to keep a log of the fillers they hear people use in conversation and generalize about the function of fillers in speech. The

activities are definitely doable and accomplish the purpose of engaging students in wide exploration on many aspects of language, including spelling, dialects, and semantics as well as word meanings and speech.

Weaver, C. (1998). *Lessons to share: On teaching grammar in context.* Portsmouth, NH: Boynton/Cook.

Several chapters in this book show teachers teaching some principles of grammar. Although the examples aren't always as detailed as I would like and some of them are more geared to elementary level than secondary level, they give an idea of what integrated grammar instruction could look like and provide some examples of student work in response to the described lessons. The end of Weaver's chapter shows three "extended mini-lessons" (pp. 26–33). Chapter 5 by Sarah Woltjer, chapter 6 by Sue Rowe, and chapter 7 by Renee Callies come the closest to showing what integration looks like, as opposed to just telling about it.

APPENDIX B

A Brief Note About Foundational Grammar Knowledge

Some readers might want to know what rules and definitions form a basic knowledge of grammar for teachers. I don't think I can give rules or definitions. As Schuster (2003) argues effectively, they often don't work. I will be frank and say that I learned, mostly, from teaching my students out of their eighth- and ninth-grade textbooks. So I learned the rules and definitions first. Then, as I helped students work through the activities we engaged in, I found myself thinking more and more about the ways the definitions and rules didn't work; as a result, I had to learn more, ask questions, read, expand on what our book said, and allow students to modify what we used to explain ourselves. So, what follows is my own way of explaining what I think, at the start, a teacher should know.

Parts of speech: Although I hesitate to put too much emphasis on this, teachers should probably have a sense of what constitutes the concepts of nouns, verbs, adjectives, adverbs, prepositions, conjunctions, and pronouns. Teachers can consider forms as part of understanding parts of speech rather than definitions: Verbs can have *to* in front of them and may change form for past, present, or future time. Nouns take a determiner: *a, an, the*. Prepositions show relationships and come at the beginning of a group of words. Once teachers have an understanding of the parts of speech, they should think about issues related to traditional explanations. Have students play around to figure out what we mean by parts of speech. For instance, I help students see that a word doesn't belong to only one part of speech by having them think of one word that could be multiple parts of speech. My students see that *dog* might usually be a noun, but it can also be an adjective (*dog* house) or with changes in form it could be a verb (to *dog* someone) or an adverb (*doggedly*). I have them write stories with no pronouns so that they come to see the value of having shortcuts in language—but also the problem if we don't have a clear referent for a pronoun. What I'm trying to say is that this knowledge of parts of speech isn't about definitions so much as it is about concepts. Understanding parts of speech gives me and my students a vocabulary to talk about language—when we read and write and speak.

Terms: Students need to be familiar with some terms in order for me to talk to them about their writing—both about the problems they have and the ways they could be more effective. So, teachers should know these concepts as well. These terms include *phrase* and *clause*. A *phrase* is a group of words that go together. The group might have a noun or a verb, or even both, but not as subjects and predicates, not in the sense of a sentence (see how hard it is to define?). Some types of phrases I might address are these:

- prepositional phrase
- noun phrase
- verb phrase
- verbal phrases—infinitive, gerund, and participial

A *clause* is a group of words with both a subject and a predicate. Some types of clauses I might address are these:

- dependent/subordinate—although I sometimes address different kinds of clauses (adjective, adverb, and noun), I generally don't get too specific. We do talk about clauses as part of sentence structure (understanding ineffective fragments, for instance, requires an understanding of dependent clauses) and as part of style (moving adverbial clauses around, for example).
- independent—if students have trouble with sentence boundaries, an understanding of "stand alone" clauses is essential.

After I explain, as best as I can, the difference between phrases and clauses. I give examples and then I play "Thumbs" with my students: I take a well-known text and break it up into phrases and clauses listed on an overhead transparency. Then as I show the groups of words, one at a time, my students put their thumbs up if it's a phrase and their thumbs down if it's a clause. For example, one year I used the poem "'Twas the Night Before Christmas" (Moore, 2002) just before the winter break. "All through the house?" A phrase—thumbs up. "Not a creature was stirring?" A clause—thumbs down. I vary the way I break up the text so that students don't think clauses are long and phrases are short—so that they really have to look at them and get a sense of them. Repeating this activity, or one like it, usually gets my students to understand phrases and clauses about as well as they need to for our work in class. The knowledge is reinforced by my referring to phrases and clauses when we read and write.

Sentence structure: I learned most about sentence structure from diagramming—but I know it has a bad reputation now. However teachers learn about structure, they should pay attention to sentences, to how they work and how writers use them. I sometimes teach my students about simple, compound, complex, and compound–complex sentences. I have a simple process they follow: looking first for coordinate conjunctions and checking to see if they join "whole sentences" (if they find them, the sentence is either compound or compound–complex) and then looking for subordinate conjunctions and checking to see if they are acting as starts to clauses or phrases (if they start clauses, the sentence is either complex or compound–complex). Process of elimination determines the answer. With the conjunctions listed on posters on the walls, students can follow the quick process and identify most sentences. Knowing something about these types and about how sentences are structured allows teachers to address correctness issues as well as rhetorical issues (style) and sentence effectiveness.

The rest of what I come to know comes from the needs of my students and my own interests. I see sentences with structures I find interesting, so I look up the pattern in a book and find out its name: *appositives*, *participial phrases*, *polysyndeton*, *anaphora*, and so forth. I read a grammar rant about how language is used, so I look up usage issues: *shall* vs. *will*, *continuously* vs. *continually*, *hopefully*, and so forth. I find a person's use of language noticeable in a particular situation, so I research levels of formality and bring it to the classroom talk on language. I see a sign with a play on words, so I go through my grammar books until I find a name for it: *paragram*. Each new thing I learn, each interesting example of language I hear or see around me—all of it becomes part of what I bring to the classroom. And each year what I am able to bring is more than the year before.

REFERENCES

Alvarez, J. (1998). Ten of my writing commandments. *English Journal, 88*(2), 36–41.

Anderson, J. (2005). *Mechanically inclined: Building grammar, usage, and style into writer's workshop.* Portland, ME: Stenhouse.

Anderson, L. (2005, August 29). Making a fit stop. *Sports Illustrated, 103,* 32.

Andrews, L. (2006). *Language exploration and awareness: A resource book for teachers* (3rd ed.). Mahwah, NJ: Erlbaum.

Angelillo, J. (2002). *A fresh approach to teaching punctuation: Helping young writers use conventions with precision and purpose.* New York: Scholastic.

Atwell, N. (2002). *Lessons that change writers.* Portsmouth, NH: Heinemann.

Barry, D. (1993). What is and ain't grammatical. In D. Barry, *Dave Barry's bad habits: A 100% fact-free book* (pp. 191–193). New York: Owl Books.

Battistella, E. (1999). The persistence of traditional grammar. In R.S. Wheeler (Ed.), *Language alive in the classroom* (pp. 13–21). Westport, CT: Praeger.

Beers, K. (2001). Contextualizing grammar. *Voices From the Middle, 8*(3), 4.

Benjamin, A. (2004). Grammar teaches literature. *Syntax in the Schools, 20*(2), 2–5.

Berger, J. (2006). Transforming writers through grammar study. *English Journal, 95*(5), 53–59.

Bex, T., & Watts, R.J. (Eds.). (1999). Introduction. In *Standard English: The widening debate* (pp. 1–10). London: Routledge.

Beyond grammar drills: How language works in learning to write. (2006, October 25). *The Council Chronicle Online.* Retrieved November 6, 2006, from www.ncte.org/pubs/chron/highlights/125935.htm

Birch, B.M. (2005). *Learning and teaching English grammar, K–12.* Upper Saddle River, NJ: Pearson Education.

Bomer, R. (2006). Reading with the mind's ear: Listening to text as a mental action. *Journal of Adolescent & Adult Literacy, 49,* 524–535.

Braddock, R., Lloyd-Jones, R., & Schoer, L. (1963). *Research in written composition.* Urbana, IL: National Council of Teachers of English. Retrieved February 27, 2006, from education.nyu.edu/teachlearn/research/ncrll/Braddock_et_al.pdf

Bresler, K. (2004). Playing the synonym game. In R.H. Fiske (Ed.), *Vocabula bound: Outbursts, insights, explanations, and oddities* (pp. 67–71). Oak Park, IL: Marion Street Press.

Bryson, B. (1990). *The mother tongue: English and how it got that way.* New York: Avon.

Burke, J. (2001). Developing students' textual intelligence through grammar. *Voices From the Middle, 8*(3), 56–61.

Burke, J. (2004). Learning the language of academic study. *Voices From the Middle, 11*(4), 37–42.

California Department of Education. (2005). *California standards test, grade 9 English-language arts.* Retrieved November 2, 2006, from www.cde.ca.gov/ta/tg/sr/documents/rtqgr9ela.pdf

Canby, H.S. (1937). Preface. In H.A. Treble & G.H. Vallins (Eds.), *An A.B.C. of English usage* (pp. 5–9). New York: Oxford University Press.

Carroll, P.S., & Hasson, D.J. (2004). Helping ELLs look at stories through literary lenses. *Voices From the Middle, 11*(4), 20–26.

Christy, J. (2005). *Helping English language learners in the English and language arts classroom.* New York: Glencoe/McGraw-Hill. Retrieved November 8, 2006, from www.glencoe.com/sec/teachingtoday/subject/help_ELL_lit_la.phtml

Collins, V. (2004). Words of a feather. In R.H. Fiske (Ed.), *Vocabula bound: Outbursts, insights, explanations, and oddities* (pp. 125–132). Oak Park, IL: Marion Street Press.

Corbett, E.P.J., & Connors, R.J. (1999). *Classical rhetoric for the modern student* (4th ed.). New York: Oxford University Press.

Cordeiro, P. (1998). Dora learns to write and in the process encounters punctuation. In C. Weaver (Ed.), *Lessons to share: On teaching grammar in context* (pp. 39–66). Portsmouth, NH: Boynton/Cook.

Cruz, M.C. (2004). Can English language learners acquire academic English? *English Journal, 93*(4), 14–17.

Crystal, D. (2004). *The stories of English*. Woodstock, NY: Overlook Press.

Curzan, A. (2005). Spelling stories: A way to teach the history of English. In K. Denham & A. Lobeck (Eds.), *Language in the schools: Integrating linguistic knowledge into K–12 teaching* (pp. 139–148). Mahwah, NJ: Erlbaum.

Curzan, A., & Adams, M. (2006). *How English works: A linguistic introduction*. Upper Saddle River, NJ: Pearson Education.

Dean, D. (2000). Going public: Letters to the world. *Voices From the Middle, 8*(1), 42–47.

Dean, D. (2002). Underground, out the door, in disguise: Teaching grammar after 1963. *The English Record, 52*(2), 27–35.

Dean, D. (2006). *Strategic writing: The writing process and beyond in the secondary English classroom*. Urbana, IL: National Council of Teachers of English.

Denham, K. (2005). Teaching students about language change, language endangerment, and language death. In K. Denham & A. Lobeck (Eds.), *Language in the schools: Integrating linguistic knowledge into K–12 teaching* (pp. 149–160). Mahwah, NJ: Erlbaum.

deVise, D. (2007, July 13). Montgomery finds racial slur offends, no matter the context. *Washington Post*, p. A01.

Dillard, A. (1989). *The writing life*. New York: Harper and Row.

Dong, Y.R. (2004). Don't keep them in the dark! Teaching metaphors to English language learners. *English Journal, 93*(4), 29–35.

Doniger, P. (2004). Shakespeare through grammar. *Syntax in the Schools, 20*(2), 6–11.

Donna, J.M. (1999). Linguistics is for kids. In R.S. Wheeler (Ed.), *Language alive in the classroom* (pp. 67–80). Westport, CT: Praeger.

Dunn, P.A., & Lindblom, K. (2003). Why revitalize grammar? *English Journal, 92*(3), 43–50.

Dunn, P.A., & Lindblom, K. (2005). Developing savvy writers by analyzing grammar rants. In K. Denham & A. Lobeck (Eds.), *Language in the schools: Integrating linguistic knowledge into K–12 teaching* (pp. 191–207). Mahwah, NJ: Erlbaum.

Edlund, J.R. (1995). The rainbow and the stream: Grammar as system versus language in use. In S. Hunter & R. Wallace (Eds.), *The place of grammar in writing instruction: Past, present, future* (pp. 89–102). Portsmouth, NH: Boynton/Cook.

Ehrenworth, M. (2003). Grammar—comma—a new beginning. *English Journal, 92*(3), 90–96.

Ehrenworth, M., & Vinton, V. (2005). *The power of grammar: Unconventional approaches to the conventions of language*. Portsmouth, NH: Heinemann.

Fagan, B. (2003). Scaffolds to help ELL readers. *Voices From the Middle, 11*(1), 38–42.

Faigley, L. (2006). *The brief penguin handbook* (2nd ed.). New York: Pearson Education.

Fravel, L.A. (2005). The role of talk in the refinement of writing: Positive effects that accrue to both native speakers and English language learners. *The Virginia English Bulletin, 55*(1), 67–76.

Frey, N. (2007). Side trip: Using robust minilessons. *Voices From the Middle, 14*(3), 26.

Fuchs, H. (1991). Fantasy objects. In J.M. Curran & M.S. Johlas (Eds.), *Ideas plus: Book nine* (p. 57). Urbana, IL: National Council of Teachers of English.

Gates, H.L., Jr. (1998). Afterword. In Z.N. Hurston, *Their eyes were watching God* (pp. 195–205). New York: Perennial.

Gold, D. (2006). "But when do you teach grammar?" Allaying community concerns about pedagogy. *English Journal, 95*(6), 42–47.

Graff, G., & Birkenstein, C. (2006). *They say/I say: The moves that matter in academic writing*. New York: W.W. Norton.

Graham, S., & Perin, D. (2007). *Writing next: Effective strategies to improve writing of adolescents in middle and high schools—A report to Carnegie Corporation of New York*. Washington, DC: Alliance for Excellent Education.

Gray, R. (2004). Grammar correction in ESL/EFL writing classes may not be effective. *The Internet TESL Journal, 10*(11). Retrieved July 15, 2006, from iteslj.org/Techniques/Gray-WritingCorrection.html

Hagemann, J.A. (2001). Bridge from home to school: Helping working class students acquire school literacy. *English Journal, 90*(4), 74–81.

Hagemann, J.A. (2003a). Balancing content and form in the writing workshop. *English Journal, 92*(3), 73–79.

Hagemann, J.A. (2003b). *Teaching grammar: A reader and workbook.* Boston: Allyn & Bacon.

Hale, C. (1999). *Sin and syntax: How to craft wickedly effective prose.* New York: Broadway.

Harmon, M.R., & Wilson, M.J. (2006). *Beyond grammar: Language, power, and the classroom.* Mahwah, NJ: Erlbaum.

Hartwell, P. (1985). Grammar, grammars, and the teaching of grammar. *College English, 47,* 105–127.

Haussamen, B. (with Benjamin, A., Kolln, M., & Wheeler, R.S.). (2003). *Grammar alive! A guide for teachers.* Urbana, IL: National Council of Teachers of English.

Hazen, K. (2005). English LIVEs: Language in variation exercises for today's classroom. In K. Denham & A. Lobeck (Eds.), *Language in the schools: Integrating linguistic knowledge into K–12 teaching* (pp. 181–189). Mahwah, NJ: Erlbaum.

Heck, S.K. (1999). Writing standard English IS acquiring a second language. In R.S. Wheeler (Ed.), *Language alive in the classroom* (pp. 115–120). Westport, CT: Praeger.

Hillocks, G., Jr. (1986). *Research on written composition: New directions for teaching.* Urbana, IL: National Council of Teachers of English.

Hillocks, G., Jr., & Smith, M.W. (2003).Grammars and literacy learning. In J. Flood, D. Lapp, J.R. Squire, & J.M. Jensen (Eds.), *Handbook of research on teaching the English language arts* (2nd ed., pp. 721–737). Mahwah, NJ: Erlbaum.

Horning, A. (1987). *Teaching writing as a second language.* Carbondale, IL: Southern Illinois University Press.

Hudson, R. (1999). Grammar teaching is dead—NOT! In R.S. Wheeler (Ed.), *Language alive in the classroom* (pp. 101–112). Westport, CT: Praeger.

International Reading Association & National Council of Teachers of English. (1996). *Standards for the English language arts.* Newark, DE; Urbana, IL: Authors. Retrieved February 24, 2006, from www.ncte.org/about/over/standards/110846.htm (Also available: www.reading.org/downloads/publications/books/bk889.pdf)

Iyer, P. (2000). In praise of the humble comma. In J. Loughery (Ed.), *The eloquent essay: An anthology of classic and creative nonfiction* (pp. 93–96). New York: Persea Books.

Johnson, T.R. (2003). *A rhetoric of pleasure: Prose style and today's composition classroom.* Portsmouth, NH: Boynton/Cook.

Kennedy, J.F. (1999). Inaugural address. In E.P.J. Corbett & R.J. Connor (Eds.), *Classical rhetoric for the modern student* (4th ed., pp. 459–461). New York: Oxford University Press.

Killgallon, D. (1997). *Sentence composing for middle school.* Portsmouth, NH: Heinemann.

Kolln, M. (2003). *Rhetorical grammar: Grammatical choices, rhetorical effects* (4th ed.). New York: Longman.

Kolln, M., & Funk, R. (2006). *Understanding English grammar* (7th ed.). New York: Longman.

Kooy, M., & Chiu, A. (1998). Language, literature, and learning in the ESL classroom. *English Journal, 88*(2), 78–84.

Lederer, R. (1994). *Adventures of a verbivore.* New York: Pocket.

Lee, J.S. (2005). Embracing diversity through the understanding of pragmatics. In K. Denham & A. Lobeck (Eds.), *Language in the schools: Integrating linguistic knowledge into K–12 teaching* (pp. 17–27). Mahwah, NJ: Erlbaum.

Lobeck, A. (2005). A critical approach to standard English. In K. Denham & A. Lobeck (Eds.), *Language in the schools: Integrating linguistic knowledge into K–12 teaching* (pp. 97–108). Mahwah, NJ: Erlbaum.

Loewen, S. (1998). Grammar correction in ESL student writing: How effective is it? *Schuylkill.* Retrieved July 15, 2006, from www.temple.edu/gradmag/fall98/loewen.htm

McDougal, Littell English (Teacher's ed.). (1989). Evanston, IL: Author.

McQuain, J., & Malless, S. (1998). *Coined by Shakespeare: Words and meanings first penned by the bard.* Springfield, MA: Merriam-Webster.

McWhorter, J. (2001). *The power of Babel: A natural history of language.* New York: Henry Holt.

Meyer, J. (2003). Living with competing goals: State frameworks vs. understanding of linguistics. *English Journal, 92*(3), 38–42.

Micciche, L.R. (2004). Making a case for rhetorical grammar. *College Composition and Communication*, *55*(4), 716–737.

Milroy, J., & Milroy, L. (1991). *Authority in language: Investigating language prescription and standardization* (2nd ed.). London: Routledge.

Mulroy, D. (2003). *The war against grammar*. Portsmouth, NH: Boynton/Cook.

Murfin, R., & Ray, S.M. (2003). *The Bedford glossary of critical and literary terms* (2nd ed.). Boston: Bedford/St. Martin's.

Myers, M. (2006). Review of the book *Artful sentences: Syntax as style*. *ATEG Journal, 22*(1), 17–18.

Napoli, D.J. (2005). Linguistics as a tool in teaching fiction writing. In K. Denham & A. Lobeck (Eds.), *Language in the schools: Integrating linguistic knowledge into K–12 teaching* (pp. 209–221). Mahwah, NJ: Erlbaum.

National Council of Teachers of English. (2006). *NCTE position paper on the role of English teachers in educating English language learners (ELLs)*. Urbana, IL: Author. Retrieved November 8, 2006, from www.ncte.org/about/over/positions/category/div/124545.htm

Naylor, G. (1999). The meanings of a word. In J.E. Aaron (Ed.), *The compact reader: Short essays by method and theme* (6th ed., pp. 266–269). Boston: Bedford/St. Martin's.

Nilsen, A.P., & Nilsen, D.L.F. (2004). Working under lucky stars: Language lessons for multilingual classrooms. *Voices From the Middle, 11*(4), 27–32.

Noden, H. (1999). *Image grammar: Using grammatical structures to teach writing*. Portsmouth, NH: Boynton/Cook.

Noden, H. (2006). Teacher to teacher: What is your most compelling reason for teaching grammar? *English Journal, 95*(5), 18–21.

Noguchi, R.R. (1991). *Grammar and the teaching of writing: Limits and possibilities*. Urbana, IL: National Council of Teachers of English.

Noguchi, R.R. (2002). Rethinking the teaching of grammar. *The English Record, 52*(2), 22–26.

Nunan, S.L. (2005). Forgiving ourselves and forging ahead: Teaching grammar in a new millennium. *English Journal, 94*(4), 70–75.

Oakley, T. (1999). Copious reasoning: The student writer as an astute observer of language. In R.S. Wheeler (Ed.), *Language alive in the classroom* (pp. 129–138). Westport, CT: Praeger.

O'Conner, P.T. (2003). *Woe is I: The grammarphobe's guide to better English in plain English*. New York: Riverhead Books.

Oxford English Dictionary Online. New York: Oxford University Press. Available: www.oed.com/

Paraskevas, C. (2006). Grammar apprenticeship. *English Journal, 95*(5), 65–70.

Parkes, M.B. (1993). *Pause and effect: An introduction to the history of punctuation in the West*. Berkeley, CA: University of California Press.

Patterson, N., & Pipkin, G. (2001). Grammar in the labyrinth: Resources on the World Wide Web. *Voices From the Middle, 8*(3), 63–67.

Penha, J. (2006). Teacher to teacher: What is your most compelling reason for teaching grammar? *English Journal, 95*(5), 18–21.

Perrin, R. (2007). Words, words, words: Helping students discover the power of language. *English Journal, 96*(3), 36–39.

Petit, A. (2003). The stylish semicolon: Teaching punctuation as rhetorical choice. *English Journal, 92*(3), 66–72.

Postman, N. (1995). *The end of education: Redefining the value of school*. New York: Vintage.

Poth, J. (2006). Nontraditional grammar and learning transfer. *ATEG Journal, 21*(2), 11–13.

Pugh, S.L., Hicks, J.W., & Davis, M. (1997). *Metaphorical ways of knowing: The imaginative nature of thought and expression*. Urbana, IL: National Council of Teachers of English.

Raub, A.N. (1880). *Lessons in English: A practical course of language lessons and elementary grammar*. Philadelphia: Porter and Coates.

Ray, K.W. (1999). *Wondrous words: Writers and writing in the elementary classroom*. Urbana, IL: National Council of Teachers of English.

Ray, K.W. (2006). *Study driven: A framework for planning units of study in the writing workshop*. Portsmouth, NH: Heinemann.

Reid, L. (2005). Teaching grammar in contexts for writing. In F. Claggett (Ed.), *Teaching writing: Craft, art, genre* (pp. 136–151). Urbana, IL: National Council of Teachers of English.

Roberts, D.R., & Langer, J.A. (2000). *Supporting the process of literary understanding: Analysis of a classroom discussion*. Albany, NY: National Research Center on English Learning and Achievement. (ERIC Document Reproduction Service No. ED 337780) Retrieved July 26, 2007, from www.kokken.go.jp/public/world/mirror/cela.albany.edu/support/index.html

Romaine, S. (1994). *Language in society: An introduction to sociolinguistics*. New York: Oxford University Press.

Romano, T. (2004). *Crafting authentic voice*. Portsmouth, NH: Heinemann.

Schuster, E.H. (2003). *Breaking the rules: Liberating writers through innovative grammar instruction*. Portsmouth, NH: Heinemann.

Schuster, E.H. (2006). A fresh look at sentence fragments. *English Journal, 95*(5), 78–83.

Shafer, G. (2001). Standard English and the migrant community. *English Journal, 90*(4), 37–43.

Simmons, J.S. (1998). The study of language for adolescents: A U.S. historical perspective. In. J.S. Simmons & L. Baines (Eds.), *Language study in middle school, high school, and beyond: Views on enhancing the study of language* (pp. 6–18). Newark, DE: International Reading Association.

Sjolie, D. (2006). Phrase and clause grammar tactics for the ESL/ELL writing classroom. *English Journal, 95*(5), 35–40.

Smoot, W.S. (2001). An experiment in teaching grammar in context. *Voices From the Middle, 8*(3), 34–42.

Sorenson, S. (1996). What is integrated language arts? In Prentice Hall, *Literature: World masterpieces* (4th ed., pp. T3–T5). Upper Saddle River, NJ: Author.

Strong, W. (2001). *Coaching writing: The power of guided practice*. Portsmouth, NH: Heinemann.

Tan, A. (2000). Mother tongue. In J. Loughery (Ed.), *The eloquent essay: An anthology of classic and creative nonfiction* (pp. 112–119). New York: Persea Books.

Townsend, J.S. (2005). Language arts: Explore, create, discover through inquiry. In R.H. Audet & L.K. Jordan (Eds.), *Integrating inquiry across the curriculum* (pp. 111–135). Thousand Oaks, CA: Corwin Press.

Traugott, E.C. (1999). In fiction, whose speech, whose vision? In R.S. Wheeler (Ed.), *Language alive in the classroom* (pp. 167–177). Westport, CT: Praeger.

Trudgill, P. (1999). Standard English: What it isn't. In T. Bex & R.J. Watts (Eds.), *Standard English: The widening debate* (pp. 117–128). London: Routledge.

Truss, L. (2003). *Eats, shoots & leaves: The zero tolerance approach to punctuation*. New York: Gotham.

Truss, L. (2006). *Eats, shoots & leaves: Why, commas really do make a difference!* New York: Putnam.

Tufte, V. (2006). *Artful sentences: Syntax as style*. Cheshire, CT: Graphics Press.

Umbach, D.B. (1999). Grammar, tradition, and the living language. In R.S. Wheeler (Ed.), *Language alive in the classroom* (pp. 3–11). Westport, CT: Praeger.

Wallace, R. (1995). Introduction: Reexamining the place of grammar in writing instruction. In S. Hunter & R. Wallace (Eds.), *The place of grammar in writing instruction: Past, present, future* (pp. 1–5). Portsmouth, NH: Boynton/Cook.

Warne, B.M. (2006). Teaching conventions in a state-mandated testing context. *English Journal, 95*(5), 22–27.

Washington, M.H. (1998). Foreword. In Z.N. Hurston, *Their eyes were watching God* (pp. ix–xvii). New York: Perennial.

Weaver, C. (1996a). *Teaching grammar in context*. Portsmouth, NH: Boynton/Cook.

Weaver, C. (1996b). Teaching grammar in the context of writing. *English Journal, 85*(7), 15–23.

Weaver, C. (1998). *Lessons to share: On teaching grammar in context*. Portsmouth, NH: Boynton/Cook.

Weaver, C. (2007). *The grammar plan book: A guide to smart teaching* . Portsmouth, NH: Heinemann.

Wheeler, R.S. (Ed.). (1999). *Language alive in the classroom*. Westport, CT: Praeger.

Wheeler, R.S., & Swords, R. (2006). *Code-switching: Teaching Standard English in urban classrooms*. Urbana, IL: National Council of Teachers of English.

Wiesel, E. (2007). Why I write: Making no become yes. In L.Z. Bloom (Ed.), *The essay connection: Readings for writers* (8th ed., pp. 23–27). Boston: Houghton Mifflin.

Williams, D.R. (2004). Snobs and slobs. In R.H. Fiske (Ed.), *Vocabula bound: Outbursts, insights, explanations, and oddities* (pp. 64–66). Oak Park, IL: Marion Street Press.

Williams, J. (2003). *Style: Ten lessons in clarity and grace* (7th ed.). New York: Addison-Wesley.

Winchester, S. (2003). *The meaning of everything: The story of the* Oxford English Dictionary. New York: Oxford University Press.

Wolfram, W. (1998). Linguistic and sociolinguistic requisites for teaching language. In J.S. Simmons & L. Baines (Eds.), *Language study in middle school, high school, and beyond: Views on enhancing the study of language* (pp. 79–109). Newark, DE: International Reading Association.

Wolfram, W. (1999). Dialect awareness programs in the school and community. In R.S. Wheeler (Ed.), *Language alive in the classroom* (pp. 47–66). Westport, CT: Praeger.

Literature Cited

Angelou, M. (1969). *I know why the caged bird sings*. New York: Bantam.

Austen, J. (2005). *Pride and prejudice*. New York: Viking.

Bedard, M. (1998). *Sitting ducks*. New York: Puffin.

Borden, L. (2005). *The journey that saved Curious George: The true wartime escape of Margret and H.A. Rey*. Boston: Houghton Mifflin.

Bronte, E. (1988). *Wuthering heights*. New York: TOR Books.

Brown, M.W. (1949). *The important book*. New York: HarperCollins.

Burns, O.A. (1984). *Cold sassy tree*. New York: Dell.

Cather, W. (1954). *My Antonia*. Boston: Houghton Mifflin.

Cazet, D. (2005). *The perfect pumpkin pie*. New York: Atheneum Books for Young Readers.

Charlip, R. (1964). *Fortunately*. New York: Aladdin.

Cisneros, S. (1984). *The house on Mango Street*. New York: Vintage.

Crowe, C. (2002). *Mississippi trial, 1955*. New York: Phyllis Fogelman.

Cuyler, M. (1991). *That's good! That's bad!* New York: Henry Holt.

Dickens, C. (1963). *Great expectations*. New York: Signet.

Dickens, C. (1997). *A tale of two cities*. New York: Signet.

Dillard, A. (1987). *An American childhood*. New York: Harper & Row.

Dunphy, M. (2006a). *Here is the African savanna*. Berkeley, CA: Web of Life Children's Books.

Dunphy, M. (2006b). *Here is the tropical rain forest*. Berkeley, CA: Web of Life Children's Books.

Fitzgerald, F.S. (1925). *The great Gatsby*. New York: Scribner.

Fritz, J. (2001). *Leonardo's horse*. New York: G.P. Putnam's Sons.

Gall, C. (2006). *Dear fish*. New York: Little, Brown.

Golding, W. (1954). *Lord of the flies*. New York: Paragon Books.

Hawthorne, N. (1986). *The scarlet letter*. New York: Bantam.

Hesse, K. (1999). *Come on, rain!* New York: Scholastic.

Hurston, Z.N. (1998). *Their eyes were watching God*. New York: Perennial Classics.

Kingsolver, B. (1988). *The bean trees*. New York: Harpertorch.

Kingston, M.H. (1989). *The woman warrior*. New York: Vintage.

Knowles, J. (1959). *A separate peace*. New York: Bantam.

Lee, H. (1960). *To kill a mockingbird*. New York: Warner.

Marshall, J. (1999). *Swine lake*. New York: HarperCollins.

McKissack, P.C. (1986). *Flossie and the fox*. New York: Dial Books for Young Readers.

Miller, A. (1976). *The crucible*. New York: Penguin.

Monceaux, M. (1994). *Jazz: My music, my people*. New York: Knopf.

Moore, C.C. (2002). *'Twas the night before Christmas, or, account of a visit from St. Nicholas*. Cambridge, MA: Candlewick.

Moss, T. (1993). *I want to be*. New York: Dial Books for Young Readers.

Myers, W.D. (1999). *Monster*. New York: Amistad.

Park, L.S., & Durango, J. (2005). *Yum! Yuck!* Watertown, MA: Charlesbridge.

Peck, R.N. (1972). *A day no pigs would die*. New York: Random House.

Philbrick, R. (2001). *Freak the mighty*. New York: Scholastic.

Pinkney, A.D. (1998). *Duke Ellington*. New York: Hyperion.

Prelutsky, J. (2004). *If not for the cat*. New York: Greenwillow.

Prentice Hall. (1996). *Literature: World masterpieces* (4th ed.). Upper Saddle River, NJ: Author.

Rawls, W. (1961). *Where the red fern grows*. New York: Bantam.

Robinson, M. (1993). *Cock-a-doodle doo! What does it sound like to you?* New York: Stewart, Tabori, & Chang.

Rylant, C. (1998). *Scarecrow*. San Diego, CA: Voyager.

Rylant, C. (2004). *Long night moon*. Ill. M. Siegel. New York: Simon & Schuster.

Salinger, J.D. (1991). *Catcher in the rye*. New York: Little, Brown.

Sendak, M. (1991). *Where the wild things are*. New York: HarperCollins.

Shakespeare, W. (1969). *Romeo and Juliet*. New York: Scholastic.

Steinbeck, J. (2002). *The grapes of wrath*. New York: Penguin.

Stoker, B. (1988). *Dracula*. New York: Tom Doherty Associates.

Swift, J. (1996). A modest proposal. In Prentice Hall, *Literature: World masterpieces* (4th ed., pp. 801–809). Upper Saddle River, NJ: Author.

Taback, S. (2005). *Kibitzers and fools: Tales my zayda told me*. New York: Penguin.

Taylor, M. (1976). *Roll of thunder, hear my cry*. New York: Scholastic.

Taylor, M. (2003). *The land*. New York: Penguin.

Thoreau, H.D. (1980). *Walden and civil disobedience*. New York: New American Library.

Tunnell, M.O. (1999). *Halloween pie*. New York: Lothrop, Lee & Shepard.

Twain, M. (1988). *The adventures of Huckleberry Finn*. Berkeley: University of California Press.

Tyson, L.A. (2003). *An interview with Harry the Tarantula*. Washington, DC: National Geographic Society.

White, E.B. (1970). *The trumpet of the swan*. New York: Scholastic.

Wiesel, E. (2006). *Night*. New York: Hill and Wang.

Williams, C.L. (1999). *My Angelica*. New York: Random House.

Woodson, J. (2005). *Show way*. New York: Putnam.

Wordsworth, W. (1996). Ode: Intimations of immortality. In Prentice Hall, *Literature: World Masterpieces* (4th ed., pp. 896–899). Upper Saddle River, NJ: Prentice Hall.

Young, J. (2005). *R is for rhyme: A poetry alphabet*. Chelsea, MI: Sleeping Bear Press.

INDEX

Note. Page numbers followed by *f*, *b*, or *t* indicate figures, boxes, or tables, respectively.

Y

Learning Team